Gerald H. Anderson

Reg new copy
4/15/92

**The Gospel and
contemporary culture**

86 – "Hick's theory of religion is, like other theories of pluralism, in
many respects, the precise opposite. ... Here is an example of
the homogenization of religion which does its utmost to
reduce the different faiths to a kind of lowest common denominator."

95   Hick says, "The Real cannot be said to be personal.
For this would presuppose that the real is eternally in
relation to other persons. Whilst this is of course
conceivable, it constitutes a pure <u>ad hoc</u> speculation..."

The Gospel and
contemporary culture

Edited with an introduction by

HUGH MONTEFIORE

MOWBRAY

Mowbray
A Cassell imprint

Villiers House,   387 Park Avenue South
41/47 Strand,   New York
London WC2N 5JE,   NY 10016–8810
England   USA

© Mowbray, a Cassell imprint 1992

First published 1992

British Library Cataloguing-in-Publication Data
A catalogue record for this book is available from the British Library.

ISBN 0–264–67259–3

Typeset by Colset Private Limited, Singapore.
Printed and bound in Great Britain by
Biddles Ltd, Guildford and King's Lynn.

Contents

The lines from Edmund Blunden, 'Report on Experience', on pp. 34–5 are reproduced by permission of Peters Fraser Dunlop.

Gunton is giving the 1982 Bampton Lectures at Oxford on Trinity.

The contributors

Eric Ives is Professor of English History in the University of Birmingham. His principal expertise is in the fields of early modern legal history and political history. He is a Baptist by denomination. Recent works include *Anne Boleyn* (Blackwell, 1986) and articles on the relation between Christianity and history, as well as *God in History* (Lion, 1979).

Mary Midgley is a professional philosopher with a special interest in the frontiers between human and other animals and between science and religion. She is author of *Beast and Man, Wickedness, Evolution As a Religion* and *Salvation Through Science*.

Jeremy Begbie is Director of Academic Studies and Tutor in Doctrine at Ridley Hall, Cambridge. His keen and active interest in music has led him to found an orchestra at Cambridge. He was musical editor of *Anglican Praise* (Oxford University Press), author of *Music in God's Purposes* (Handsel Press) and *Voicing Creation's Praise: Towards a Theology of the Arts* (T. & T. Clark).

Colin Gunton has been Professor of Christian Doctrine at King's College, University of London, since 1984, and is a minister of the United Reformed Church. The nature and justification of claims to knowledge have always been at the centre of his interests. Recent discussion of the topics are to be found in his *Enlightenment and Alienation: An Essay Towards a Trinitarian Theology* (Marshall, Morgan and Scott, 1985) and *The Actuality of Atonement: A Study of Metaphor, Rationality and the Christian Tradition* (T. & T. Clark, 1989).

Jane Collier is Lecturer in Management Studies in the University of Cambridge, and Fellow and Director of Studies in Economics at Lucy Cavendish College. She is also a Roman Catholic Eucharistic minister and involved with chaplaincy work at Addenbrookes Hospital in Cambridge. She has lectured and published in economics over a number of years.

Brenda Watson is a part-time academic consultant to the Farmington Trust. She is a sometime teacher, lecturer at Didsbury College of Education, and Director of the Farmington Institute in Oxford, and is in constant contact with a range of schools and teachers. She is author of *Education and Belief* (Blackwell, 1987) and is currently writing a book for Longman's *Effective Teacher Series* and editing a book on *Priorities for Religious Education* (Falmer).

John Young was a medical doctor and a priest, and Director of the Churches' Council for Health and Healing. He was a Reader for nineteen years before his ordination, and worked as a GP before becoming a Fellow of the Royal College of Psychiatrists. He died in 1991.

Jim McDonnell has spent the last ten years at the international Jesuit research institute, the Centre for the Study of Communication and Culture, researching and writing on all aspects of religious communication. He has had a particular interest in the influence of media technologies on contemporary cultures and has made a special study of public broadcasting in Britain. He was joint editor of a series of essays entitled *Communicating Faith in a Technological Age* (St Paul Publications, 1990). He is now Director of the Catholic Communications Centre.

Introduction

HUGH MONTEFIORE

Many Christian writers in the past have written penetrating books about the relationship between faith and culture, as Richard Niebuhr did in his celebrated book entitled *Christ and Culture*. This collection of essays, however, differs strikingly from all such books because it is closely connected with mission.

Lesslie Newbigin has forcefully reminded us that missionaries who go from their home base to share their Christian faith with those who speak a foreign tongue in a far country commonly examine the culture of that country as an essential preliminary of their task. The process of expressing the Gospel in terms of that foreign culture is commonly called 'inculturation'. Pope John Paul II, in his encyclical *Redemptoris Missio*, explains how this should function:

> Through inculturation the Church makes the Gospel incarnate in different cultures and at the same time introduces people, together with their cultures, into her own community. She transmits to them her own values, at the same time taking the good elements that already exist in them and renewing them from within (52).

This assumes that the inculturation of the Gospel is concerned with the Christian mission to foreign cultures, and the encyclical specifically mentions missionaries in this connection (52, 53).

It is comparatively easy to ask awkward questions about the suitability of another culture as the vehicle for communicating the Gospel; but it is very difficult to ask them about one's own. This is what has been attempted here. This book constitutes a searching enquiry into some fundamental aspects of modern Western culture in the light of the Christian Gospel. It is frankly missionary in its orientation. How can the credibility of the Gospel be established in this secular age? First it is necessary to analyse what makes it seem incredible or irrelevant to so many people today. Such an enquiry is fundamental for all the churches at the commencement of a Decade of Evangelism, although in fact the initial thinking of which this book is the fruit

1

began long before that Decade was on anyone's agenda.

'Culture' is not an easy word to handle. Its meaning is often vague and soft at the edges. It is sometimes used to mean education, as when we speak of a cultured person. No doubt it was in that sense that Hermann Goering allegedly said: 'When I hear someone talking about Culture, I reach for my revolver'.

According to a dictionary definition culture is 'the intellectual side of civilisation, the training and refinement of mind, tastes and manners'. It was in this sense that Matthew Arnold wrote that 'the great aim of culture [is] the aim of setting ourselves to ascertain what perfection is and to make it prevail'. Such a remark illuminates a common problem about the discussion of the subject: people commonly speak about culture in general under the influence of the particular culture to which they happen to belong.

Every age has its own distinctive culture, and every country too. It forms the background of the lives of people who live in a country, and it is compounded of its dominant religion (or lack of it), its ethics and ideology, its literature and art, its science and technology, its philosophical and ethical traditions, and its ethos and way of life. This complexity makes it difficult adequately to describe. To make it even more difficult, there are also complex cultural interrelationships between countries, and between generations. British culture, for example, has been influenced by French, German and American cultures, and of course every culture bears marks of its inheritance from the past. Since no society is monolithic, there are also subcultures among different ethnic groups and among teenagers in most societies, not to mention contemporary 'pop cultures'.

How then is it possible to generalize about contemporary culture? Among the most important of its ingredients are the unconscious assumptions which underlie the thinking of a society and by which its members live their lives. Anthropologists call these 'root paradigms', which may be described as a set of assumptions about the fundamental nature of the universe, humankind, or the way in which people behave, which are so deeply held by the members of a society as to be essentially unquestioned by them. It is these 'root paradigms' which are subjected to a Christian critique in the chapters of this book. These 'root paradigms' are not only prevalent in the particular culture in which this volume has been written: they are also prevalent in Western Europe as a whole and in North America. They are being adopted in the name of 'modernization' by many leaders of opinion throughout the world. So we hope that our work may fit a larger context than that of one country.

Over the last twenty years the Christian mission has made little progress in the West. And yet there has hardly been a period in the long history of Christian mission when the Church at the parochial level has seemed to be better equipped for mission. The clergy (for the most part) have been theologically educated, are pastorally minded, and conscientious in their duties, while lay men and women probably play a greater part in the life of the Church than ever before, and they are often thirsting for more training in Christian life and spirituality. Christian literature abounds, and Christians are becoming more and more aware of the importance of communication in this era of mass media. Missions and evangelistic outreach have become a common part of the Christian life; but for all their trumpeted 'success', it seems that they can do little more than replace those who have lapsed from the Christian faith.

The result of all this Christian activity seems to have been comparatively slight. Statistics show that over the last twenty years there has been a progressive decline, or at best a plateau. Certainly in 1988 Church of England numbers 'bucked the trend', and the statistics of other churches showed a corresponding slowdown in the decline; but we do not yet know if this is a momentary blink, or if it is the beginning of a new trend. The position in Western Europe is in stark contrast to that in Africa, where during the last century the Christian mission has registered the greatest advance in all its long history, and also to the position in Eastern Europe or China, where the Church has emerged from a long period of state repression with greatly increased energies and vastly increased numbers.

What are the reasons for these contrasts? So far as lack of response to the Gospel in Western Europe is concerned, they are complex. In the first place, society has become more pluralist, in the sense that there are now minorities of considerable size claiming allegiance to non-Christian religions (or to no religious faith at all), so that the compelling nature of the Christian faith is no longer apparent. Even though it still has a privileged position, Christianity is often seen as one religious option among many, which is intrinsically neither better nor truer than any of the other options, among which must be included both atheism and agnosticism. Secondly, there has been a tendency for all mainstream churches to become more sect-like. The characteristic of a sect is to look inwards to itself rather than outwards to the society of which it forms a part, and this tends to make people outside its membership disregard it. Thirdly, there has been a growing secularization in the West over a period of years, in the sense that religious thinking, practices and institutions have been losing their social significance, and there has been a tendency to marginalize their leaders, so that religious institutions are not regarded with the same respect as they used to enjoy on the part of those outside the community of faith.

There is however a further very important although usually neglected reason for the malaise of the Christian faith; and it is with this that our volume is particularly concerned. The reception of the Christian faith within a country is bound up with the 'root paradigms' of that country's culture. If the underlying assumptions and attitudes are not 'Gospel-friendly', the Gospel in that country will not prosper. Here lies the chief reason for the relative failure of our Christian mission.

This vital truth, unless it is taken seriously to heart, will frustrate the Decade of Evangelism which is just beginning. It is supported by sociological evidence. Those whose discipline lies in assessing social attitudes have often noted that statistics of different Churches and denominations rise and fall at the same time. This demonstrates that 'success' or 'failure' is not to be laid at the door of a particular Church or denomination, but that it is simply illustrative of a social trend. And what influences such social trends? No doubt a full answer to this question is complex, but the unconscious assumptions of people play a major part.

To say that a culture is not 'Gospel-friendly' is quite different from suggesting that there are not good people who live within such a society, an idea which can be manifestly shown to be false. Nor is it to suggest that our particular society does not share with other societies certain common values. Of course it does, for without those common values no society can exist, and part of the task of the Christian Church is to reinforce such values for the common good.

It ill behoves the Christian Church to despise the culture in which it finds itself. It is within this culture that the Christian life must be lived. Unless people are to be hermits, or to live in enclosed communities which keep modern culture at bay, it has to come to terms with society. This book of essays has come into being at the start of the Decade of Evangelism, and unless the Gospel is expressed in a way that is meaningful to those who live within a culture, they will be deaf to the Good News which it is bringing, because it makes no contact with the way in which they think and act. (It is no good preaching Christ as the good shepherd within the culture of those who live exclusively by hunting.) Hence the concern among missionaries for 'inculturation', the expression of the Gospel within the cultural forms of those to whom it is brought.

In any case, there are many aspects of our culture which most of us greatly value. For all that is said against the Enlightenment (and a lot will rightly be said in this volume), we prefer to live at the end of the twentieth century rather than during the fourteenth century, when superstition, dirt, and poverty were prevalent, when a high proportion of the population was being killed off through ignorance about plague, and when the Church's authority was unchallenged and matters of ethics and belief were directed from the centre. Our modern technological society has many advantages, our deepened knowledge and understanding about the world can enrich and enliven our lives, while our better insight into psychological processes has at least the potential of helping us to accept ourselves. This list of benefits could be greatly extended. At the same time, there are grave criticisms of our culture to be made. What is being asserted here is that many of its assumptions, presuppositions, and values are contrary to the fundamental assumptions, presuppositions and values of the Christian Gospel.

It follows that a mission to our culture is needed quite as much as a mission to the individuals who live within that culture. The first step in a mission to a culture is to analyse its 'root paradigms' in the light of the message and values of the Gospel; and it is with such an analysis that this collection of essays is concerned. Such a mission to culture is well founded in the Christian Scriptures. St Paul frequently in his letters referred to the 'principalities and powers'. Although, as a man of his time, he probably regarded these powers as the work of semi-angelic beings who were thought to control the destinies of peoples, in fact when he wrote of these powers he was referring to the impersonal structures which play so large a part in shaping society as a whole, and which must include the 'root paradigms' of particular cultures.

The cultural ways of thinking which ordinary people hold have 'trickled down' from the intellectual thinking of those who have set the tone for the spirit of the age. To change the culture of a country is therefore a considerable undertaking. Some people think that it will take a century or more for the culture of a country to change. But things move nowadays very swiftly in our age of mass media and instant communication. There is nothing static about our unwritten assumptions or our way of life. They have been changing rapidly in the past, and they can alter again rapidly in the future. Change is assisted by those with public influence in the intellectual or artistic world. If one thinks of Karl Marx labouring alone in the British Museum, and then assesses the impact that his thought has had for so many millions worldwide, it is clear that the effect of 'trickle down' can be very powerful indeed. But ordinary Christians can also assist change. The impact of a minority (such as Christians now constitute) on the 'root paradigms' of society can be very considerable, providing that individual church members are aware of the need to challenge their own cultural ways of thinking and believing, and are not afraid of stating their convictions forcefully and publicly.

* * *

The purpose of the essays in this book is to examine certain key areas of our cultural thought in the light of the Christian Gospel. There are many subjects which might have been chosen, and many ways in which they might have been treated. We have chosen eight which we regard as most important, because their presuppositions and assumptions so greatly influence people's receptivity to the Christian faith. Each subject is large enough to have a whole volume devoted to it (and we hope that this book may help to stimulate such future writing). Here each contributor in a single essay has been able to concentrate only on the fundamental issues at stake.

Because Christianity is about events in history, this theme must come first. Professor Ives points out the chimera of 'objective history', the impossibility of writing history as a meaningless jumble of events, and the fallacies involved in viewing history as disclosing a pattern of progress, or response to challenge, or conflict, or revealing a cyclic pattern. Noticing the comparative strength of the evidence for Christian origins, he shows how impossible it is to interpret history without any values, and that purpose, morality and grace, the three pillars of a Christian metaphysic of history, are perfectly proper categories through which history may be interpreted by those who have the commitment of faith.

Science is also to be given high priority in this volume, if only because we are living in a scientific age, and it is a popular belief that science has made religion redundant, because it can provide the answers to so many of our problems. But the assumption that religion can be dismissed on grounds of scientism can be shown to be very fragile indeed. Mary Midgley points out how strangely the notion of 'science' has been extended, far beyond the establishment of facts, to provide a comforting kind of pseudo-religion. It has thus seemed to have a peculiar, all-powerful authority. She shows that religion is not the only sufferer from this inflated idea of 'science'. She concludes that 'exaggerated faith in "science", along with a very confused idea of what science is, distorts a wide area of Western thought'.

Important as these subjects are to the formation of culture, they do not provide its only ingredients. For human beings, the impact of non-verbal communication can be very great. The effect upon us of the unquestioned assumptions about the form as well as the content of literature can be very considerable. Dr Begbie examines some of the assumptions which have tended to alienate the arts in Western culture, and suggests that, for the arts (as Professor Gunton suggests for epistemology), there are resources within Christian theology, especially Trinitarian theology, which provide a fresh and fruitful basis for the renewal of the arts today.

On any reckoning epistemology is of key importance. In the discussions which have preceded these chapters we have found ourselves again and again coming back to this subject. What are the assumptions on which it can be known that something is true, or indeed on which knowledge itself is based? Professor Gunton locates the heart of the problem in the relation of the particular to the general, and, pointing out that there is no dis-carnate rationality, he argues that the basis of knowledge is by acquain-tance rather than conceptual. He distances himself from empiricism and idealism, insisting on the material basis, particularity, freedom and falli-bility of all our systems of thought and science. He suggests that in God's world the key to the fundamental problem of knowledge is to be found not in the philosophical assumptions of contemporary culture, but in the relations of the Persons of the Blessed Trinity.

Included also in this book are four subjects which could be called 'second-order' but which all nonetheless have a great impact on our 'root paradigms'. For example, we are bombarded with information about economics, and, rather like an over-anxious person when he becomes ill, the country seems to be continually taking its economic temperature. The influence of economics is transmitted in the first place by the presupposi-tions, values and norms which are basic to the way in which we think about the economy. Dr Collier points out that the basic image of a 'culture of economism' is that of a self-regulating machine which ignores the reali-ties of human relationships and human needs, encouraging us to adopt 'value-neutral' attitudes to what happens around us. Our lives and actions are affected by the decisions of those who seek to put into practice economic policies which put material welfare above human welfare in general, and which value today's welfare above that of future generations.

If economics tends to condition the way in which we evaluate so many aspects of our existence, education is almost equally important, because it tends to influence at an early age the formation of our adult attitudes. Brenda Watson, after looking at five different approaches to schooling, concludes that, whatever be the intention of educators, the pressing requirements of the educational system result in consumerism and prag-matism being the major lessons that are actually learnt, and those more often by default than by official pronouncements, and that the moral humanism inculcated in many schools is grounded in social convenience rather than on moral principle, while the role of religious education in schools has been marginalized.

When the National Health Service was first introduced, it was hoped to improve the level of health throughout the country. This has not happened, and to judge from the concern which is generally felt about the present state of the Health Service, as well as by the spread of private medicine, it seems that, despite the allocation of more resources, the need is greater than ever. This suggests that a deeper analysis is needed of our modern attitudes to health and healing. Dr Young, himself a practising doctor as well as a priest, explains the confusion in the popular mind between cure and healing. Pointing out the fallacy of regarding the body as a machine, and also the falseness of some exaggerated claims for alternative therapies, he shows that a more truly holistic approach is needed and that healing involves the whole person, not merely the alleviation of physical conditions.

The media are influential elements in our daily lives. Dr McDonnell examines our assumptions about them and surveys the philosophies of those who have shaped media policy. He shows how the media are affected by the growth of commercialism and how they tend both to fragment our experience and to reinforce the cultural diversity of society. They also reflect, and to a certain extent reinforce, the confusions and contradictions of a pluralistic and increasingly secular society, including the 'vacuum of meaning' which lies at its heart. Nonetheless there are still Gospel values to be found in the media, even if not easily discerned. Both for appreciation and critical appraisal of the media, he emphasizes the need of a certain detachment, the very condition which the media threaten to overwhelm.

The assumptions underlying these eight subjects, under the expert analysis of those whose professional lives are (or have been) spent in their pursuit, lead to a massive indictment of some of the more important 'root paradigms' of contemporary culture, when they are subjected to the critique of the Christian Gospel. Such a critique is seldom attempted, if only because academic studies are usually considered to be 'objective', while Christianity is considered to be partisan.

This contrast deserves some further exploration. No subject can be pursued without presuppositions. Today we take it for granted that academic subjects are rationally pursued. This appeal to reason, which in our culture can be traced back ultimately to the Enlightenment, is in fact an appeal to a particular form of rationality greatly influenced by the cultural assumptions of the period concerned. The Enlightenment is certainly not the cause of all our evils, and in fact nihilism could be said today to be the chief cultural opponent to the Christian Gospel. We are indebted to the Enlightenment in many ways, and none of us would wish to turn back to an age of superstition. But, nonetheless, it is the case that what appears to those under the influence of the Enlightenment to be an appeal to reason is in fact an appeal to a particular form of rationality which takes its origin in the Enlightenment, and which presupposes that the unaided reason is the sole means of true knowledge.

Christianity has a long tradition of a different type of rationality, which seems entirely reasonable to Christians, and which presupposes a belief in human reason purified and assisted by revelation, and in particular by the final self-revelation of God in Jesus Christ, culminating in his death and resurrection. Reason, as Christians understand it, refers, as Tillich has put it, to 'the structure of the mind which enables it to grasp and shape reality'. Because we are surrounded by mystery, we can never fully understand what is revealed. We even may have to employ paradox, or to make use of a seemingly contradictory *ensemble* of models, in order to apprehend more adequately the full splendour of divine revelation. Despite our human limitations, the Christian structure of rationality does enable us to have some real understanding of our relationship with God: its framework of discourse allows us to have a coherent view of God's world which seems to correspond to the real world around us. This is made possible because there is a corresponding structure in reality itself which enables us to understand it in this way.

At the end of the day, a choice must be made between two world-views. As Newbigin has well put it, 'the true opposition is not between reason and revelation as sources and criteria of truth. It is between two uses to which reason is put.' A choice must be made between the Christian tradition of rationality and that of secularism. In the same way, a choice has to be made between the Christian tradition of rationalism and that of other faiths, as well as the view that different faiths are equally valid expressions on the one unknowable Reality.

The basis of such a choice should be a judgement about which world-view (with its accompanying form of rationality) is most adequate. A religious view, to be true, must be adequate to the strangeness of the universe in which we find ourselves. The credentials of the divine revelation which forms the basis of faith must be adequate for belief. Such a faith must be adequate to an individual's religious experience, and at the same time it must do justice to the religious experiences of adherents to other faiths. It must cohere within a structure of rationality in a way which corresponds to the truth as it is perceived. In a historical religion, the interpretation of divine revelation must be seen to rest upon an adequate historical base. Such a faith must be adequate to the human condition as a whole, in the sense that it adequately measures up to fundamental human needs. It must adequately cohere with our understanding of the physical universe as well as with our understanding of psychological and sociological aspects of humanity. No two people are likely to hold exactly the same interpretation of their common faith; but since it is intrinsically improbable that the truth about human life has been hidden down the ages but has been lately revealed to an individual, personal belief must be shared by others within the tradition to which a person belongs.

According to the continuing Christian tradition, Christians believe that their faith is adequate in terms of these criteria. This faith is wholly compatible with the greatest respect for the faith of those who follow the other mainstream religions of the world. Christians believe that the Christian faith provides a more adequate basis for life and thought than a secular world-view which regards the world as lacking an ultimate purpose and values other than those which individuals may ascribe to it. They recognize that they cannot *prove* the truth of their faith, but they equally realize that adherents of other world-views cannot prove the truth of what they believe. They are convinced that they inherit a tradition of rationality which is adequate for them to claim with integrity God's full and personal self-disclosure in Christ, to challenge with confidence the secular values of the world, and warmly to commend their faith to other individuals and to the society to which they belong. They are prepared, as the contributors to this book have done, to expose themselves by subjecting their own disciplines to the critique of their faith.

The Gospel, in the light of which the subjects in this collection have been examined, is not to be identified with the writings of the Christian Scriptures, although it is certainly to be found within their pages; nor is it to be identified with the Church, although it can certainly be found within the Church. The Gospel is God's gracious action in creating the world, and recreating the lives of men and women, and restoring them to a loving relationship with himself. It is God's saving activity within human history, foreshadowed in the writings of the Old Testament, embodied in the event of Christ, particularly in his death and resurrection. It is the acceptance of Christ as the way, the truth and the life. It is our means of access through Christ to God's Kingdom. It is the good news that God has freed us to be our true selves. It is the power of God to renew lives in the strength of his Spirit and to weld people together in a true community. So the Gospel is for society as well as individuals. Society itself needs renewal, redemption and reconciliation. Since the presuppositions of contemporary culture are opposed in many ways to the Gospel, it is hardly surprising that we find ourselves living in an increasingly frustrated and unsatisfied society.

*   *   *

The seeds of 'The Gospel and Our Culture' programme are to be found in a sermon by the late Sydney Evans, when he was Dean of Salisbury, to the effect that the progress of the Gospel has been greatly affected by the culture of a country where it has been preached. In July 1981 the Executive of the British Council of Churches approved a large National Conference on this theme to take place in 1984, and appointed the Revd Dr Kenneth Slack as chairman of a planning group to set up the conference. This group came to realize that the subject had not been given reflection at sufficient depth, so the 1984 Conference was abandoned and Bishop Lesslie Newbigin was invited to write a booklet to get people thinking.

This booklet was published in 1983 under the title *The Other Side of 1984*, and immediately it became a bestseller: it was translated into many languages, including Chinese. This was followed by more substantial books by Bishop Newbigin, *Foolishness to the Greeks* (1986) and *The Gospel in a Pluralist Society* (1989). Meanwhile the Revd Dr Dan Beeby, formerly Principal of St Andrew's Hall, Selly Oak Colleges, had been appointed Co-ordinator of 'The Gospel and Our Culture' programme, and after Dr Slack's premature death in 1987 I took over as chairman of the management group until 1990, when the editorship of this volume made it expedient for me to resign, and the Revd Dr Philip Morgan became chairman.

Although there has been no public advertising of 'The Gospel and Our Culture', it seems like an idea whose time has come. It seems to have grown into a Movement involving those who realize that we are living in a culture which is not 'Gospel-friendly', and who realize the need for Christian mission in this country. Interest is ecumenical. The Superior General of the English Jesuits invited Fr John Coventry SJ to join the Birmingham team. The Mennonite Church in the USA has seconded Dr Wilbert Schenk, Professor of Missions, for three years on a six-monthly basis to follow up contacts on the continent of Europe and in the United States of America. A printed British newsletter was initiated in 1989 and within a year and without advertising it has over 1,000 subscribers; and there is also a newsletter published in the USA. Various books on the theme have been published. The Bible Society has already sponsored one Conference on the subject at High Leigh, which was oversubscribed, and two more regional conferences will be held before the National Consultation at Swanwick in mid-1992. This collection of essays is published as a permanent contribution to the theme, and also to provide material for consideration at the National Consultation.

Very careful consideration has gone into the making of this book. Selected groups have met for Discussion Days on each of its themes, and discussion papers have been circulated to corresponding members as well. After this, I invited a team of men and women to contribute, and they have consulted together before publication. I have to report with great sadness that the Revd Dr John Young, priest, consultant psychiatrist and Director of the Churches' Council for Health and Healing, was taken ill after completing the first draft of his essay, and subsequently died before he could revise it as he wished to do. I have edited it and included it in this collection in its unrevised form.

Among the contributors there are represented many Churches and none: the United Reformed Church, the Baptist Church, the Methodist Church, the Roman Catholic Church and the Church of England. I regret that there was no Presbyterian in the team, especially as members of the Church of Scotland participated fully in the consultative process. In fact, matters of churchmanship have never entered into the debate at all; and we find among ourselves Barthians, traditional Catholics, conservative Evangelicals and central Churchmen. All the Churches in this land, and all church people, are now living within a culture which has some excellent characteristics, but which is also in many ways hostile to the Christian Gospel. In Paul VI's encyclical *Evangelii Nuntiandi* evangelization is described as 'bringing the good news into every strata of humanity, and through its influence transforming humanity from within and making it new' (18). We offer this book as a small contribution towards this end.

The Gospel and history

ERIC IVES

If the Christian Gospel is anything, it is Good News in history and about history. The central place which it gives to this is distinctive among the major religions, even in comparison with Judaism and Islam with which it shares common historical roots. In the Jewish *sh*^e*ma'*, affirmation of the oneness of God is accompanied by an announcement of what is required from humans, in the Islamic *shahādah*, by a confession of Mohammed as his prophet.[1] But in the Christian creeds, that affirmation prefaces a recital of the historic events of the life of Jesus Christ and culminates in the proclamation of his impending return and rule. The truth of Christianity is an event in history, the career and personality of a first-century Middle Eastern Jew.

Although from the fourth century to the seventeenth Western historians thought and wrote within the framework of this Christian revelation, today the fracture between historical study and the Gospel is virtually complete. The Christian understanding of history is categorized as supernatural and dismissed accordingly. This chapter will explore the reason for this, and will argue that the exclusion from history of metaphysical and partly metaphysical issues, including the Christian interpretation, does not arise from the nature of the discipline but from *a priori* assumptions as to its parameters. The further argument will be developed that unless the broader issues of meaning and explanation in history are faced, understanding of the subject is severely disabled.

Academic history

It is a curiosity of British scholarship that history is written by historians, but thinking about history is left to philosophers. There are notable exceptions, but the generalization is overwhelmingly true. Historians, indeed, are generally unaware and certainly uninterested in the theoretical problems about their discipline which have exercised philosophers for at least three centuries. Even though most history degree syllabuses will include a course in historiography, this will rarely get further than a discussion of past and present practice. J. H. Plumb wrote:

> It would be profitless to enter into a philosophic discussion of the nature of history or of its capacity to establish objective truth. The practising historian is like the practising scientist. Just as the latter has no great interest in or use for the philosophy of science, so the active historian is not much concerned with the philosophy of history. He knows history exists and he has been trained in the methods necessary for its investigation.[2]

What is true of the professional is still more true of the general public. It rarely appreciates even the practical realities of historical study—witness the invincible expectation that history is a compendium of self-sufficient facts—a myth which significantly influenced the 1990 debate in England on history within the National Curriculum in schools.

There are several reasons for this restricted thinking. One, as Plumb suggests, is that philosophical speculation seems to be irrelevant to what historians do—in trying to explain a particular episode in the past, the researcher is not helped by a digression into what 'explanation' means. His sympathies will be with the

> *faith healer from Deal*
> *Who said, although pain isn't real,*
> *When I sit on a pin,*
> *And it punctures my skin,*
> *I dislike what I fancy I feel.*[3]

The realistic course is always to ignore the philosophy and get on with the matter in hand.

Another disincentive is that philosophical speculation is alien to the 'practical, common sense' approach which characterizes both historians and the history they write and teach; explanation seems only to require the application of self-evident, normal criteria of analysis and logic—indeed it is this normality which, it is argued, gives history a pedagogic value as a training in 'problem-solving'. Another factor is the incompatibility of abstract theorizing and the concern of history with real people in actual situations as revealed by physical survivals—artefacts, buildings, landscape, books, paper and parchment. Then, too, there is time, or, rather, priority in allocating it; few historians would expect time spent on the philosophy of history to yield much in the way of a useful conclusion.

But behind what philosophers may see as wilful ignorance, there is a more fundamental reason for the gulf in Britain between studying history and thinking about the nature of history. This is the character of the scientific study of the subject which dominates Western scholarship. Of course people have been writing history for thousands of years in many parts of the globe, with widely different understandings of what they were doing—which should make us at least pause before claiming that ours is the only valid way to understand the past. But for the genesis of the contemporary Western approach, we have to go no further than eighteenth-century France, then the intellectual leader of Europe.

At the start of the century, history there was dominated by the *érudits*, or antiquarians, who understood history to be a matter of establishing atomistic facts about the past. Soon, however, they came under vigorous attack from the increasingly prominent thinkers of the Enlightenment such as Voltaire for being nothing but purposeless pedants. As one of his correspondents had asked:

> What is the point for a Frenchwoman like myself of knowing that in Sweden Egli succeeded Haquin and that Ottoman was the son of Ortogul?[4]

Hence the French Enlightenment demanded a new history which would *explain*—be written '*en philosophe*'—and with attention to the broad context of civilization and culture; Montesquieu with his *De l'Esprit des Lois* led the way.

The polarization of *érudition* and *philosophie* was, in fact, somewhat unreal, and the evident need to fuse the values of the two schools was certainly well understood by the English *philosophe* Edward Gibbon. Integration, however, really came about in Germany early in the next century. Personified by the Berlin scholar Leopold Ranke, a new 'scientific' history claimed to be able to explain objectively what actually happened in the past because it was based on archival research and nothing but archival research—it was both 'philosophical' and 'erudite'. Ranke's own approach to the writing of history undoubtedly claimed too much and, as we shall see, was less value-free than is often supposed. The 'historicist' approach which he exemplified argued that all cultures are moulded, almost determined, by the past, and that view remained dominant in Germany until after the Second World War. However, outside Germany, Ranke's importance was not in philosophy but in his principles of archival enquiry.

It was as technique that the new history was accepted in Britain in the second half of the nineteenth century, a methodology for acquiring, assessing and interpreting evidence. The result was academic history as we know it today, a system closed by the parameters of data, positivist in being preoccupied with archivally substantiated fact, dominated by the rational criteria for analysis, occupied with limited problems and concerned to establish cause and effect in as concrete a fashion as is possible.

This new approach to history left little room for the philosophy of history. To advance the discipline it was necessary to adhere to a rigorous epistemology which ruled out speculative questions. The system was intrinsically secular, had little time for 'meaning' and wholly excluded the numinous and still more any participation of a deity in history. God, if he did exist, was outside the system of knowing and must be ignored. The treatment of religion in history thus tended to become reductionist, as did the historical criticism of religious texts, biblical and otherwise. Those prominent historians who were Christians accepted that it was a professional duty to insulate their faith from their scholarship, satisfied, perhaps, with William Cowper, that 'God moves in a mysterious way his wonders to perform'. Those who were unbelievers, an increasing number, dismissed God's wonders as archivally unsupported.

As a closed intellectual system, the modern Western way of studying history is formidable. It has also proved to be a highly effective way of approaching the past. But it is important to recognize the conceptual restrictions in the system and the consequent restrictions on the statements historians can legitimately make. Kierkegaard remarked 'Life can only be understood backwards, but it must be lived forwards'. But how can we understand backwards? For example, how can we know about an event without direct access to it? If the answer is that we cannot know but can only interpret evidence, does not the nature and character of that evidence determine what can be known of the real past? If every historical document produced during a particular century reflected the affairs and attitudes of a priestly caste, this would not imply that priests had been equally dominant at the time. The caste, however, would necessarily loom large in any history that was written. An inescapable gap exists between the past as it occurred and the past as it is knowable by us through the surviving evidence. What would we understand a pea to be if all we had was a tin of the processed kind?

Evidence, moreover, requires interpretation. Dr Johnson was being overbearing and perverse (not for the first or last time) when he remarked:

> Great abilities are not requisite for an Historian. He has the facts ready to his hand.[5]

The 'facts' of history are certainly not 'ready to hand'. Even the simplest has to be particularized by a historian from among the raw data from the past; the majority, and certainly those of most interest, have to be inferred by the historian from a scrutiny and comparison of several, possibly contradictory, items of data. History cannot exist 'untouched by human hand'.

It is, of course, the case that the totality of historical evidence is independent of the historian. He or she can neither invent evidence nor ignore it; the historian does not write fiction. But the independence of the past is only a limited guarantee of objectivity. For all but the last century or century-and-a-half of human existence, evidence has survived in a partial and frequently random fashion. This means that history has to be hypothesized like a jigsaw puzzle which has lost its picture and also has many of its pieces missing. Students of more recent history face the opposite problem: a surfeit of material. This again requires historians to assert their authority, this time to select what is, that is *what appears to them to be*, important. Intervention and interpretation by the historian is a necessary and integral part of the study of history. What happened, happened—the past itself is an objective absolute—but that is not true of the way we know it.

This creates an obvious quandary. Historians have always had the goal of objectivity. Cicero asked:

> Who does not know History's first law to be that an author must not dare to tell anything but the truth? And its second that he must make bold to tell the whole truth? That there must be no suggestion of partiality anywhere in his writings? Nor of malice?[6]

But how can objectivity be attained if writing history is impossible without the personal involvement of the historian? The sixteenth-century historian John Foxe expressed the creed well when he wrote:

> Diligence is required, and great searching out of books and authors . . . the records must be sought, the registers must be turned over, letters also and ancient instruments ought to be perused, and authors with the same compared; finally the writers amongst themselves, one to be conferred with another; and so with judgement matters are to be weighed; with diligence to be laboured; and with simplicity, pure from all addition and partiality, to be uttered.[7]

And Foxe practised what he preached. But what he produced was *The Book of Martyrs*, as avowedly propagandist a work as it is possible to imagine! In other words, it is not enough for historians to interpret as faithfully as they can what they see in the evidence; because the eyes are theirs, what they see will be theirs as well. It is this which negates the endeavours of countless historians to achieve neutrality. Mechanistic objectivity is, of course mandatory: dates must be accurate; documents transcribed correctly; bias—that is, deliberate distortion—will disqualify utterly. But even the most scrupulous interpretation of the evidence is bound to be influenced by subjective considerations. Even the vocabulary the historian selects will be affected. How should the conflict in Britain's North American colonies between 1776 and 1783 be described—rebellion or revolution?

However—and it is an important point, not to be overlooked—history does not differ in this from life in general. Total neutrality is an artificial condition; men and women are human when they have attitudes and values, not when they do not. Indeed, unless I bring to the interpretation of the past my own understanding of life, I cannot breathe life into the past. Empathy, as a distinguished tradition of historical thinkers has held, plays an essential part in writing history. An illustration from R. G. Collingwood will make the point. He supposed a historian reading an edict by the Emperor Theodosius:

> Merely reading the words and being able to translate them does not amount to knowing their historical significance. In order to do that he must envisage the situation with which the emperor was trying to deal . . . as that emperor envisaged it. Then he must see for himself, just as if the emperor's situation were his own, how such a situation might be dealt with, . . . see the possible alternatives, . . . and thus he must go through the process which the emperor went through in deciding on this particular course.[8]

What is more, when a historian claims to be disengaged, he deceives his readers as well as himself. Value-structures permeate the sub-conscious as well as the conscious, and if the historian overtly shuts out the latter, the former remain unrecognized. Lord Acton, the inspiration of the original *Cambridge Modern History*, was firm in his assertion of neutrality:

> Our scheme requires that nothing shall reveal the country, the religion, or the party to which the writers belong . . . that nobody can tell, without examining the list of authors, where the [Anglican] Bishop of Oxford laid down his pen, and whether Fairburn [Congregational scholar] or [Cardinal] Gasquet, Liebermann [Jewish scholar] or Harrison [British positivist] took it up.[9]

But Acton himself could not keep his personal value system out of his writings; the assumptions of the old English Roman Catholic community and the convictions of the nineteenth-century liberal come out together, loud and clear. Commitment is not a mask to be donned or taken off at will, and readers are less likely to be misled if they know that no historian can claim to speak *ex cathedra*.

The closed system of archive-based history practised in the West has, therefore, to be recognized as giving a limited understanding of the past, consisting of inferences drawn from evidence which historians interpret honestly but necessarily under the influence of their own personal value-structures. Recognizing this now makes it possible to go further, to establish the nature of the history and the process the historian follows.

The analogy closest to the activity of the historian is the detection and trial of crime. What matters is the evidence, and what that is worth. The detective cannot answer the question 'Did he do it?'; he can establish only that there is a prima facie case to be answered. Similarly, despite the conventional language of the court, a prosecutor does not, indeed cannot, set out to provide a proof of guilt; he only structures and presents whatever evidence he sees as indicative in an attempt to persuade the jury that it reaches a high degree of probability. Nor does the jury have first-hand knowledge of what happened; it considers only such evidence as has been presented—and decides on the basis of 'beyond reasonable doubt'. All this mirrors exactly the work of the historian. In his or her pocket there is a policeman's warrant card, a barrister's wig, and a summons to jury service, and at the end of the day the historian's goal also is probability.

A particular kind of probability which is frequently before a court concerns cause and effect, and this requires the judge and jury to make inferences on matters such as *mens rea* ('guilty intent') and 'the reasonable man'. History likewise is centrally concerned to establish relationships, and in precisely the same way can never offer more than inferences. Indeed, the cogency of the inferences it can achieve is usually less than a court's, for the latter often has living witnesses to cross-examine. All historical explanations, even the best attested, are in strict reality no more than estimates on the available evidence. For the many which are only moderately attested, the quality of that estimate may, perforce, be low.

Historical explanations are also necessarily conditional. Even the most careful scholarship cannot provide against deficiencies in the evidence—a relationship which is not recorded, or a key document which has not survived or as yet lies unrecognized in some archive. The reality of chance and accident must not be overlooked either; they are inescapable incidents of historical events. Bernard Shaw was in no way far-fetched when he had his professional 'Chocolate Soldier' defeated by a Byronic cavalry charge because his machine guns had been supplied with wrong-sized ammunition. Suppose Winston Churchill had been killed, not merely injured, in his New York street accident of 1931?

History, therefore, is not the simple factual narrative which the naïve suppose—along with many who should know better. Yet it is also important to deny the other extreme, that history is a welter of subjective speculation, the kind of assessment typified by Samuel Butler's remark that 'though God cannot alter the past, historians can'.[10] The intrinsic difficulties in the subject have long been recognized and guarded against. Subjectivity is controlled by mutual scholarly criticism and competitive cross-checking. The difficulty of arguing backwards from effect to cause has created a requirement for rigorous scepticism and a demand for counter-factual analysis which attempts to scrutinize the alternative possibility that did not happen—even, testing this, where feasible, by means of a computer simulation. The classic example here is the problem of how to estimate the influence of the coming of railways on the opening-up of the American West without knowing how that development would have progressed without them.

Historical ingenuity achieves, indeed, a high level of sophistication overall. It is also adept at scholarly osmosis. Anthropologists have shown that the meaning of behaviour and language depends on the matrix of myth, symbol and significance in which action and words exist. Structuralist ideas propounded by Foucault and others draw attention to the way in which concepts are historically conditioned and socially programmed, so that the face value of language is determined by the sub-text. History, therefore, has ceased to debate the Reformation exclusively in terms of doctrines, philosophies and politics; the Mass is now recognized to have a sociological and anthropological dimension, so too the message of Luther. Even concepts apparently antipathetic to history have value for it, as with theories of literary 'deconstruction' associated with Derrida. The assertion that a text is realizable only in the mind of the immediate reader is a fundamental challenge to the historian to explain how evidence can be understood in its original context.

The value of recognizing conceptual difficulties implicit in historical study is, thus, not to discredit the discipline. It is, rather, to establish that the essence of the historical statement is probability, and that the role of the historian is to achieve the highest level of probability congruent with the state of the evidence. Not that this should be surprising. As the comparison with detection and criminal trial illustrates, history's concern with probability, not certainty, makes it one with the normal way of knowing. In the famous words of Bishop Butler, 'probability is the very guide of life'.[11]

Jesus Christ: the historical record

It is to the bar of this historical tribunal that Christianity has to bring its claims to be based on a historical person and historical events in first-century Palestine. The broader philosophical issues of a Christian understanding of history are a different matter and will be considered later, but the Christ event was an event in history and stands or falls as such.

Judged by historical criteria, the evidence relating to Jesus Christ is impressive. The essential Christian claims are clearly documented in hostile Jewish and pagan sources within seventy or eighty years of his execution in Jerusalem in either AD 30 or 33. Letters to Christian communities in Greece can be dated within twenty years of that event. What is particularly striking, by comparison with the exiguous sources for contemporary non-Christian events, is the variety and range of the documentary evidence for Jesus Christ which can be dated before the end of the first century, including the Gospel narratives. The comparison made by the historian of ancient Rome A. N. Sherwin-White is worth quoting at length:

> . . . the more advanced exponents of [the study of the Gospel narratives] apparently maintain that the historical Christ is unknowable and the history of his mission cannot be written. This seems very curious when one compares the case for the best known contemporary of Christ, who like Christ is a well-documented figure—Tiberius Caesar [died AD 37]. The story is known from four sources, the *Annals* of Tacitus and the biography of Suetonius, written some eighty or ninety years later, the brief contemporary record of Velleius Paterculus, and the third-century . . . Cassius Dio. These disagree amongst themselves in the wildest possible fashion, both in major matters . . . and in specific details.[12]

The Congregationalist scholar C. H. Dodd went even further:

> I believe that a sober and instructed criticism of the Gospels justifies the belief that in their central and dominant tradition they represent the testimony of those who stood nearest to the facts, and whose life and outlook had been moulded by them.[13]

Evidence of this quality would normally cause the historian no difficulty. That the opposite is the case is because this evidence is very specific not only about the career and sayings of Jesus of Nazareth, but in insisting that he was the author of a number of acts which are represented as miraculous. Nor is this an instance where a core of truth has become surrounded by myth. The miraculous is integral to the story and, according to the texts, demonstrates that Christ, while fully human, was 'God among men'. Even this might not throw the historian. There is no difficulty in recognizing that sources put a contemporary gloss or construction on the evidence they describe. Mediaeval claims that miracles took place at the shrine of this saint or that are a comment on the way 'miracle' was then understood.

What, however, the historian cannot dismiss is the fact that at the heart of the evidence about Jesus Christ is the report that despite crucifixion and burial he was later seen alive. Here we have a Christian assertion that a specific event took place in history, with the corollary that if it did not, then Christianity is founded on a delusion.

The response of many people to the notion of a resurrection is to deny the possibility. The Scottish philosopher of the Enlightenment, David Hume, wrote of miracles:

> There must be a uniform experience against every miraculous event, otherwise the event would not be miraculous. And as an uniform experience amounts to a proof, there is here a direct and full proof from the nature of the fact, against the evidence of miracle.[14]

In other words, to be a miracle, an event would need to be wholly unexpected. That is only possible if uniformity is the norm in nature. If uniformity is the norm, that in itself is good reason to believe that miracles do not happen. Two comments, however, must be made. The first is that Hume's argument is a reflection of his Enlightenment understanding of nature as a machine. When science today attempts to explain nature, far from repudiating randomness, it actually has to invoke it. In the second place, on Hume's own terms, the one point at which nature cannot be uniform is at a moment of creation, and early Christians understood the resurrection of Christ precisely as a creative act by God—they called Christ 'the second Adam'.[15]

But neither logic nor science can shield the historian from the question 'Is "the resurrection of Christ" capable of historical demonstration?' As we have seen, what history can say will not be more than an estimate of probabilities and will depend on the data available.[16] That caveat made, the question can be answered if broken down into three elements.

The first is 'Did anything happen?' Here the answer 'Yes' has a high probability. The establishing of Christian communities a thousand miles away, so soon after the execution of Jesus Christ, indicates that some dynamic was in operation. That this was belief in the resurrection is clear in the letters to these churches. Indeed, the rapid emergence and drive of Christianity is a phenomenon impossible to explain adequately if this impetus is excluded.

The second question to ask is 'What happened to make people believe that Christ was alive'. This is much more difficult to answer in purely historical terms. The evidence consists of eye-witness accounts which are very striking. As Gordon Davis wrote:

> The accounts of the resurrection experiences, impossible though it may be to reconcile them, are evidence that Jesus's followers were convinced that they

had seen him risen and had had a personal encounter not with a ghost but with one who had died and was now alive, having broken the power of death.[17]

There is, nevertheless, little here for the historian. The accounts are evidence only of belief in a resurrection. What is more, it is hard to see what kind of evidence a historian would need in order to be able to suggest what happened. Conceive, for example, what he could say of the reason for the catastrophe of Hiroshima in August 1945 if no evidence had survived to document the principles, the manufacture or the dropping of the atomic bomb. A totally unprecedented event without data leaves the historian with nothing to say.

What, of course, the historian at Hiroshima could do, is to look at the consequences of the event. Analysis of reports from survivors would soon point to some kind of explosion, and if it was then established that Japan at the time was at war and under massive aerial attack, the probability would be high that some new kind of offensive device was to blame— though what, it would be impossible to say. The third element in the question, therefore, is 'Are there consequences which throw light on the event?'

The consequence of a resurrection which is susceptible to historical analysis is the claim that Christ's grave was empty. The import of this is often misunderstood, as though in a world where graves are frequently emptied, an empty grave would somehow prove the case. The real signifi-cance is negative: that Christ could not have come alive in the way the early Christians believed if his body remained interred.[18]

However, the probability that the grave was empty is high. The key source—not the Gospel stories (relying on them easily leads to circular-ity), but again the letters to the early Christian churches—show that the empty tomb was an important element in the belief of the first Christian communities.[19] The belief had also become identified with the rite of baptism, one of the two original cult acts of the Christian community.[20] The date of these pieces of evidence is twenty years after the supposed event, which disposes of the notion that the story was a late elaboration. It also follows that for the story to have reached Europe in such a rela-tively short time after starting in Jerusalem, the story must have origi-nated soon after the alleged event.

Faced with the challenge to explain why there was this firm early conviction that the grave was empty, history has little to suggest. The first-century Jewish tradition that the disciples removed the body neces-sarily involves their conspiring to fabricate a new religion, which they then proceeded to die for.[21] It also implies that it had not been possible to discredit the story by producing the corpse, which suggests that it was not there to be produced, while the absence of any attempt to make a substitution, indicates that its disappearance was common knowledge. Nor are modern explanations of the disappearance any more convincing. There is little merit in the suggestion that the wrong tomb was examined—the correct one would still be available for inspection—or that the authorities removed the body to defuse possible trouble. Neither does the notion that the execution squad left Jesus alive carry much conviction. A convincing natural explanation is yet to be found.

It may, of course, be felt that if the events alleged are without rational explanation, the whole business must in some way be fiction or a pious hallucination. If so, it is important to recognize that this is not a historical judgement. It is a response to presuppositions which, in the words of Archbishop Michael Ramsey, 'demand that Jesus Christ be fitted into certain naturalistic beliefs about the world, man and religion'.[22]

Numerous attempts have, in fact, been made to account for the dynamic of the resurrection while rejecting the notion of a physical resurrection, usually by suggesting some kind of psychological impact on Christ's followers. All share three difficulties. First, they require Christ's disciples to be convinced of the resurrection and at the same time aware that the body lay undisturbed. As again Ramsey wrote:

> It is hard to see how the Apostles or their converts could have been convinced of a redemptive victory over death by Jesus had they believed that his body was corrupted in the grave.[23]

Second, there is the speed with which, as we have seen, the story of a resurrection spread. There was little time for the belief to develop gradually, or grow out of the worship practices of the early Church. The more time an explanation requires between the event and the emergence of the belief, the less it explains.[24] Third, the force of the psychological impact required to produce the dynamic of early Christianity must be reckoned hardly less exceptional than a physical resurrection.

The attempts to produce a psychological explanation of the resurrection do, however, point to one thing, that there *is* a problem to be explained. The historical evidence for the appearance and spread of a Christian community which proclaimed the resurrection story, and for the possibility that the body of Christ did not remain where it had been placed, point in the same direction. The probabilities are firmly against the notion that what ensued after Christ's death can be brushed aside as myth or legend. And after several centuries of the most searching enquiry have failed to produce a convincing 'normal' explanation, perhaps it may be right to accept that there is none.

Approaches to explanation

Within its closed parameters, history as studied in the modern Western world is an effective way to understand the past, though one limited by necessary assumptions and techniques. It remains the case, however, that the self-contained character of the system is a convenient postulate; we have merely chosen to define history thus. Philosophical issues have not been answered; they have been excluded from consideration, *a priori*. An analogy from science will make the point. In the laboratory, scientific method rejects ecological considerations as wholly irrelevant either to the aim or the conduct of research; the concept of technical rationality operates. However, those environmental issues still exist. They wait outside the laboratory and will not go away. In a similar way, challenges lurk outside the laboratory of historical method. One of the most notable— and specially relevant to the theme of this book—is 'significance'.

The problem of significance can be simply put. Suppose we can be satisfied that it is technically possible to 'understand life backwards', do we discover anything more than a chronological sequence? If that is the case, understanding of the past is a very low-grade activity. The *érudits* were right; 'history', in words attributed to H.A.L. Fisher, 'is one damn fact after another'.

Significance is not a topic many historians like to speak about. Fisher, even, was brave enough to deny that it exists. He wrote:

> Men wiser than I have discerned in history a plot, a rhythm, a predetermined pattern. These harmonies are concealed from me. I can see only one emergency following upon another as wave follows upon wave, one great fact with respect to which, since it is unique, there can be no generalisations, only one safe rule for the historian: that he should recognise in the development of human destinies the play of the contingent and the unforeseen.[25]

Popular belief credits Ranke, the father of scientific history, with equal detachment. His famous credo of 1824 has been quoted again and again:

> To history has been assigned the office of judging the past, of instructing the present for the benefit of future ages. To such high offices this work does not aspire; it wants only to show what actually happened [*wie es eigentlich gewesen*].[26]

Yet, is such a position tenable? The answer must be 'no'. If all historians do is to list the details of chaos, there are better things to do with life.

Historians, at the very least, have to set the past in some minimum order. And if they accept even this, the question must then be, how far does this extend? Where is the ordering no longer valid? The contempt is overt in A. J. Toynbee's demonstration that modern Western historians who see 'a chaotic disorderly, fortuitous flux in which there is no pattern or rhythm of any kind to be discerned' are guilty of self-deception:

> We may be sure that they do see some order, pattern, and shape in History at some level of the Psyche; for if they saw no shape in History, they could have no vision of it. When they protest that they see no shape, what they are really doing is to refuse to bring a latent picture of the Universe up and out into the light of consciousness; and in making this refusal they are allowing their historical thought to be governed by some pattern embedded in their minds at the subconscious level . . . and a mental pattern that is not consciously criticized is likely to be archaic, infantile, and crude.[27]

The criticism certainly applies to Fisher. His avowal of agnosticism is contradicted by the books he wrote which show that he saw progress as the theme of history, not continuous linear progress but a pattern of the ebb and flow of liberal values.

> The fact of progress is written plain and large on the page of history; but progress is not a law of nature. The ground gained by one generation may be lost by the next. The thoughts of men may flow into the channels which lead to disaster and barbarism.[28]

As for Ranke, his 'what actually happened' was not an early version of the once-notorious catch-phrase, 'the facts, Ma'am, just the facts'. In early nineteenth-century German, the adverb *eigentlich* meant 'essentially', so that the agenda Ranke set himself was not to amass facts but to demonstrate the underlying realities in history, which for him were the truths of historicism.

Only if they imitate the ostrich can historians escape the need to think about meaning in history. There are, however, several models on offer. One would interpret the past in terms of humanity's struggle against the environment, another in terms of socio-economic struggle within society.[29] What has undoubtedly been the most common interpretation of history is that it operates in cycles. This notion remains ubiquitous in the Anglo-Saxon world in the weak proverbial form that 'history repeats itself', but is found as far back as Ancient Greece and China.[30]

The obvious model of significance to examine in some detail is the one Fisher chose—'progress'—for the feeling that this in some way or other makes the best sense, or at least some sense, of the past is common to many, perhaps most Western historians. A century ago the belief was often in an ongoing dynamic of humane advancement. The Roman Catholic Acton made this an article of faith: 'Not to believe in Progress is to question the divine government'; the agnostic Herbert Spencer proclaimed 'progress is not an accident but a necessity . . . It is part of nature.'[31] Certainty of a teleology of progress was largely destroyed by the experience and memories of 1914–18—hence Fisher's pessimism, which appeared amply warranted in the Europe of 1936. But in the confidence engendered by the Second World War, Julian Huxley could again offer the hope of evolutionary biology directed by human reason:

> Man can now see himself as the sole agent of further evolutionary advance on this planet, and one of the few possible instruments of progress in the universe at large. He finds himself in the unexpected position of business manager for the cosmic process of evolution.[32]

The historian E. H. Carr fully accepted the need to see a significance in the human past:

> History properly so-called can be written only by those who find and accept a sense of direction in history itself. The belief that we have come from somewhere is closely linked with the belief that we are going somewhere.[33]

He was equally clear as to what this significance was:

> I profess no belief in the perfectibility of man or in a future paradise on earth. . . . But I shall be content with the possibility of unlimited progress— or progress subject to no limits that we can or need envisage—towards goals which can be defined only as we advance towards them, and the validity of which can be verified only in a process of attaining them. Nor do I know how, without some such conception of progress, society can survive. Every civilized society imposes sacrifices on the living generation, for the sake of generations yet unborn. . . . In Bury's words, 'the principle of duty to posterity is a direct corollary of the idea of progress'.[34]

That history is a record of human progress is, as Fisher said, beyond any question. One has only to reflect on the greater real wealth of the world today, whether in terms of productive capacity or personal assets which enhance 'the quality of life'. Advances in medical science, transport and communication have substantially reduced human limitations. Moral improvement is evident in development such as the growth of a commitment to the peaceful settlement of disputes, concern for the Third World and for famine, anxiety about pollution and the repudiation of cruelties such as torture or capital punishment. Despite the romance of the past, there are few who would choose not to live in the present.

But confidence in progress is very much a Western point of view. By no means all the advances in this list would be true elsewhere. Indeed, there is good reason to argue that material progress in the West has been at the relative, sometimes even at the absolute, expense of the rest of the world. A good example is atmospheric pollution and the problem of global warming. The notion of material progress also appears to have a future only for the West.[35] It is highly improbable that the average per capita income of the underdeveloped world can ever be raised to that, say, of the United States. This is not to deny that some benefits have been more widely shared, notably improvement in health, but even this has the corollary of creating a monstrous problem of overpopulation.

Equally open to challenge is the extent of moral improvement. The savagery of Hitler, Stalin and Pol Pot had nothing to learn from the frightfulness of ancient Assyrian imperialism or the wiping out of aboriginal peoples by colonizing Europeans. Equally, the history of armaments seems to indicate that the human race has always pressed the development of the means of destruction to the maximum level of sophistication technically possible at the time in question. It is arguable, too, that force is no less institutionalized in the modern state than it was in the Roman Empire. But it may be asked 'Has the social conscience not become more sensitive?' No doubt this is so on certain issues in certain communities—in Britain, for example, the preservation of particular animal species—but it is harder to demonstrate overall progress in social responsibility, than changes in fashion.

Over and beyond the difficulty of demonstrating progress there is a more fundamental problem. On the face of it, 'material' and 'moral progress' appear terms which can be sensibly debated, but the only reason for this is the existence of an unstated common understanding as to what they might mean to the people discussing them. 'Progress', like 'beauty', is in the eye of the beholder; contemporary values are being imposed on the past. As for Carr's belief in 'progress . . . towards goals which can be defined only as we advance towards them', which he also describes as 'a sense of direction which alone enables us to order and interpret the events of the past', this is perilously close to *1984* and the Record Department of the Ministry of Truth, continuously revising the past to justify Big Brother's latest position. The development of the American Mid-West is a story of progress—unless you are a Red Indian.

'Progress', therefore, is less the obvious theme of history than some have imagined. Those who advance it are at least in part expressing their own value structure or the value structure of their contemporary society. But in this, 'progress' is merely an illustration. Much the same would be found to be the case were any other of the suggested general significances in history to be put under scrutiny. The reality is that significance is not intrinsic in history; significance is something the historian assigns to the past.

The historian is, therefore, in a quandary. We have established that some notion of significance in history is inescapable. Without this the historian's position becomes morally untenable. As Kant said, it is 'repugnant' to view the past:

> as if the whole web of human history were woven out of folly and childish vanity and the frenzy of destruction, so that one hardly knows in the end what idea to form of our race, for all that it is so proud of its prerogatives.[36]

On the other hand, a scrutiny of possible answers would suggest that none can be wholly warranted by history. It is not surprising, therefore, that most historians choose to endure Toynbee's berating and keep silent.

What, then, is the resolution of this dilemma? The answer is, 'a conscious choice of commitment'. The position of the historian requires the classic existentialist leap of faith; there is no guarantee that the significance he commits himself to will be wholly convincing, but he can retain no integrity if he refuses to choose. We can turn, for an example, to J. H. Plumb. Despite the difficulties involved in the concept, he announced that his conviction was that history does demonstrate progress through human reason.

> It is to me the one truth of history—that the condition of mankind has improved, materially, alas, more than morally, but nevertheless both have improved. Progress has come by fits and starts; retrogressions are common. Man's success has derived from his application of reason, whether this has been to technical or social questions.[37]

Plumb's declaration of faith is even followed by a call to evangelize: 'It is the duty of the historian to teach this'. E. H. Carr was equally clear of his commitment. He wrote:

> For myself, I remain an optimist; and when Sir Lewis Namier warns me to eschew programmes and ideals, and Professor Oakeshott tells me that we are going nowhere in particular . . . I shall look out on a world in tumult and a world in travail, and shall answer in the well-worn words of a great scientist: 'And yet—it moves'.[38]

The existential nature of his choice could not be plainer.

The conclusion, therefore, is threefold. Meaning in history is not self-evident; no historian can be professionally agnostic and retain his integrity; every historian must make his own philosophical commitment.

Value systems vary from individual to individual, and other historians will see things differently and adopt different positions from Plumb and Carr; later in this chapter we shall look at what a Christian interpretation of history has to offer. But first we must ask whether the conclusion which has been arrived at means that there is nothing to choose between one view and another, and whether, because the significance which a historian embraces for history reflects his other personal value structure, individual historians are, in effect, free to pick whatever interpretation of the past happens to please them. But if that were the case, there would be no necessary connection between the substance of history and the significance assigned to it. The historian's view would be mere caprice or even something more dangerous. In Hitler's Germany the historical establishment embraced the racial interpretations of National Socialism and thereby committed history to giving a disastrous intellectual respectability to Nazi propaganda. The traducing of German national figures even became a punishable offence!

Philosophical commitment which is influenced by assumptions outside history must, therefore, in some way be validated by history. How is this possible? The example of the Third Reich suggests the answer. What went wrong was a failure to cross-check with the closed scholarly system which we have seen gives academic history its authority. Theory was advanced without reference to analysis—even more, it was used to pre-determine the results of that analysis. To return to the analogy of science having to exclude ecological issues from the laboratory, what was done in the history written in Nazi Germany was equivalent to allowing ecological theory to decide in advance what the result of an experiment would be.

The way, therefore, to separate admissible answers to the question 'What is the significance of history?' from those which are fantasy or worse is to test philosophical answers against academic analysis. The force of any such test will, of course, only be partial. As we have seen, a hypothesis such as 'progress' cannot be wholly demonstrated by historical method. What, however, we can expect a test to show is whether there are grounds to support the hypothesis. That is, the requirement is not that the theory shall be proved, but that it is historically tenable.

A sound application of that test would certainly have disqualified Aryan superiority as a motif which properly deserved consideration. Nothing in the record of the past would have supported such a theory. As it was, the point was left to be made by the world's athletes in the 1936 Olympic Games. In contrast, the hypothesis of progress embraced by Plumb and Carr is, prima facie, supported by some evidence, and is at least a possibility to which a degree of probability can be assigned. The historian, indeed, owes a moral responsibility to his community to test broad interpretations in this way and to demonstrate the level of plausibility which they achieve. The power of the assertion 'history proves that. . .' is not to be let loose lightly.

Christian approaches

The idea that history demonstrates human progress originated in the Enlightenment, but it did not spring fully armed from the head of Voltaire and his colleagues. It was, in fact, a secularized offshoot of the much older Christian understanding of history, and its characteristic linear pattern, confidence in the future and certainty as to unchanging moral values were features which it took over from its rejected parent.

The Christian metaphysic of history begins with words which have been recited for two millennia:

> I believe in one God, the Father, the Almighty, maker of heaven and earth, of all that is seen and unseen; and in one Lord Jesus Christ, the only Son of God. . . . For us men and for our salvation he came down from heaven . . . and was made man. For our sake he was crucified . . . and was buried. On the third day he rose again . . .; he ascended into heaven, and is seated at the right hand of the Father. He will come again in glory to judge the living and the dead and his kingdom will have no end.[39]

At first hearing this may seem a bare catalogue, but underlying it is a unifying concept—the idea of 'providence'. According to this, the universe as well as events of history operates by the continuous will of God, either positively or by permission.[40] In other words, belief in providence is not a conclusion drawn from observation of the human past, but from the postulated nature of a supreme deity, and from the Christian conviction that such a deity must necessarily be continuously involved in the world as creator and sustainer. Given that, the world and human society must reflect both the activity of God and the nature of God.

Christians understand the activity of God to be both linear (i.e. sequential) and particular, much as, in classical wave mechanics, light can be considered as a wave and as a particle. The linear dimension is an ongoing process of divine action in history which reached a climax in the Christ event and will culminate in an act of final divine self-revelation and triumph. The particular dimension is the interim significance of providential action; meaning does not wait for the final curtain—it exists also in each line of the script. Hence what Christians believe about God leads them to conclude that history must have a divine purpose.

In the same way as his activity, the impact of the nature of God is both through time and at each point in time. That impact is first of all ethical. If we conceive of the deity as consistent and of necessity characterized by integrity, it is impossible to conceive of his calling into existence or tolerating an ethically neutral order of creation, or acting in providence in a way which is not at the same time ethically directed. Again, therefore, what is believed about God leads to a conclusion about history—that it must exhibit the operation of morality.

The Christian understanding of the nature of God is, however, not limited to an ethical dimension. It is also seen as redemptive, that is, God's nature leads to activity positively directed to the benefit of the world and in particular to the rescue of men and women from their disastrous tendency to self-destruction. The name given to this divine commitment is 'grace'. Again it is sequential—evidenced in the centuries of preparation for the coming of Jesus Christ, the Son of God, in his life, death and resurrection, and in his ongoing life in the Church. Again, too, grace is immediate. It is experienced in particular instances and is in principle available in every circumstance.

Thus, the three pillars of a Christian view of history are purpose, morality and grace. To begin with 'purpose'. The Christian understanding is that the intention of God is to bring into existence 'the Kingdom of God', which, in relation to this chapter, can be described as nothing less than the re-creation of the human race and its environment. This calls for a new and expanding community of conviction, which consists of individuals who progressively develop, personally and collectively, the characteristics of Jesus Christ whom they follow. The operation of divine purpose, therefore, must be measured by the progress of personal and corporate spirituality and commitment, in the day-to-day decisions which individuals and groups of Christians make and in their orientation to issues and circumstances which from time to time face them.

Looking for evidence of this is, of course, difficult. The data required for this level of understanding are far too minute for the historian normally to detect. But one can, nevertheless, note possible consequences. The expansion of Christian belief shows no sign of slackening; it is the secularism of the West today which is out of line with the global trend. One can note, too, the resilience of Christian belief under pressure—even generations of pressure by the modern secular state. It is also possible to see throughout history a recurring tendency among Christians to move towards increased depth in their involvement, that is, towards commitment to the Gospel, not mere assent. One might also point to increased respect between Christians for diversities within human experience of the numinous, or their recognition of spirituality shared across barriers of tradition and culture.

The Christian claim that divine purpose, as well as functioning overall, functions in the particular, is closely associated with the second of the elements in the Christian view of history, the belief that morality operates in the world. This is not a crude notion of sin and retribution, but the conviction that, as Dietrich Bonhoeffer said:

> The world *is* simply ordered in such a way that a profound respect for the absolute laws and human rights is also the best means of self-preservation.[41]

That is, self-preservation demands a respect for morality or, put in the negative, disregard for morality brings its own penalty.

Historical examples of morality operating in this way are not hard to find. Herbert Butterfield argued that the catastrophic end of Hitlerite Germany was the penalty for Prussian militarism; it was certainly an actual consequence.[42] We might also say that the more widespread disaster produced by the Second World War was in part the penalty of vindictiveness at Versailles and national self-interestedness afterwards. It is also possible to suggest more long-term patterns of moral judgement. That 'the sins of the fathers are visited on the children to the third and fourth generation' is very evident in the struggles of the United States to cope with the consequences of slavery and the slave trade.

'Purpose', 'morality'—there remains the question of 'grace'. How can this be understood as operating in history? Natural disasters there have been in plenty, likewise, monstrous acts of human folly; it is entirely possible to sympathize with Voltaire when he wrote: 'History is nothing but a tableau of crimes and misfortunes'.[43] But humanity's errors have not had fatal results overall, despite its destructive capacity and selfish temper. No historian can do other than marvel at the capacity of the human spirit to survive. Nor is the past short of what earlier generations would have called 'special providences'. The historian may rightly point out that geography and advantages in raw material supply and industrial capacity meant that the Allies and not the Axis won the race to produce an atom bomb. But it is not patriotic nostalgia to feel that it was of profound importance for humanity that the West did get there first.

What is more, the record of history shows that human disaster has again and again been redeemed by becoming a base for something better. The Black Death led to the collapse of villeinage. The exhaustion of religious war produced religious toleration. Not that this somehow cancels out or mitigates the disaster. No one can deny that the Second World War was 'a sum total of virtually unimaginable human misery'.[44] But it is also undeniable that that war and its aftermath has put an end to the inter-state violence which has characterized Western Europe since the fifteenth century; partners in an integrated economy may quarrel, but they are unable to fight. And over and beyond the disasters of history there has been the ordinary business of mankind. As Butterfield observed:

> Millions of men in a given century, conscious of nothing save going about their own business, have together woven a fabric better in many respects than any of them knew.[45]

The Christian view of history is, thus, historically tenable, but in the light of the earlier discussion, it is not to be expected that its providential interpretation will present no difficulty. The notion of divine purpose is commonly questioned because persons claiming to be motivated by Christ have done a great deal of harm in history—although this can be countered by the observation that Christians have no entitlement to claim to be other than sinners needing salvation. A more fundamental doubt about divine purpose is posed by the situation which is the theme of this book—the marginalizing of religious issues in the very culture in which Christianity is rooted looks more like the demise than the progress of any Kingdom of God. There are conceptual problems too. It could, for example, be objected that divine purpose in the terms described has yet to have much impact on the vast continent of Asia.

The claim that morality operates in history has attracted very many sceptics. The cynicism: 'God is on the side of the big battalions' has been known since the days of Tacitus, while Machiavelli's argument that morality is a positive disadvantage to a ruler, except as a disguise, is certainly plausible. The Bible itself admits that the unrighteous frequently get away with it. As for the suggestion that morality operates as consequence: this seems to offend against justice; the sufferers are so often innocent victims. But, of course, if the Christian emphasis on the corporate entity of humanity is correct, and so too its understanding that human disobedience does corrupt the structure of society, the innocent will suffer; a plague is no respecter of virtue.

The concept of 'grace' is also easy to question. Edmund Blunden wrote:

> *I have been young, and now am not too old,*
> *And I have seen the righteous forsaken,*
> *His health, his honour and his quality taken.*
> *This is not what we were formerly told.*
>
> *I have seen a green country, useful to the race,*

Knocked silly with guns and mines, its villages vanished,
Even the last rat and last kestrel banished—
God bless us all, this was peculiar grace.[46]

Given Blunden's experience in the Flanders trenches, such cynicism is all too understandable. But the concept of divine 'grace' does not imply an insurance policy. The heart of the Christian understanding of history is that the supreme manifestation of grace was a crucifixion.

One must note, however, that the problems which the providential interpretation of history faces are the very ones which challenge the interpretation of history as 'progress', or, rather, the problems of each view arise from common sources. One such is human freedom. Progress 'is not a law of nature'; 'retrogressions are common'.[47] Nor is providence a law, imposing determinism; to deny choice, responsibility and the possibility of human error would reduce human beings to automata. 'Grace' likewise, is resistible; it is not a cocoon which protects men and women from the consequences of humanity or from the fact that they live in an environment they do not control—or even more dangerous, imagine that they do. Then there is the reality of the selfish and atavistic instincts in individuals and societies. That 'the thoughts of men may flow into the channels which lead to disaster and barbarism' is a challenge to 'progress' and 'providence' alike.[48]

The contention of this chapter has been that a Christian understanding of history is a serious interpretative option. That it is so often ignored is not because of instrinsic improbability but because of two elements in contemporary thinking: the domination of naturalistic and materialistic presuppositions, and the refusal even of historians who would question such assumptions to venture outside their academic specialisms.

A sceptic, of course, may say that the argument has amounted to demonstrating that there are deficiencies in all interpretations and that the holes in the Christian case are no worse than in any other. He may further assert that the rational position is that whatever people may wish or feel a need to believe about 'significance' or 'purpose' in the past, history has nothing to say about it. The subject does not exist at that macro-level of explanation; that is the province of philosophy and theology. Meaning in history is a concept which only makes sense at the micro-level, within the confines of the academic discipline. The general public must accept that history will not give it the broad interpretative hypotheses it is looking for.

An objection of this kind promises a quiet life, but the cost will be far more serious than a loss of popular respect for the subject. A reductionist approach imposes total detachment. This, at first hearing, may appear to be no bad thing. The goal of history is objectivity. The subject can, as we have seen, never be entirely unsubjective, but if historians firmly refuse to entertain anything above the micro-level of explanation, that danger might for practical purposes become insignificant. The siren voice is clear. But consider the implications.

The *locus classicus* is the Jewish Holocaust. Historians who turn their back on meaning will, along with the rest of their colleagues, be expected to discuss the philosophy and planning behind the 'Final Solution', the numbers involved, the development and refinement of the necessary techniques, transport, the bureaucratic machinery which was set up (and its efficiency), management, staffing, staff psychology and motivation, the pros and cons of the operation in relation to the war-effort of the Third Reich, the handling of propaganda, the cost, and the profit or loss. But they cannot say that this was a monstrous evil. Colleagues may, who do not share this detachment, but professionalism requires the former to be totally indifferent between the SS and their victims; since they deny that there is any significance in history, what was done or not done is wholly immaterial.

Simply to state the position is to demonstrate its impossibility. To adopt it would be an affront to the historian's humanity. What is more, it would amount to a surrender to the Nazi way of looking at the issue. On the Holocaust, detachment is not a civilized option. And only the Holocaust? The conclusion is inescapable. History only becomes a possible humane activity if it does recognize values.[49]

It is here that the Christian interpretation of history has a very distinct advantage. It is appalled by the Holocaust, but it is not surprised. If 'progress' is the theme of history, such episodes, as we have seen, deny, not demonstrate, the hypothesis; human potential seems to be one of the great 'might-have-beens'. Alternatively, if history is the story of man's struggle against the environment, here was mankind turned upon itself.

In contrast, the Christian understanding of history comprehends both the good and the bad. It expects nothing of man; it has neither hopes nor illusions. History reveals men and women as it knows them to be; it does not need them to be rational and humane. Indeed, it recognizes that the non-rational and the irrational is natural in man. It starts not with man as he ought to be, but man as he is; it allows for, even expects evil as well as glory from a flawed humanity. Spinoza pointed out that the requirement is 'not to laugh at human actions, not to weep at them, nor to hate them, but to understand them'.[50] This the Christian approach to history does. And, something more. Not only does it understand women and men, both as individuals and in society, comprehensively and realistically, it believes that something has been done about, rather, done for them and their follies, and is being done and will be done. The Christian understanding of history, while it is the least optimistic, offers the greatest hope.

The argument of this chapter has been that the Christian interpretation of history vindicates the essential morality of existence and gives shape and purpose to history. Of course the Christian hypothesis requires faith—but so does any other interpretation of history. The widespread ignoring of the Christian approach is not because faith is not necessary, but because religious faith is ruled out of consideration. It is by-passed because of the dominance of secular thought-patterns, not because of a careful scrutiny of what it says.

But the Christian understanding of history does not merely require faith, like all the rest. It gives historical grounds for faith. It stands or falls by the historicity of the life, death and resurrection of Jesus Christ, an issue which will not go away. And in consequence the commitment it requires is more than intellectual preference. Faith echoes the existential commitment of a first-century Jew who threw himself away in the faith that the world and human affairs were in the hands of God, and in so doing revolutionized both.

Notes

1 'Hear, O Israel, the Lord is our God, the Lord is our one God; and you must love the Lord your God . . .'; 'There is no God but Allah, and Mohammed is his prophet'.

2 J.H. Plumb, *The Death of the Past* (1973), p. 84.

3 Anon. in R.L. Green (ed.), *A Century of Humorous Verse, 1850–1950* (1959).

4 Quoted in D.W. Bebbington, *Patterns in History* (1979), p. 74.

5 James Boswell, *Life of Johnson*, ed. L.B. Powell (1934), i.424.

6 Cicero, *De Oratore* (Loeb, 1917), p. 234.

7 John Foxe, *Acts and Monuments* (1869), iii.373.

8 R.G. Collingwood, *The Idea of History* (Oxford, 1946), quoted from P. Gardiner (ed.), *Theories of History* (Glencoe, IL, 1959), p. 255. It is not necessary in recognizing the truth of Collingwood's illustration to follow him in his assertion that '*only in so far as*' the historian re-enacts 'in his own mind the experience of the emperor . . . has he any historical knowledge, as distinct from a merely philological knowledge of the edict'.

9 J.E.E.D.-Acton, on the proposed Cambridge Modern History, quoted in F. Stern (ed.), *The Varieties of History* (1956), p. 249.

10 Samuel Butler, *Erewhon Revisited*.

11 Joseph Butler, *The Analogy of Religion* (1756).

12 A.N. Sherwin-White, *Roman Society and Roman Law in the New Testament* (Oxford, 1963), pp. 187–8.

13 C.H. Dodd, *The Apostolic Preaching and Its Development* (1963), p. 56.

14 D. Hume, *Essays Moral, Political and Literary*, ed. T.H. Green and T.H. Grose (1875), ii.93.

15 M. Ramsey, *The Resurrection of Christ* (1945), pp. 30–3.

16 The eighteenth-century German thinker Gotthold Lessing has been credited with undermining the assurance of the Church by his dictum that, because they are only probabilities, 'accidental truths of history can never become the proof of necessary truths of reason': H. Chadwick, *Lessing's Theological Writings* (1956), p. 31. The remark had an impact only because of Enlightenment assumptions that truths could be proved. I would agree that history does deal in probabilities.

17 J.G. Davies, *The Early Christian Church* (1965), p. 28.

18 NB: the argument that knowledge advances by being disproved, not by being proved. Countless sightings of white swans will not establish that 'all swans are white'; a single sighting of a black swan will disprove it.

19 The claim that the very early Christian formula or *kerygma* 'Christ died . . . was buried . . . raised' (1 Corinthians 15.3–4) indicates belief in his death and resurrection but not in an empty tomb appears perverse; cf. the earliest Gospel account 'He has been raised; he is not here; look, there is the place where they laid him' (Mark 16.6). The limited attention which the early Church gave to the empty tomb was because at most that was only corroborative of the truth which really mattered—that Christ was alive.

20 Paul's interpretation of baptizing a convert (by immersion) as a symbol of being united with Christ in burial and raised to share his new life (Romans 6.3–5) necessarily implies belief that Christ left the tomb.

21 The tradition is known by the rebuttal attempted in Matthew 28.11–15.

22 Ramsey, *Resurrection of Christ*, p. 53.

23 Ibid., p. 55.

24 It is this which makes improbable the theory that a handful of disciples kept their delusions alive in secret until, with the link with the original events broken, the Christian myth became a convenient vehicle to express sociological and other pressures in the Roman world.

25 H.A.L. Fisher, *History of Europe* (1936), p. v.

26 Leopold Ranke, *Histories of the Latin and Germanic Nations, 1494–1514* (1824), quoted in Stern (ed.), *Varieties of History*, p. 57.

27 A.J. Toynbee, *An Historian's Approach to Religion* 2nd edn (Oxford, 1979), pp. 13–14.

28 Fisher, *History*, p. v.

29 A.J. Toynbee, *A Study of History* (1934–54) argued that history operated by a natural process of challenge and response, either physical or intellectual/spiritual: 'the greater the challenge, the greater the stimulus' (quoted in *Theories of History*, p. 310). Marx's 'materialist conception of history' argued that socio-economic struggle was the dynamic of history (*Communist Manifesto* (1848)). He derived part of his thinking from Hegel, who argued that the goal of history was freedom (i.e. a rationally organized society with which each citizen identified and so experienced neither alienation nor constraint) and that history progressed towards this by the operation of dialectic. The status quo ('thesis') engenders a challenge ('antithesis') producing a new situation ('synthesis') which is challenged in turn, etc. Thus struggle, for Hegel, was the means by which progress was achieved.

30 Toynbee also argued in *A Study of History* for a pattern of the growth, breakdown and dissolution of civilizations, of which he identified 21. Most critics concluded that this was a heroic effort of selectivity.

31 Acton, quoted in Bebbington, *Patterns in History*, p. 88; H. Spencer, *Social Statics* (1850), i.4.

32 J. Huxley, *Evolution in Action* (1963), p. 139.

33 E.H. Carr, *What Is History?* (1964), p. 132.

34 Ibid., p. 119.

35 World Watch Institute, *Progress Towards a Sustainable Society* (New York, 1991), p. 188.

36 I. Kant, *Idea of a Universal History from a Cosmopolitan Point of View* (1784), repr. in Gardiner (ed.), *Theories of History*, p. 23.

37 Plumb, *Death of the Past*, p. 113.

38 Carr, *What Is History?*, p. 156.

39 Version promoted by the International Consultation on English Texts.

40 The key words in the Creed are 'maker of heaven and earth', which imply continuous action, not a single creation.

41 D. Bonhoeffer, *Letters . . . from Prison*, ed. E. Bethge (1959), pp. 141–2.

42 H. Butterfield, *Christianity and History* (1949), pp. 49–50.

43 Voltaire, *L'Ingénu* (1767), ch. 10.

44 J.A.S. Grenville, *A World History of the Twentieth Century, 1900–45* (1980), p. 526.

45 Butterfield, *Christianity and History*, p. 96.

46 E. Blunden, 'Report on Experience', from J. Hayward (ed.), *The Penguin Book of English Verse* (1956), p. 450.

47 See above, notes 28, 37.

48 See above, note 28.

49 It is noticeable, however, that historians are much more detached about suffering in the more distant past.

50 Baruch Spinoza, *Tractatus Politicus* (1677), 1.iv.

Strange contest: science versus religion

MARY MIDGLEY

Does it make sense for science and religion to be seen as competitors, struggling for a single position? Their functions might seem too different for this conflict to be possible. Yet in our culture at present people often take it for granted that they are so, and suppose that it is clear which boxer is the current world champion. I would like here to look more closely at the assumptions which make this strange view possible.

I shall attend chiefly to assumptions about the nature and position of science, because these seem to me much odder, much wilder than is usually noticed. We are used to the idea that *religion* is logically insecure, and people who say this tend to have the unspoken feeling 'Why can't it be more like science?' But should an elephant try to be like a concrete-mixer? And are we clear about just what kind of a concrete-mixer science is meant to be anyway? Let us have a brief look at some things that this approach confidently takes for granted.

The standing of knowledge

First, why is knowledge so important to us? Why does our culture value it so peculiarly highly? Of course we are not alone in esteeming knowledge, nor in using very sophisticated thinking to reach it. What is unique about us is simply the high priority that we officially set on knowledge over various other values or ideals, along with a narrow view of its nature which separates it off fairly sharply from them. Knowledge, in this isolation, becomes no longer a part of other values, but a rival competing for supremacy with them. This competition tends to splinter our lives into a set of disconnected activities, pursuing divergent aims. The intellect is exalted, but no longer knows how it should relate to the rest of the personality.

I am not saying anything new in mentioning this danger. The Greeks saw it as soon as they began the special intellectual development which has marked European culture, and it already alarmed Aristotle. He made impressive efforts to bring intellectual ideals back into harmony with other human aims by stressing the interdependence of mind and body, reason and feeling, form and matter, divinity and the physical cosmos, in a way that has been quite widely followed.

But many on both sides of the divide have not wanted to pay the costs of his reconciling methods. The gap between champions of intellectual skills and those devoted to other aspects of life has continued to widen, and in the last two centuries bridging it has grown much harder. This has meant that the concept of knowledge itself has changed. The old, wide notion of knowledge or learning as an aspect of wisdom—an element in the whole spiritual life which the West once largely shared with other cultures, has gradually shifted and narrowed to crystallize in the ideal of science. This too has been narrowed, so that it is now often conceived as simply exact information about the physical world, acquired professionally by experts using experimental methods.

At a glance, this shift might have been expected to lower the public prestige of science automatically, since the scientific aim has now become something evidently smaller, and something that far fewer people even pretend to understand or appreciate. It might have seemed natural for science to appear no longer as something vast, sacred and mysterious, near the top of the hierarchy of values, but merely—like the study of history or language—as an impressive sectional interest with some very useful spin-offs.

If the public status of science had been seen as contracting in this way, it would of course have been much less likely to appear as competing with religion. But it was not so seen; it still held its high place. This continued high respect was no doubt largely a result of its enormous usefulness. Champions of modern science have indeed quite rightly stressed its usefulness as well as its splendour. (Galileo himself was, after all, an engineer working on the flight of cannonballs, and Bacon dwelt much on the hope of truly scientific medicine.) But there has also been, equally from the start, a strong claim that, in itself and apart from consequences, scientific activity has a very high spiritual value, that it is an end in itself. And it is this that is most obviously liable to bring science—or at least 'the scientific world-view'—into competition with religion.

The notion of a high spiritual value for science did not need to be invented by the scientific propagandists of the Renaissance; it existed already in the tradition. Plato and Aristotle bequeathed to later scholars a tremendous reverence for thought as such, an exaltation of contemplation over outward action as the highest human function. They believed that it contained the true end of life. In their tradition, indeed, that reverence was explained by the still greater exaltation of the objects that were being contemplated.[1] The Platonic Forms and Aristotle's ensouled universe were themselves venerated as effectively divine; to contemplate and wonder at them was also to worship. Knowledge was not separated from love. And at the Renaissance this aspect of learning did not vanish, since the physical world was still seen as God's creation and to study it was still to contemplate his glory—a point central to Newton.

This rationale for venerating science has, however, gradually been lost, until finally the whole value has come to be attributed to human thought itself. The emphasis is no longer on knowing things that are themselves of special value, but simply on knowing *something* securely, exactly, with absolute certainty. Increasingly, too, this value has been treated as self-evident, self-justifying, needing no explanation. Today, accordingly, we quite often find a strange situation where knowledge about the physical universe is treated as obviously the supreme human achievement, although the thing known—the physical universe itself—is regarded as mere dead matter, having no value at all, and no creator behind it. What is venerated is then simply the human scientific intellect. Science is thus revered by people who, in theory at least, do not revere anything else, not even the object of science.[2] Its value is displayed, not as part of a wider pattern of human ideals, but in stark isolation.

The shrinking pedestal

Examples of this process are very common, but I must content myself with two, divided by a generation and showing two distinct phases of its development. In *The Scientific Attitude*, published in 1941, Conrad Waddington wrote:

> Science *by itself* is able to provide mankind with a way of life which is, firstly, self-consistent and harmonious, and secondly, free for the exercise of that objective reason on which our material progress depends. So far as I can see, the scientific attitude of mind is *the only* one which is, at the present day, adequate in both these respects. There are many other worthy ideals which might supplement it; but I cannot see that any of them could take its place as the basis of a progressive and rich society.
>
> (*The Scientific Attitude*, Penguin, 1941, p. 170. Emphases mine)

At this stage, Waddington still allowed other aspects of life to play some part in supplementing science. Moreover, what he counted as germane to 'science' itself was much wider than would be generally allowed today. It included, for instance, much of Freudian and some of Marxist theory, and—most emphatically—modern art, especially architecture, also modern poetry. It was a general attitude to life. Nevertheless, as the words I have italicized make clear, he saw it as only one among several possible quite distinct attitudes, faced by rivals that would wrest the supreme position from it if they were allowed to. These were what he saw as traditional humanistic and religious approaches to life. Instead of trying to relate these to the scientific attitude within a larger whole, Waddington saw them as rival horses which had failed in the race, and which must now give place to the winner.

Thirty years later, however, the isolation and exaltation of science had grown much more complete than this. Describing it, Jacques Monod painted in the darkest possible colours the Existentialist picture of humanity abandoned by its gods and stripped of all its 'animist' hopes:

> Man must wake out of his millennary dream, and discover his total solitude, his fundamental isolation. He must realise that, like a gypsy, he lives on the boundary of an alien world; a world that is deaf to his music, and as indifferent to his hopes as it is to his sufferings or his crimes.
>
> Who then is to define crime? Who decides what is good and what is evil? . . . Now he is master of (values) they seem to be dissolving in the uncaring emptiness of the universe.[3]
>
> (*Chance and Necessity*, tr. Austryn Wainhouse, Collins/Fontana, 1974, p. 160)

Astonishingly enough, however, Monod, having tied himself in this desperate knot, suddenly gives one bound and is free. There is, he explains, just one value that still keeps its reality while all the rest dissolve, namely knowledge. How can knowledge do this? Monod's explanations are not particularly lucid:

> True knowledge is ignorant of values, but it has to be grounded on a value judgment, or rather on an *axiomatic* value . . . In order to establish the *norm* for knowledge, the objectivity principle defines a *value*; that value is objective knowledge itself . . . The ethic of knowledge . . . puts forward a transcendent value, true knowledge, not for the use of man, but for man to serve from deliberate and conscious choice.
>
> (Ibid., pp. 163–5. The emphases this time are Monod's, and are part of a somewhat frantic typographical display designed to make sure that everything is perfectly clear.)

What about other values?

By his absolute isolation of science, Monod saved scientists the trouble of even attempting—as Waddington had done—to relate the importance of their activity to other human aims and ideals. That isolation is what now makes discussion of the actual value of science so hard. The claim to supremacy is treated as self-evident and unchallengeable. But, as usually happens with claims to self-evidence, the plausibility is actually due to a long tradition of argument which once explained the basis of the judgement, and which has now made it habitual. ('We hold these truths to be self-evident', cried the authors of the American Declaration of Independence—stating claims that would certainly not look self-evident in most cultures.) As usual, too, this claim carries a considerable burden of humbug. Hardly anybody, in their actual lives, treats the quest for scientific truth as a project entitled to prevail over all other values—say, over art, over freedom, over justice, over love—or thinks that other people ought to do so. And many of the greatest scientists, notably Einstein, have devoted much of their lives to other aims that they thought more important.

The refuge of scepticism

How do we, and how should we, really relate the goals of science to other human goals? This is a difficult question, because, in our time, the whole business of comparing and relating values in a disciplined way has dropped out of the academic scene. We live in a culture with a tremendous devotion to means, and an extremely poor vocabulary for talking about ends. The sort of moral discussion that came perfectly naturally not just to Victorians like T. H. Huxley but also to the great generation of Marxist savants that includes Needham, Bernal, Waddington, J. B. S. Haldane—is now so sternly excluded from the curriculum of most respectable scientists that they haven't the faintest idea how to conduct it even when they want to. Philosophers also (to their shame) have allowed themselves to become so over-specialized that they too are liable to mutter 'not my subject'. Moral philosophy, which might seem the one discipline unable to evade these questions, was conducted in English-speaking countries for much of this century on sceptical, irrationalist lines which were designed to exclude them. (There is now a welcome revival of 'applied ethics' and some other signs of returning health.)

This withdrawal has not just been a by-product of academic specialization; more profoundly, it expresses current popular moral ideas. Here official scepticism acts (as it always does) as a cover for undisciplined dogmatism. A general sense that moral confusion is incurable has resulted in a loose mix of positions in which (social) relativism, (individual) subjectivism and a general sceptical destructiveness are used equally and uncritically to marginalize other people's moral and metaphysical judgements by treating them as undiscussable personal quirks. ('It's all a matter of your own subjective point of view.'[4])

In this painful confusion, 'science' has seemed to provide a refuge, because it is supposed to be—by definition—certain and clear. Indeed, it is even supposed to be unanimous, odd though that may be in the presence of so much scientific doubt and controversy. There is therefore enormous pressure to use it somehow as a base for an ideology that will be able to fill the agonizing gap by providing practical guidance. Already in the last century, ideologies began to claim to be 'scientific'. Prophets such as Comte, Marx, Freud, J.B. Watson and H.G. Wells convinced themselves and their followers that they were not only using scientific data, but were extending the actual methods of science to deal with vital central areas of life traditionally handled by faith. Questions about what we are and how we ought to live would now (they said) no longer need religious solutions, no longer involve agonizing personal doubts and struggles. They could be settled vicariously and impersonally by suitably trained experts.

This hope could not last. The mere number of different, conflicting supposedly scientific solutions to life's vaster problems soon undermined all their claims to final, impersonal authority. Many scholars, too, did not want to see themselves as ideologists at all but as scientists in a narrower sense, and saw the supposed extension of scientific methods to problems of salvation as moonshine. But if they wanted to say that it was moonshine—to cut off science securely from all such speculations—they could not just speak in scientific terms, for science in their narrow sense contains no language for such questions. They too needed philosophical arguments, in fact they too needed an ideology. They moved gradually from traditional Comtian Positivism, which claimed to bring spiritual matters under the dominion of science, to logical-positivist positions which put such matters outside the province of thought altogether. The resulting muddled metaphysic still underlies many of our problems today.

Separating facts from values: the Boo—Hurray theory

With disarming simplicity, logical positivism claimed that only statements which could be verified in sense-perception had meaning; these alone described facts. Value-judgements, along with religious judgements and many other kinds of pronouncement, had no meaning and could properly be called nonsensical. Their function was purely emotive; to express feelings and to rouse the feelings of others. Science, by summing up the factual data derived from sense-perception, would then ideally codify all that could meaningfully be said. All discourse about anything else such as values or religious matters was not only rigidly excluded from this well-lit realm; it was also radically disconnected from it. There could (it was ruled) be no reasoning from facts to values. Thus, any statement about a particular set of facts (for instance, 'He wants to crush and dominate the entire universe') was in principle perfectly compatible with any value-judgement about them (for instance, 'Hurrah; what a wise and constructive policy'). The attribution of values did not involve the intellect at all.[5]

These bizarre views on the way that human life and human language work were never put in a very coherent form. Like other confused ideologies, they got a fairly cold reception from the learned. But the public liked them, and they are still surprisingly influential, especially among scientists. It is interesting to ask why this should be. What did the sharp, unrealistic division between facts and values offer that was really needed?

It appeared, I think, as a much-needed attempt at a traffic regulation which would stop the authority of science from being misused to back all sorts of irrelevant propaganda and which would, among other advantages, save science from being brought into bogus conflicts with religion. But this project was crippled from the start by the fact that many of the participants still half-wanted those conflicts to take place, and to be won by science. Scepticism about value-judgements, if it were thoroughgoing, would make it impossible to go on laying down one's own value-judgements as simple matters of fact, as both Waddington and Monod did. The partiality which was ready to use the emotive word 'nonsense' for everything non-scientific was not compatible with a genuine division of spheres. If that division was to be attempted, it had to be made in a much more sensitive, realistic manner. Facts can indeed often be separated from values for convenience of argument. But it makes no sense to suggest that these facts are only found in science, nor that they are permanently separated from values by an ultimate, unbridgeable logical and conceptual gulf.

Facts and the law

To explain: there are many circumstances where we need to separate off decisions about 'the facts'—the data—from decisions about how we should now react to them. The most obvious one, and a prime model for the fact–value distinction, is in the law courts. The jury decides the facts; the judge then says how the law directs us to treat them. But this situation is completely different from the one suggested for facts and values. Law courts don't radically divide off the province of reason from the province of action. Nobody supposes that the function of law is merely to shout boo and hurray at random. Judges, as well as juries, use a complex intellectual system—the law—with rules referring to both elements. And the relation between that system and the one which establishes 'the facts' is not some mysterious existential gap, as Monod suggested. It comes from a background culture, and underlying that culture a community of species, in which all parties share. Jurors are also voters. It is not just by some arbitrary chance that the law considers deliberate killing—rather than sneezing or using china plates—to be a crime. It does so because of a publicly understood set of reasons that can in principle be explained.

By contrast, *the division between facts and values is conceived as placed at the extreme border of the rational.* The emotivist-style ethics used here treats all value-judgements as simply arbitrary, individual, existential leaps in the dark. It dismisses the apparent moral arguments that may be used to support them as not real arguments but either just persuasive techniques—manipulative moves in social engineering (Ayer and C.L. Stevenson)—or concealed calculations of consequences (R.M. Hare).[6] It recognizes no standards of validity in moral reasoning; indeed, no such thing as moral reasoning at all.

Another oddity of this total separation of facts from values is that it treats all 'facts' as scientific facts. Thus, while all practical thinking is pushed right off the platform of serious thought, all theoretical truths— including presumably, those of history, geography and so forth—count as science. The boundaries of science then embrace everything that thought can handle at all. This is really quite incompatible with the much narrower official conception of 'science' (evolved largely by Karl Popper) that is in vogue today, the conception in which controlled experimental method is central. By that narrow criterion, most facts are not part of any science. Historical and geographical knowledge and most of anthropology, as well as the simple direct certainties of the senses and memory in daily life, are then non-scientific, and the firm boundary of 'facts' becomes utterly misty. Yet the inertia of reverence for science—the hope that it can supply a safe ship to carry us through all our confusions—is so strong that contradictions like these are scarcely noticed.

And so on. It may seem tiresome, at this time of day, to dwell further on the weaknesses of logical-positivist thinking. Academics have indeed long ceased to defend its confusions, but it is still powerful. Though its logic was quickly exposed, its general message was never refuted in a manner understandable to the heart. Part of the reason for this persistence was no doubt the insight we started from—a sense that there should indeed be *some* division made between the province of science and that of the faiths by which we live.

The problems of bias

Can we do better?

It may help us to begin with the most obvious cases—the places where we now see fairly clearly that there has been trespass. On one side, we can see that the Church authorities did indeed mistake their function in so far as they tried to decide the facts about the Copernican hypothesis on theological grounds, against Galileo;[7] and that Creationists are doing so today about the age of the earth. On the other side, scientists who have claimed to justify racism, sexism and economic injustice by producing scientific arguments to establish the natural inferiority of oppressed classes have equally mistaken the function of science by trying to use it to shore up a weak moral position.

These particular excesses may indeed strike us as just internal offences, breaches of the disciplines to which they officially belong. Racism is surely bad science; equally, creationism is bad theology. Here, however, we begin to see difficulties, because these judgements do depend partly on the way in which those disciplines are themselves conceived, and that involves a moral, metaphysical and factual background. For instance, should we say that, if one were a thoroughly convinced racist, one ought no more to think racist propaganda irrelevant in biology textbooks than we now think medical textbooks are propagandist because they assume that the purpose of medicine is to heal, rather than to be used by torturers? In a trivial sense this is true: that is, it does describe the racist's view. But this does *not* mean—as people are now inclined to think—that we therefore cannot argue against racism. That argument is a different argument with a different background, a wider field of action. To deal with it, we would need to move right away from the particular controversy (about IQs, or skull sizes, or the like) to general considerations about what people are and how we ought to treat them. Today, academic specialization makes it terribly hard for the learned to do this.

Unconscious metaphysics

Things grow even harder when we move away to more doubtful and less obvious cases, which often concern large-scale metaphysical problems. Sweeping views on how the world actually is are unconsciously adopted because they are thought to be implied by scientific method. They are in fact *presuppositions* of that method, made for its convenience, but they are taken to be its results—facts 'proved by science'.

A very interesting example is determinism. Many people in the West believe or suspect—even if unwillingly—that science has proved that we do not really have free will, that our apparent experiences of choosing are just an illusion. Quite what this means is obscure, but the general idea is that science has revealed a kind of cast-iron necessity by which our thoughts and actions are merely effects forced on us by outside causes—perhaps by movements of molecules in our bodies, or by our state of health, or by economic factors, or by social conditioning. We ourselves are therefore somehow deluded and powerless.

Now causal necessity is certainly not a fact; it is a metaphysical pre-supposition. As many empiricists have pointed out (notably Hume),[8] it is actually a rather extravagant and mysterious presupposition which is quite hard to justify. Experience, said Hume, only tells us what (up till now) *has* happened; it cannot possibly tell us that what must happen, nor indeed what words like 'must' could possibly mean. Necessity, he concluded, is the work of the mind.

Hume's position is itself by no means a clear one, but he is surely right to raise sharp questions about the highly dramatized concept of necessity on which the determinist is so confidently relying. To make use of these questions, we do not have to plunge into the vortex of general scepticism for which Hume was headed. We only have to ask what is really involved in this notion of being *forced*. The idea of a cause as meaning that something is *forced* to happen is surely confused and anthropomorphic. The scientific idea of a force, as used in physics, is not the idea of a dramatized power struggle—of compulsion prevailing over a will or driving a helpless being or an unconscious machine—but simply a generalization about regular sequences of events. It is quite as correct, or more so, to say that our molecules, or our social conditioning or whatever, provide the material for our choices as that they force them on us.

The question about determinism is much more one about the language we choose to use—meaning not just the words but the whole conceptual scheme that goes with them—than about how the world really is. There is not just one right way of thinking about human choice. We need to think about it in different ways for different purposes. For instance, we need to think very differently when we are trying to understand what brought about particular choices made by other people in the past, and when we are wondering what choice our own group ought to make now. It has been said that it is best to believe in free will for oneself and determinism for other people, and this is not half so silly a remark as it may sound. All conceptual schemes are incomplete, and for each kind of problem we need to choose the one which brings out the kind of point most relevant for the particular difficulties before us.

When we are discussing cases where the effect of certain causes is specially important and has been neglected, we may indeed want to speak of people being forced. But then we are doing so in the ordinary sense. Thus prophets such as Hobbes, Marx, Skinner and Freud are trying to make us aware of factors, both outside and inside our own motivation, that affect us much more than we suppose. And it is true that if one is being moved by something one is quite unaware of, one is indeed being forced into action without one's proper consent.

In modern times, these prophets tend to make their point by using that potent Renaissance metaphor of machines—clockwork—a set of cogs that, once started, pushes the grass or wood or whatever into place by an implacable 'force'. This, however, is a metaphor, not a literal statement of fact, and like other metaphors it is incomplete and tendentious. Machines are by definition things designed by someone, and all machinery can in principle be stopped or redirected. This is important, because prophets like these are actually calling on us to take action which will *change* this ineluctable course of events. This causes logical confusion in their writing, which they deal with as best they can, but which always continues to stand out as a clear sign that this metaphysic has been distorted by its own metaphors.

Is the useful always true?

Trying to think it out a little better, we must of course ask: How far does the fact that a presupposition—for instance, determinism—has been successfully used for science, imply that it is actually true? In general, successful use plainly does imply that a proposition contains some truth, but not that it is true as a whole. People who live near a tar-well and believe strongly enough that it contains a malignant demon will be saved from its dangers, but that does not make the demon real. Again, flat-earthers for whom the sun moves across a solid firmament can conduct their lives as successfully as the rest of us, and better than people who suppose that, because they live on a round earth out in space, they are in constant danger of falling off or being attacked by alien beings. Again—to take an example from within science itself—chemistry based on a belief in phlogiston endowed with negative weight was in many ways mistaken, but it helped to make possible a clearer notion of chemical elements.

In cases like these, we shall probably want to say that what made the mistaken belief useful was that it contained a part of the real truth. But it is often quite hard to say just what that part is, even after the mistake is located. The whole truth is usually something so large and complicated that we will never have stated it properly. A couple more examples may make it a little clearer how this works with the metaphysical presuppositions of science.

The negative path

One very interesting case concerns the attitude of contemporary physicists to cosmic questions involving purpose. Until quite lately, it was widely held that what made modern physics so superior to its Greek and mediaeval predecessors was largely—perhaps chiefly—its determined refusal to raise questions about purpose at all. The dramatic success of Galileo, Newton and the rest was held to grow from their rejection of teleology and final causes. Quite suddenly of late, however, thoughts about the Big Bang have begun to raise such questions. The drama has been put back into cosmology.

Current theories are held to show that, when that bang took place, it was highly improbable that events should be such as to lead to the present state of the universe. Now one might respond to this information in various ways. We might simply point out that all existing total states of affairs are highly and perhaps equally improbable. Or we might get, suspicious about the account of bangery which shows this sequel to be specially improbable. What we would *not* be expected to do, if we grasped the methods of the science, is to revive the argument from design, suddenly and without much apology, under the name of the Strong Anthropic Principle—to conclude blandly that the whole cosmic performance must be somehow designed to make possible the eventual existence of human beings who, by doing physics, will bring the cosmos finally to its consummation in an orgy of information-storage, thus:

> At the instant the Omega Point is reached, life will have gained control of *all* matter and forces not only in a single universe, but in all universes whose existence is logically possible; life will have spread into *all* spatial regions of all universes which could logically exist, and will have stored an infinite amount of information, including *all* bits of information which it is logically possible to know. And this is the end.
>
> *Footnote.* A modern-day theologian might wish to say that the totality of life at the Omega Point is omnipotent, omnipresent and omniscient!
>
> (John D. Barrow and Frank R. Tipler, *The Anthropic Cosmological Principle*, Oxford University Press, 1986, concluding passage. Emphases are the authors'.)

Still less would one expect serious cosmologists to claim that a solution to their problems would reveal 'the mind of God',[9] without even discussing the word 'God' or adding it to the terms they explain in their glossary.

This is not just teleology; it is bad, careless, quite undisciplined teleology. It is a huge, vague, unconsidered metaphysical move. Psychologically speaking, it is not a surprising move, because it shows how natural and perhaps unavoidable teleological thinking is to us. But in relation to the official doctrines that excluded purpose from physics, it is a real explosion. For those doctrines had been widely regarded, up till now, not just as expedient conventions about method, but as statements of scientifically discovered truth. The fact that physicists did not investigate purpose in the universe was commonly taken as meaning that they had proved that it was not there.

This is a typical example of a main way in which the methods of science have been seen as settling metaphysical issues—the negative path. If a science (or at least a particular science, or at least physics) excludes something from its considerations, this tends to be taken as showing that that thing does not really exist. When, by contrast, people practising this same science begin to talk as if cosmic purpose exists, there is at once a widespread impression that they have proved it does so. But all that they have actually done is to change their presupposition, in many cases without, apparently, even noticing it.

Another obvious example is, of course, the mind or soul. Modern biology rightly separated body from soul for the limited purpose of understanding the 'mechanisms' of the body. In this it relied on parsimony, and it did—after a long delay—finally succeed, during the nineteenth century, in producing some effective treatment of disease. Many, accordingly, took the success of these methods to prove that the soul or mind did not exist, and the early Behaviourists delightedly expanded this by adding that consciousness did not exist either. This conclusion turned out to raise marked difficulties. ('How am I? You're very well thank you . . .', etc.) Yet the reasons for arriving at the Behaviourist dead-end were every bit as good as the earlier ones—namely, that consciousness was something not mentioned in biological science. The ill-effects of trying to deal with bodies as if no minds or souls were entangled with them have become clear in many areas of medicine, and indeed in other departments of life.

In fact, the success of the physical sciences always depends on their deliberately limiting their scope, on their refraining from mentioning most of what goes on, so as to concentrate their methods on the limited aspects that they are able to handle. Currently fashionable metaphysics, however, is structured throughout by treating these omissions of the sciences as if they were proofs of non-existence, by treating Occam's razor, not just as a methodological device, but as the sole tool needed to describe the world.

Another example which may be briefly mentioned is social atomism, the idea that the scientific way to consider communities is as loose assemblies of egoistic individuals held together only by contract: 'the state is a logical construction out of its members'. While there are of course many other reasons for the popularity of this idea—some of them indeed laudable ones—the notion that it is always scientific to explain large wholes by dissecting them and examining their smallest elements has certainly contributed.

Religion does not stand alone

All these are examples of ways in which people in our culture manage to see science as shaping their whole conceptual schemes, as dictating what ways of thinking are legitimate for them to use even on their widest and most practically important problems. This idea still persists, even though they also suppose it to deal only in proven facts about the physical world. The fact–value division does not prevent this confusion, because metaphysical assumptions are treated as facts, and the apparent new-found ability of the physical sciences to prove these vast facts—indeed, to absorb metaphysics into physics—is seen as just one more sign of its amazing powers.

How, then, does all this affect Christianity? Not very differently, I suggest, from how it affects a great mass of other vital human concerns, for instance, metaphysics and ethics, literature and literary criticism, history, geography, psychology and anthropology, politics and political theory and child-rearing. In all these provinces of life and many others, the unconsidered pursuit of a supposedly 'scientific' ideal—often quite remotely related to any actual science—simply enforces a paradigm of thinking that cuts out concepts which are needed if these things are to be realistically thought about at all. Exaggerated faith in 'science', along with a very confused idea of what science is, distorts a wide area of Western thought. It is outstandingly disastrous in moral philosophy and in the psychology of motive (which happen to be my home territories), because the ideal of supposedly scientific method that is its Procrustes' Bed is notably unusable in both of them. But all over the range of what are ominously called the social *sciences* (ominously, because they need not to be tied to such a model) a similar distortion prevails, and even remoter studies such as history and literary criticism are badly infected with the idea that it is necessary in some way to imitate 'science'. Even biology becomes distorted by an insistence on trying to make it look like physics.

Nor does this plague infect only academic work. The idea that natural affection is in some way *unscientific* was vigorously promoted by the early Behaviourists. J.B. Watson severely vetoed the kissing and hugging of small children on these grounds,[10] and B.F. Skinner has steadily promoted what he calls an 'objective' attitude in all personal relations—that is, an approach modelled as closely as possible on the way in which we treat lifeless objects. These malign fantasies were never in any true sense scientific at all; they never arose out of empirical evidence. They sprang *a priori* from their inventors' notion of what sort of person a scientist ought to be. Genuine empirical studies of infants have since that time luckily shown how disastrous such attitudes are. But this is only one example of many where the notion of *objectivity* as characteristic of science has licensed an extension far beyond its proper province. Objectivity is a widely respected ideal, and also a somewhat obscure one. Where it is treated as synonymous with both 'scientific' and 'unemotional', there is scope for a great mass of dangerous confusions.

This has important tactical consequences. *We need to avoid the kind of discussion in which 'science' and 'religion' appear as sole protagonists, confronting each other in a vacuum.* When the scene is set up in that way, it is almost impossible, in the present climate, to relate them intelligibly, and if they are related, the links will usually be stated in terms dictated by science. Then (1) the discussion at once becomes epistemological, becomes a competition for what is officially supposed to be the function of science—the acquiring of knowledge.[11] Here (2) the epistemological position of science is treated as obviously secure. (This step has begun to be threatened by a better understanding of its history, but not in a way that reaches a wide public.) After this, (3) enquiry naturally centres on how religion can be made more fit to perform this function, by becoming more 'scientific'.

What we surely need is a quite different kind of discussion. It might take various forms, and the first thing needed is to ask ourselves 'Just why, in the present context, do we want to relate these two things? What relations are coming in question?' There could be many possibilities, but a central one will surely be the enquiry which compares and relates the roles that various kinds of concern, and their accompanying activities, play in life as a whole. Here one would naturally bring in such things as the arts, personal affection, political activity, response to non-human nature and so forth, as well as religion. In this wide field, it would seem natural to speak of 'learning' or 'academic enquiry', rather than 'science' which is, after all, only a small part of our knowledge. (Technology is a different matter and might need a separate heading.)

The next question would then be 'What do these various concerns or elements in life do for us? Why are they needed?', and 'If these needs cannot all be satisfied, how should we handle the conflicts that arise between them? What are our priorities?' In discussing this, epistemological issues would certainly arise, but not particularly often. The first point is not 'How securely do we know this particular thing?' but 'Why is this particular thing worth doing or knowing?' For instance, it is surely very important to *know people*. The fact that our judgements about them are fallible and often mistaken does not make this a futile enterprise. It would indeed be possible to raise Behaviourist doubts about whether we can ever know anything except their overt behaviour, or even about whether anything else actually exists. But we do not have to raise these doubts unless they *arise*, unless we have first seen reason to take up the peculiar standpoint which makes them relevant. Not all doubts are sensible. The Behaviourists had distinct aims and assumptions which we may well see reason to reject.

What would gradually emerge from the discussion I am suggesting would be the need to hammer out some sort of priority system. If, during this enterprise, anybody said that religion should not be on this list at all because it is a discredited or empty occupation, they should surely be answered by simply pointing to the persistent flourishing of religious attitudes even in the absence of any proper object or institution for them.[12] People, except for some fairly mean and muck-rake-ridden characters, simply do not abandon reverence. They just reverence very odd things, such as technology. The heathen in his blindness bows down to wood and stone—or rather, as has been pointed out, always to some power supposed to inhabit these materials. Flying saucers fascinate, not just because it is clever of them to stay up, but because they are supposed to contain benign, alien beings bringing salvation. Again, through a strange tradition unfortunately launched by Nietzsche, 'the future' is worshipped—meaning, of course, not what is actually going to happen but a projection of selected hopes—as if it were a real thing. The vast credulity poured out on this Western cargo-cult makes the kind of faith demanded by the traditional religions look quite trifling. Superstition does not vanish or even weaken with the removal of serious religion; instead it expands with even less discipline than before.

Envoi

This discussion has been somewhat destructive: an attempt to diagnose
diseases rather than a proposal for cure. It has been so because I think that
at present our attitudes to questions about the role of religion are distorted by the notion that we are getting along perfectly all right without
it—that we have a secular world-view, safely centred on the notion of
science, which is quite straightforward and, as Waddington put it, perfectly 'self-consistent and harmonious'. I have been suggesting that, far
from this, our current conception of how to relate our various aims is
chaotic. And although we use the word 'science' to make this conception
look more orderly, the meaning we attach to that word is variable and
obscure. I also think that many elements of a religious attitude have been
quietly preserved as parts of this supposedly secular culture, and that
some of them do a lot more harm in this unnoticed situation than they
would do if they were recognized.

This diagnosis does not, of course, mean that we have only to slot all
the traditional forms of religion back into their accustomed places to get
things right. Things have changed too much for that, in any case. But it
surely does mean that all of us, even people quite disinclined to religious
solutions, need to make a more serious attempt to see the gaps and confusions in our supposedly 'scientific' outlook, and to think what is necessary
if we are to remedy them. It is my impression that the kind of boxing-
match relation which has for so long been seen as holding between something called 'science' and religion is a radically misleading model. To
make sense of our lives, we are certainly going to need many ideas from
both contexts, as well as others from different sources altogether. The
confrontational picture needs to be finally buried.

Notes

1 Thus Aristotle: 'This activity [philosophic contemplation] is the best, since not only is
   reason the best thing in us, but the objects of reason are the best of knowable objects'
   (*Nicomachean Ethics*, Book X, ch. 7, 1177a).

2 A general, rather puritanical abstention from reverence is indeed often professed as a
   mark of a properly modern or scientific attitude. Thus Maynard Keynes, discussing
   sensitively the criticism D. H. Lawrence had made of him and his friends, noted as
   central the charge that 'We lacked reverence, as Lawrence observed and as Ludwig
   [Wittgenstein] also used to say, for everything and everyone'. He accepts this charge as
   partly justified, but is not disturbed by it. 'So far as I am concerned, it is too late to
   change. I remain, and always will remain, an immoralist' ('My early beliefs' in *Two
   Memoirs* (Rupert Hart-Davis, 1949), pp. 99, 98). This claim is actually quite inconsistent with the deep reverence for certain aspects of art, beauty and personal relations
   which Keynes also professes in this very memoir. The function of *professed* irrever-
   ence is therefore very interesting.

3 I have discussed these views of Monod's more fully in my book *Evolution as a Religion* (Methuen, 1985): see index s.v. Monod.

4 See my little book *Can't We Make Moral Judgments?* (Bristol Classical Press, 1990; 'Mind Matters' series) for the surprising difficulties of this widely fancied position.

5 In Britain, the chief source for this colourful doctrine was A.J. Ayer's best-seller *Language, Truth and Logic* (Gollancz, 1936). In the United States, cross-fertilization with the Pragmatist tradition produced C.L. Stevenson's *Ethics and Language* (Yale University Press, 1944), which gives a noticeably less brutal version of the doctrine, but no modification of its basic irrationalism. Anyone interested in really clearing up the philosophical mistakes involved in the whole approach should read Julius Kovesi's *Moral Notions* (Routledge and Kegan Paul, 1967). I have also discussed them myself in my *Beast and Man* (Methuen Paperback, 1980), ch. nine.

6 See Hare's *The Language of Morals* (Oxford University Press, 1961) and *Freedom and Reason* (Oxford University Press, 1963). Here the irrationalism is greatly modified, because deductive moral reasoning bringing a particular case under a general principle is now recognized as valid. But the way in which principles themselves are arrived at remains for Hare non-rational except where it is strictly Utilitarian.

7 Historians have now made it clear that this happened far less than has been widely supposed, much of the opposition to Galileo being either genuinely scientific or simply political. Nor, of course, was he actually persecuted to anything like the extent alleged by folklore and conveyed in, for instance, Brecht's highly fanciful play. It is as well to correct these distortions of history (which have occurred to some extent over Darwin too) because they suggest a chronic, incurable clash of approaches and discourage attempts at mutual understanding.

8 *Treatise of Human Nature*, Book 1, Part iii, section 12, 'Of the Idea of Necessary Connection' and Part iv, section 4, 'Of the Modern Philosophy'.

9 Stephen Hawking, *A Brief History of Time* (Bantam Press, 1988), concluding paragraph. See also Paul Davies, *God and the New Physics* (Dent, 1983).

10 'It is a serious question in my mind whether there should be individual homes for children—or even whether children should know their own parents. There are undoubtedly more scientific ways of bringing up children which probably mean finer and happier children'; 'Let your behaviour always be objective and kindly firm. Never hug and kiss them, never let them sit on your lap. If you must, kiss them once on the forehead when they say good-night. Shake hands with them in the morning': John B. Watson, *Psychological Care of Infant and Child* (W.W. Norton and Co., 1928), pp. 81, 82; quoted in Barbara Ehrenreich and Deirdre English, *For Her Own Good* (Pluto Press, 1979).

11 I have discussed the bad effects of this more fully in my book *Wisdom, Information and Wonder: What is Knowledge For?* (Routledge, 1989).

12 They should of course read—if they have not done so already—William James's *Varieties of Religious Experience*, and also a good deal of anthropology.

The Gospel, the arts and our culture

JEREMY BEGBIE

In a recent article in *The Daily Telegraph*, a lecturer in chemistry at Lincoln College, Oxford, writes about the potential of science to illuminate art. As his main illustration, he cites the famous 'fractal images' of Mandelbrot—elaborate and beautiful patterns which spring from a single mathematical formula. His discussion is intriguing throughout. But for our purposes, it is his opening remarks which deserve special attention. He juxtaposes what he calls the 'two Titans'—art and science—and declares: 'if I had to identify the dominant partner, I would not hesitate to name science. Science is the deeper, more encompassing activity of the brain, for it elucidates the mechanism of the world. Art, of course, illuminates too; but only by stirring the emotions and stimulating self-reflection and enjoyment.' He continues: 'science encompasses art and will, one day, explain it'.[1] As to the writer's somewhat exaggerated faith in the sciences, Dr Midgley has trenchantly dealt with views of this type in her chapter.[2] My main purpose here is to focus on the other 'Titan'—that area of human activity we loosely call 'art'. I shall question the belief that art is essentially self-directed or primarily aimed at 'stirring the emotions and stimulating self-reflection and enjoyment', and I shall do so by challenging some of the assumptions on which this belief rests, assumptions which are deeply-held and pervasive in our culture, and which, I shall argue, have severely distorted our understanding of the arts. Particular attention will be paid to the ways in which these assumptions have found expression in, and been perpetuated by art-theory (or 'aesthetics'). I shall go on to indicate some of the ways in which better progress can be made by taking as a starting point the interaction of God with the created world in Jesus Christ.

It is hazardous to generalize about so complex a matter as the place of the arts in any given society. Nonetheless, it would be hard to deny that among the more dominant features of British culture (and, we might say, of Western European culture) is a cast of mind which tends to alienate the arts and demote them in favour of other spheres of human endeavour. The notion of the artist as an essentially solitary figure with little responsibility to his or her community; the concept of 'art for art's sake'; the widespread belief that there are no universal criteria for assessing the worth or quality of art; the common assumption that the arts, though perhaps entertaining for those who can afford to enjoy them, have little (if anything) to do with the world of demonstrable knowledge and fact—all these are signs of an attitude which treats the experience of art as somehow profoundly discontinuous with the rest of our experience and as relatively unimportant in comparison with, typically, the sciences. In this light, it is not surprising that some will see art's destiny in terms of being swallowed up by science. Hence the view expressed in the opening quotation.

The phenomenon is described well (and roundly attacked) in Peter Fuller's essay *Aesthetics After Modernism*. In the West, Fuller argues, the 'aesthetic dimension' has been gradually expunged from everyday concerns, progressively weakened by technological and economic structures. From the Renaissance onwards, 'men and women were compelled to shift uneasily between an emotional participation in the world, and the pose that they were outside a system they could observe objectively'.[3] The division of labour in the eighteenth and nineteenth centuries severed the creative relationship between imagination and intellect, heart and hand. Art kept its distance from craft; the lofty Romantic poet from the common artificer. The result is, says Fuller, that the vocabulary of art, artists and aesthetics appears obsolete today because a great dimension of human life and experience is at present marginalized.

Even allowing for a degree of literary licence, the central thrust of Fuller's argument is hard to deny. But we need to specify more fully the key components and also some of the causes of this apparent marginalization of the arts if we are to deal with the issues at stake in any depth.

▌

Art and the material world

We begin by noting, in much speaking and writing about the arts in modern times, a tendency to move away from the material to the nonmaterial, to abstract aesthetic experience from physical reality. This undoubtedly has its roots in ancient Greek thought, but if the way of Plato was towards the contemplation of the eternal form of beauty, in modernity it is towards the feeling responses of the human subject. According to the philosopher Immanuel Kant (1724–1804)—in so many ways the father of modern aesthetics—aesthetic pleasure comes about when two mental faculties, the imagination and the understanding, engage in a 'free play'. It is *this* free play which we enjoy. This distinctive experience arises when we contemplate beautiful objects characterized by what Kant calls 'purposiveness without purpose'. Yet Kant holds that aesthetic judgements are based not on features of the world to which we respond but rather on features of *our response*—specifically the interplay of the imagination and understanding. Aesthetic experience and knowledge are quite distinct, so Kant believes. When someone makes an aesthetic judgement, says Kant, 'nothing in the object is signified, but [only] a feeling in the subject as it is affected by the representation'.[4] The same tendency is seen in a more acute form in Kant's great successor G. W. F. Hegel (1770–1831). For Hegel, the great drawback of art is its dependence on the external and material world. Art reaches its highest form in poetry, because poetic verse comes closest to pure thought. For the German and English Romantics, the focus is generally much less intellectualist, the main interest being in the expression of inner emotional dispositions which are themselves often seen as being in tune with a cosmic spirit or force. (The notion of art as the expression of emotion is still very much alive in one form or another. Many have told me how much they envy my ability as a practising musician to 'express my feelings' through music.) Others have construed art in terms of the contrast between inner thought and outward expression. On this view, a work of art is merely the externalization of a vision or idea in the imagination of the artist. The work itself, the object of art, can be regarded as quite distinct from the idea or 'meaning' it conveys. The very real differences between these approaches should not be glossed over. Yet what they appear to share is a tendency to subordinate the sensuous and material to the spiritual and immaterial.

Imposition of order

Closely bound up with this, and especially characteristic of modernity, is a concept of the artist as chiefly an *imposer*, rather than a *discoverer* of value and meaning. Clearly, there can be no such thing as pure discovery; all our commerce with reality involves a contribution on our part which affects the content and character of our experience. We have no quarrel with this, perhaps the most celebrated of all Kant's insights. But, as Professor Gunton reminds us, it is the Kantian stress on the mind's imposition of a *fixed* conceptual order on essentially *unknown* reality—the Enlightenment epistemology *par excellence*—which needs challenging.[5] Kant's aesthetics was not left untouched in this respect. For him, the crucial factor in the experience of beauty is the 'form of purposiveness', and by definition, 'form' is something given by the subject's mind.[6]

Aesthetic pleasure is derived from those powers which enable *us* to arrange the plurality of sense-data, not from the apprehension of order beyond ourselves. Prominent since Kant has been the view that art triumphs by working the wonders of the human mind upon the formlessness of the world, not by interacting with an order already given to hand. As Roger Lundin observes, it was this line of thinking which in time led to the view of art as a bulwark against the chaos and confusion of the world. For the Romantics, he reminds us, art 'becomes the place in which inert nature and chaotic history are brought to life by the unifying imagination. The ability of the imagination to impart beauty to objects creates a restful place for man . . . in an otherwise hostile world.'[7] The fact that Lundin can trace this conception from the early nineteenth century through modern influential critics like Northrop Frye to the 'structuralists' and beyond, indicates something of how persistent it has been.

Art and action

A further aspect of Kant's legacy concerns a divorce between art and action. In Kant's view, an aesthetic judgement is quite 'disinterested'—emancipated from scientific or moral considerations as to type, end or purpose. This was something Kant inherited from the eighteenth century, when the concept of disinterestedness began to be applied to the 'fine' (as opposed to the 'useful') arts. Essentially, it results from transferring Descartes' model of knowledge—the self impassively surveying its object—to the aesthetic realm. It has had many advocates since Kant: writers such as Arthur Schopenhauer, Edward Bullough and Roman Ingarden pursued it in different ways. If we are to treat a work of art *as art*, it is urged, we should be scrupulously careful never to regard it as a means to an end, as an instrument of action. We must fix our attention on the work itself, considering it purely for its own sake. Today, even a brief survey of what our society commonly calls 'works of art' would very likely reveal that the majority were intended, by producer or distributor, for some form of disinterested contemplation. Nicholas Wolterstorff goes as far as to say that in the West, 'No matter what the art, in each case the action that you and I tend to regard as intended is a species of . . . *perceptual contemplation*'. He continues: 'Virtually every statement concerning the purposes of the arts which comes from the hands of aestheticians, our art theorists, our critics, makes this assumption'.[8] Yet it is striking how comparatively recent and how peculiarly Western this assumption is. So important is the part played by the art gallery and museum in our approach to art today that we scarcely question it. We find it difficult to realize that no museums exist, none has ever existed, in lands where modern European civilization is, or was, unknown; and that, even amongst us, they have existed for barely two hundred and fifty years. The notion of disinterestedness in the arts is anything but universal, geographically or historically.

The autonomy of art

Often linked to disinterestedness is the doctrine of the 'autonomy' of art, a doctrine which appears with remarkable frequency over the last two centuries. Kant is again a key figure here, with his emphatic distinction between the sphere of knowledge and the sphere of aesthetic objects and aesthetic judgements. His aesthetics quickly spawned the idea of 'art for art's sake'—the view that art is answerable only to itself, has no social responsibility, and must not be evaluated according to the degree of correspondence it has to phenomena beyond itself, such as a moral order, the artist's intentions, or the circumstances of its production. In this century, essentially the same sentiment has taken many forms. A theory usually called 'formalism', reaching its clearest expression in the writings of Clive Bell, holds that what is crucial in the enjoyment of an artwork is its 'significant form'; representation has no aesthetic value at all and is, moreover, often an aesthetic disvalue.[9] (This too can be traced back to Kant, for whom formal criteria were central to the evaluation of art.) In the 1950s and 1960s, the sculptures of David Smith and Anthony Caro, the paintings of Ad Reinhardt and Robyn Denny, the music of Pierre Boulez and Karlheinz Stockhausen are all examples of artworks produced by those convinced that art should pursue its own self-referring ends, that it could only achieve its purification by eschewing external allusion and addressing no issues outside its own formal concerns. Clement Greenberg, the renowned American critic, claims in his essay on 'The New Sculpture' that 'The avant-garde poet or artist tries in effect to imitate God by creating something valid solely on its own terms, in the way nature itself is valid . . . something *given*, increate, independent of meanings, similars or originals'.[10] Similar convictions underlay an exhibition of recent 'minimal' art, where visitors were told that 'Today's real art makes no direct appeal to the emotions, nor is it involved in uplift, but instead offers itself in the form of the *simple, irreducible, irrefutable object*'.[11] (Undoubtedly, this kind of plea for the 'self-containedness' of art is in part a reaction to the commercial pressures which industrial modernization demands. The emergence of an urban culture in the nineteenth and twentieth centuries may have freed artists from aristocratic and Church patronage, but this economic autonomy brought with it the pressure to satisfy the demands of the market that mass society represented, a pressure which many artists have found themselves strenuously resisting.)

It is significant that in our own century, much avant-garde art has tried to overcome the isolation of art from everyday life by offering new visions of society in which no deep gulf separates 'art' and 'life'. The Futurists (represented by artists such as Umberto Boccioni with his massive emphasis on dynamism and action in art) and the Situationists (an alliance of European artists who emerged in the late 1950s, aiming to transform society by transforming art) are cases in point. Yet because the public invariably failed to respond to such visions, these artists quickly became not the advancing front line of a new army, but marginalized and elite. The irony is—and it is one of many ironies in the history of modern art— that today avant-garde art is quickly institutionalized, accommodated in museums of modern art, adopted into the commercialized establishment, in such a way that it is very hard for it to change prevailing attitudes in society in any significant way. As one recent commentator notes, 'the steady displacement of radical consciousness by the forces of professionalism, bureaucracy, and commercialisation has caused avant-garde art to lose its power of rebellion and crippled its impact'.[12]

Before moving on, it is worth recalling how Western and comparatively modern is this stress on the autonomy of art. It is by no means universal in other cultures where the arts have flourished. And even in the West, during some two thousand years of theoretical concern with these matters, it occurred to no thinker to claim that a human artefact is to be contemplated disinterestedly, as its own end and for its intrinsic values, without reference to things, human beings, purposes, or effects outside itself. A moment's reflection on just one of the arts—music—brings the point home. Listening to music, as distinct from reproducing it, is the product of a very late stage in musical sophistication. The composers of the Middle Ages and the Renaissance composed their music largely for church services and for secular occasions. Or else they composed it for amateurs whose relationship with it was that of the performer responding to it through active participation in its production. It is hardly overstating the case to say that 'the listener' has existed as such only for about three hundred and fifty years.

I should make clear at this point that I am not wanting to claim that the more recent a practice or idea, the less valid it is. That would be foolish. Rather my point is that the fact that many of the fundamental assumptions we make about art are relatively recent (and highly parochial) should make us ask whether they are quite as obvious as we think, and whether important aspects of the arts might have been obscured as a result.

Art and knowledge

A further factor, underlying much of what we have seen so far, concerns the disjunction of art and knowledge. Yet again, Kant emerges as a central character. As we have observed, Kant operated with a very sharp dualism between knowledge and aesthetic experience, one which he inherited from the seventeenth and eighteenth centuries. Aesthetic judgements are first and foremost concerned with a particular kind of mental experience; they do not add to our stock of knowledge of the world. Consequently, he gave philosophical credence to a picture all too familiar today, a picture vividly painted by the author of the article we quoted at the opening of this chapter: the empirical sciences grant us public, certain, clear, reliable and verifiable truth—what John Locke called 'dry truth and real knowledge'—while the arts are concerned with matters of entertainment and individual inner dispositions, with little or no bearing on the way things actually are. It is a curious picture, for it makes so little sense of the way art has actually been enjoyed and practised for the greater part of human history. Yet it has proved remarkably influential. Of course, there have been those (like a number of the nineteenth-century Romantics) who have taken up the cudgels and insisted that art—not science—offers us the supreme key to unlock the inner nature of reality. Others (like A. E. Baumgarten in the eighteenth century) have tried to give art epistemological respectability by offering a strictly 'scientific' and 'objective' aesthetics. But by far the commonest attitude today, generated in no small measure by what is perceived to be the ever-increasing success of the scientist, assigns science to the realm of certainty and art to the realm of private and individual taste. We might note that it is just this attitude which lurks behind much of the current debate about funding the arts in Britain, which is why a Herculean effort is so often needed to justify their public financial support.

One of the consequences of this kind of model is that it is hard, if not impossible, to make judgements about art which are anything more than—to use Mary Midgley's phrase—'undiscussable personal quirks'.[13] To seek even minimal objective criteria for evaluating the arts today is a courageous undertaking, and even when attempted, frequently invites charges of obscurantism and dogmatism. As Richard Bernstein observes, if we follow Kant's aesthetics, 'we are easily led down the path to relativism. And this is what did happen after Kant—so much so that today it is extraordinarily difficult to retrieve any idea of taste or aesthetic judgement that is more than the expression of personal preferences.'[14]

The lone artist

It is possible to exaggerate the extent to which individualism has affected the arts, but there are good reasons to believe that conceptions of the human person in which social relationships are seen as incidental or epiphenomenal lie behind a great deal of the contemporary language of art and art-criticism. As Lundin points out, the bulk of modern aesthetic thought stems from the Cartesian tradition which centres on the individual self as the ultimate locus of truth.[15] The outcome has been a perennial tendency to remove the artist from the untidy arena of dialogue with others; the work of art comes to be seen as the bare product of a 'creative' individual, rather than a means of personal exchange. The psychologist Paul Vitz notes how easily the word 'creative' can cloak a narcissist self-indulgence: 'Today in the secular world creativity is simply a gift from the self *to* the self, it has degenerated into a synonym for any form of personal pleasure without reference to others'.[16] The image of the artist as the lone Bohemian—misunderstood, eccentric and unconventional, oblivious of his or her audience—may be a caricature, but it is anything but dead.

It is not surprising, therefore, that an unwarranted stress on the critical distance between an artist and society should develop. In a perceptive article in *The Times*, Janet Daley remarks that in modern Britain, under governments of all complexions, it seems that for the artist, 'alienation is, as it were, part of the professional brief', that 'the only artistic productions which can be respected are those which reject, either explicitly or implicitly, their own society'. But, she continues, 'if they consistently repudiate their own society, in whatever political hands or historical mood it finds itself, then that is evidence not so much of the irretrievable evil of society as of the demoralisation of the arts'. If this trend continues, there 'will be no place any longer for an art that affirms, that contributes to a society's sense of its own worth'.[17] Along similar lines, Peter Fuller comments:

> Fine artists have been granted every freedom except the only one without which the others count as nothing: *the freedom to act socially*. It is only a mild exaggeration to say that no-one wants Fine Artists, except Fine Artists, and that neither they nor anyone else have the slightest idea of what they should be doing, or for whom they should be doing it . . . It is possible to say that a major infringement of the freedom of the artist at the moment is his lack of genuine social function.[18]

■

At this point, mention ought to be made of a cultural phenomenon of the last few decades which, at least in part, has arisen in reaction to many of the trends outlined above. The term 'postmodern' is a slippery one, to say the least. But it has come to be used to refer to a movement—if it can be called a movement—provoked by an acute awareness of the crises which Western modernity has brought. Many see the context of the emergence of postmodernism as being what Edith Wyschogrod calls 'the death event'—the rapid and terrifyingly efficient 'man-made mass death' of this century, witnessed in, for example, the two World Wars, and above all in the Holocaust. This, it is argued, has been the consequence of typically modern developments in science and technology, political, social and economic organization, and forms of 'progress' which have had disastrous global effects.

In their attempt to find a chastened, tentative and above all practical way through to something better, postmodernists are highly critical of ideals of knowledge which include claims to certainty and solid truth, theories of human progress, and rationalities which offer all-embracing explanations of the world. There is what Jean-François Lyotard has called 'an incredulity toward metanarratives';[19] that is to say, a deep suspicion of comprehensive accounts of the meaning of human history. The postmodern human subject is 'decentred', shaped essentially through particular social relations, language and culture. There is a massive stress on the variability and fallibility of all human activity; the contingency and culturally conditioned nature of all speech and action; the worthlessness of searching for fixed foundations of truth; and the futility of speaking about origins and goals in history.

Robert Hewison has recently offered penetrating comments on British postmodern visual art in *Future Tense: New Art for the Nineties*,[20] citing, among other examples, the Saatchi Gallery in St John's Wood, the Design Museum at Butlers Wharf on the south bank of the Thames, the collages of Robert Rauschenberg and Pat Steir's 'The Breughel Series'. More sympathetic in tone, in his book *What is Post-Modernism?*, Charles Jencks casts his net wider, drawing attention to painters such as David Hockney and Eric Fischl, and architects like Charles Moore, Robert Stern, Michael Graves and James Sterling. Both Hewison and Jencks believe postmodernism is inextricably linked to the plurality of post-industrial society, encouraged by the 'information explosion' and world communication. Postmodern art is intrinsically pluralistic, reflecting the absence of a single overarching value-system: it 'is fundamentally the eclectic mixture of any tradition with that of the immediate past . . . Its hybrid style is opposed to . . . all revivals which are based on an exclusive dogma or taste.'[21] Hewison argues that the key to understanding postmodern art is the 'screen'—the screen of the computer terminal or television. Quoting Angela McRobbie, he writes: 'Instead of referring to the real world, much media output devotes itself to referring to other images, other narratives. Self-referentiality is all embracing.'[22] Similarly, in postmodern art we are bombarded with a host of images. Fragments of earlier artistic styles and pictures are juxtaposed freely, producing collages of pre-existent imagery. Almost any style is, and can be, employed. We are not to ask what lies 'behind' the images or what connects them, for there is no 'master-narrative' which unites them. We must be content with the images themselves. In this way, claims Hewison, we are left with a world of pure surfaces, of face values. And, quoting Dick Hebdige, 'Because images are primary and multiple . . . space and time are discontinuous so that, in a sense, neither time nor space exist: both have been dissolved into an eternal present (the present of the image)'.[23] Hewison thinks the commercialization of art has played a key part in these developments. Postmodern art is art produced in a culture which equates money with talent and value with quick profit. In such an environment, art can no longer be allowed to affect or modify dominant attitudes because, before anything else, it must sell.

In the literary and philosophical spheres, one of postmodernism's most notorious expressions is 'deconstructionism', associated particularly with Jacques Derrida in France and Paul de Man in the United States. Although in many ways distinctively postmodern, deconstructionism finds its precursors in writers and artists such as Joyce, Heidegger, Freud and Nietzsche. It can also be seen as an offshoot of 'structuralism', a term which refers to a variety of methods which seek to understand the meaning conveyed by a text *to those who read it* rather than the meaning which the original author intended to convey. Questions about 'the original meaning' are replaced by questions about the present 'meaning effect' of the text. Deconstructionism takes the point further.[24] Insofar as its leading emphases can be formulated, it rejects any attempt to get behind a text to 'reality'. It seeks to subvert the idea that reason can somehow dispense with language and arrive at a pure, a-historical truth or method. Language is a system of signifiers detached from any stable thing or things. We simply have no way of attaining an unconditioned, a-cultural standpoint to check whether a text is being true to some 'outside' reality. We can only stand within the text. So, in Derrida's celebrated phrase: 'Il n'y a pas de hors-texte' ('There is nothing outside the text'). Texts do not point to authors or things or events. Texts point to other texts, and within this intertextuality, writing becomes a playful, ceaseless process in which writer is already reader and reader necessarily becomes writer. The boundary between 'literature' and 'criticism' disappears. Moreover, the distinction between history and fiction evaporates, for the very notion of 'the representation of reality' is misleading. Questions about the author's intention, historical circumstances and so on, become irrelevant: 'the distinction between text and context, a work and its surrounding environment is dissolved; it is all one surface, a portion of the intertext'.[25]

Postmodernist writers have exposed well the precarious confidence of modernity, the misplaced optimism of those 'total explanations' of reality offered by, for example, Marx and Freud. (It might be added that they are hardly alone in doing so.) The postmodernist reminds us of the complexity of 'authority'; the 'local' character of all truth, argument and validity; the ease with which claims to objectivity mask oppressive ideologies; the ambiguity of 'fact' and the real measure of relativity attached to all value judgements. Applied to the arts, postmodernism properly highlights the risks of over-stressing historical questions and disregarding the effect of art on the reader or hearer today, the significant degree of indeterminacy in all interpretation and the dangerous tendency to turn artworks into instruments of domination.

However, despite the important challenges postmodernism poses, in many instances it would appear to issue in even deeper and more widespread fragmentation than that associated with the philosophies of which it is so suspicious. This, of course, may not worry the deconstructionist, but a theologian with any commitment to the unity of reality (precarious as accounts of this unity might be) cannot be content with a celebration of plurality for its own sake, especially when in Western culture this plurality is in so many ways not enriching but a generator of sterile self-assertion and conflict. As far as postmodern aesthetics is concerned, it is perhaps best seen as the end result of the Kantian banishment of art from the halls of truth (even granting the acute differences between Kant and postmodernism). The artistic imagination, spurned by the world of factuality and in one sense made irrelevant to that world, now returns with a vengeance to swallow up the very world it was reluctant to describe and could not transform. Roger Lundin believes that the whole story of modern aesthetics since Kant can be seen in this light, as a struggle by aestheticians to make grand that which they have already made trivial. And Lundin sees deconstructionism as a sign of the modern triumph of language and disinterestedness over human action: 'A survey of the literary landscape since the romantic age shows the steady march of critical thinking to this position. Once the retreat from action to pleasure had been made, it was perhaps inevitable that a theory asserting language as the sole domicile of order and meaning would come to be assumed.'[26]

In its more extreme forms, postmodernism can be regarded as the ultimate expression of the dis-integration of reality, a non-relational vision of reality. Indeed, even the 'self' eventually has to collapse. Julia Kristeva sees the human condition reduced to the point where 'individuals are no more than ephemeral variables in an eternally repeating machine of identification and rejection'.[27] For some deconstructionists, the very idea of individual identity is an ideological construction, a subtle interplay of various signs and symbols. We should not be surprised by such conclusions. In the last resort, any theory which has its roots in—and effectively pushes through to its limit—the individualism implicit in the Kantian tradition will result in the destruction of personal identity. This is because, to anticipate a later point, our identity as human people is constituted, and can only be preserved by, our *active relation* to what is *distinctive* and *other* than ourselves.

Robert Hewison's verdict—and he has no theological axe to grind—is that postmodernism, at least in the visual arts, is ultimately sterile for it has no ontological roots beyond the superficiality of appearances. This may be harsh, for arguably there are forms of postmodernist art which are anything but sterile. Nevertheless, his point has substance to it. Let me end this section with Hewison's own words:

> It is no longer wise for us to rely on appearances. There has to be a different approach to experience; *the materials of the external world have to be used in a different way.*[28]

III

How, then, might the 'materials of the external world' be used by the artist in 'a different way', a way which leads not to fragmentation but to a profounder grasp of the truth of things? It is often said that there can be no return to a pre-Kantian innocence; we cannot pretend that the very real challenges which modernity has thrust before us have never arisen. Nevertheless, the Christian Gospel is predicated on certain commitments about the nature of God and the created world which, I would suggest, open up avenues arguably far more promising than those we have explored so far. In *Foolishness to the Greeks*, Lesslie Newbigin writes that 'The twin dogmas of Incarnation and the Trinity . . . form the starting point for a way of understanding reality as a whole'.[29] Much has been written in recent years which questions the usefulness (and the intelligibility) of both these doctrines. And yet, when we try to give some account of the arts, there are good grounds for believing that together they provide us with our most valuable resource.

Art and the material world

We begin with the crucial question of the goodness of the created world. In any thinking about the arts, much hinges on whether we believe the material order is *itself* a bearer of meaning, whether it has value in and of itself. Our confidence that this is a proper way of seeing creation finds its focus in the incarnation, the coming of God as man in Jesus Christ. If God the Son becomes incarnate, fleshly and material, this contains positive encouragement for treating the material world as a proper, meaningful environment for us to enjoy, explore and develop. A Judaeo-Christian account of human creativity will need to question the ancient suspicion of the goodness of physical matter, the tendency to deny its inherent value. It will need to recover the psalmists' insight that creation is *already* praising God, before we have laid a finger on it. It will need to be take seriously God's unconditional commitment to all that he has made. Further, a proper doctrine of creation reminds us that we are not disembodied spirits or intellects, but unities of spirit and matter inhabiting a physical world with which we are intimately bound up and have a large measure of continuity, and that part of what it means to be human is to interact thoroughly with this non-human reality.

From this perspective, it is far from obvious why we should construe art as concerned chiefly with moving us beyond the material world to some 'higher' realm of beauty, or see the heart of an artist's work as giving outward expression to inner, non-material realities, as if the 'real' work was carried out in the sanctuary of the self, and the piece of art merely served to externalize and convey this interior experience. I am not saying that art can be explained entirely in physical terms, or that mental activity has no place in artistic creation, or that artists are never blessed with compelling visions. But there is arguably more room today for a deeper sense of our embeddedness in creation and the rootedness of art in substance, in the human body, in pigment, in the twanging of gut and the blowing of air on reeds. Accordingly, art will be seen as an engagement with the physical world involving our senses as much as our mental and emotional faculties. The composer Igor Stravinsky has written:

very act of putting my work on paper, of, as we say, kneading the dough, inseparable from the pleasure of creation. So far as I am concerned, I arate the spiritual effort from the psychological and physical effort; me on the same level and do not present a hierarchy. The word it is most generally understood today, bestows on its bearer tual prestige, the privilege of being accepted as a pure term is in my view entirely incompatible with the role

Imposition and respect

Furthermore, if the Christian faith presents us with a vision of created existence possessing its own latent orderliness and meaning, and a crucial part of human creativity is to be attentive to that inherent order, to discover it and to bring it to light, we will need to question views of art which lay the main weight on *bringing* value and meaning *to* a reality which is regarded as essentially lacking in value and ultimately unknowable. As Oliver O'Donovan puts it: 'How can creativity function with its eyes closed upon the universe? For man does not encounter reality as an undifferentiated raw material upon which he may impose any shape that pleases him.' Love, he continues, 'achieves its creativity by being perceptive'.[31] In this connection, we need only think of Van Gogh's landscapes and interiors, Dürer's meticulously detailed drawings of the human body, and Bach's exploration of the properties of the harmonic series. The imagination creates, to be sure, but only on the basis of a prevenient divine ordering. It is not that the artist contributes meaning to something which is meaningless and formless; it is rather that he or she enables creation to take on another, hopefully richer, meaningful form.

An important part of this 'perceptiveness' concerns the way in which artists treat their materials—paint, notes, wood or whatever. They have to learn that their material will be receptive only to certain of their aims. Others it will permanently frustrate. And to others it will yield only with enormous reluctance. Serious artists will endeavour to know and honour their material, to show it a courtesy. Here a great deal depends on whether we see creation's order as something essentially constrictive or as a *gift* from God whose nature it is to love. If we take the latter course, the properties of an artist's medium can be regarded as an opportunity for, and stimulant to artistry, rather than a strait-jacket to which the artist must grudgingly yield. The novelist Dorothy Sayers insisted that the business of the artist 'is not to escape from his material medium or bully it, but to serve it; but to serve it he must love it. If he does so, he will realise that its service is perfect freedom.'[32]

The reference to freedom is significant. All too often, artistic freedom has been seen as virtually equivalent to 'unrestricted self-expression'. But, as the biblical tradition makes so clear, genuine freedom is not constituted by independent self-determination, nor by the absence of limits, nor by multiplying the number of possibilities open to us; it is realized only in *relation* to real possibilities, by acting in accordance with the way things are. We shall have more to say in due course about the artist's relationships with other people. Here we are speaking of the way artists treat their material—notes, words, stone, or whatever. Artistic freedom in this respect entails an encounter and interaction with the chosen medium in such a way that its integrity is not violated. Again, some fascinating words of Stravinsky are worth quoting:

> I have the seven notes of the scale and its chromatic intervals at my disposal . . . strong and weak accents are within my reach, and . . . in all these I possess solid and concrete elements which offer me a field of experience just as vast as the upsetting and dizzy infinitude that had just frightened me . . . What delivers me from the anguish into which an unrestricted freedom plunges me is the fact that I am always able to turn immediately to the concrete things that are here in question . . . Whatever diminishes constraint diminishes strength.[33]

Not all today would applaud Stravinsky's enthusiasm for the Western chromatic scale. But much more important is his implicit belief that his freedom as a composer is not destroyed by adapting himself to quite specific realities which are *given* to him.

It is, then, not surprising that a number of contemporary Christian writers have urged that art be re-rooted more deeply in the orderliness of creation. Ironically, the most full-blooded argument along these lines in recent years has come not from a Christian but from an atheist, Peter Fuller, in a remarkable book entitled *Theoria: Art, and the Absence of Grace*. Fuller bemoans what he calls the 'collapse of the idea of art as a channel of grace'. He looks back to the tradition embodied in Ruskin's *theoria*—a moral response to beauty rooted in the awareness of natural order—and cites evidence suggesting that in our 'postmodern age' science is 'rediscovering the aesthetic and spiritual meanings of nature'.[34] We may not totally share Fuller's estimation of recent art, nor his zest for Ruskin's 'natural theology without God'. And it is doubtful that he gives due weight to the creative contribution of the artist. Nonetheless, his call for an aesthetic grounded in natural structure is noteworthy, especially since it comes from such a distinguished art-critic and effectively overturns most of the pivotal assumptions of aesthetics in the last two hundred years. (Significantly, Fuller was deeply attracted to a Christian vision of reality but was unable to embrace it intellectually.)

Art and action

If we are to question the abstraction of art from material reality, we will also need to question the divorce of art from action so deeply rooted in Enlightenment thought. To pick up Professor Gunton's words, if we 'isolate the merely intellectual contribution to human rationality from a broader conception of the relation of a person to reality as rooted in time and space',[35] we are likely to be left with a concept of the person in which action within space and time has been marginalized. It is far from clear that such a notion of the person can claim theological support. If we take our bearings from the biblical witness to divine redemption, we will learn that God has acted to restore our *whole* being—supremely in the person of Christ—in such a way that we are able to relate actively as *whole* persons, not only to God himself, but to the world of space and time in which we are set. Instead of disengaging us from the contingencies of history, God has called us to participate in his purposes for creation as embodied agents in a history which is real, to a life of shared relationships in a world of living creatures and created things, to a life in which *all* our capacities and capabilities are to be united in obedience to him.

In this light, we need to ask whether the concept of 'disinterested' contemplation in the arts owes rather too much to modernity and too little to the Christian tradition. In his important book *Art in Action*, the Calvinist philosopher Nicholas Wolterstorff has argued that works of art are first and foremost instruments and objects of action, inextricably part of the fabric of human purposes, passions and interests, vehicles through which we carry out our intentions with respect to the world, our fellows and ourselves. Our society's institution of 'high' or 'fine' art encourages us to regard an artwork for its own sake alone. Although 'perceptual contemplation' is *one* of the uses to which some art can legitimately be put, to insist on it as the *sine qua non* of art is unduly restrictive. Art plays an enormous variety of roles—evoking emotion, expressing grief, praising, celebrating, and so on. 'Works of art equip us for action. And the range of actions for which they equip us is very nearly as broad as the range of human action itself. The purposes of art are the purposes of life . . . any aesthetic which neglects the enormous *diversity* of actions in which art plays a role, in fact and by intent, is bound to yield distortion and inscrutability.'[36] In this connection, Wolterstorff comments that the anthropologist will be only too keen to remind us of the inseparability of art and action in many other cultures—for example, in the dances and songs of the Balinese, the small clay figures made by Mexicans to accompany the dead in their after-life, the paintings of cave-dwellers scratched in stone to ensure success in hunting.

The predilection to separate art and action, is, I believe, closely related to a pervasive use of visual categories in modern art theory, and a tendency to regard painting as the epitome of art. (This is no doubt linked to the all too common assumption that authentic knowledge must conform to the pattern of optical experience.) Many Christian discussions of art move in this direction. However, by encouraging a sense of *distance* between person and world which overlooks our practical, concrete relation to (and physical continuity with) our environment, visual models will all too easily encourage the damaging alienation of artist from reality (and art-work from interpreter) which, we have seen, has vitiated so much recent theory and practice in the arts. I have written elsewhere of more productive approaches which use epistemologies not centred on visual perception (e.g. that of Michael Polanyi) and which resist the temptation to treat visual art-forms as paradigmatic for all the arts.[37]

We should add that the attempt to integrate art and action can easily be overplayed, leading to a 'functionalist' view of art, where we value a work of art solely according to its usefulness. Such a view has enjoyed much support in recent times in Britain, from both extremes of political right and left. Yet it must falter, for otherwise we would make no distinction between, say, a Rubens nude and a tabloid Page 3 photograph. Questions of aesthetic worth and excellence cannot be reduced to pragmatic questions of utility, commercial or otherwise. To say that artworks are primarily instruments and objects of action is not to say that *no* attention should ever be paid to what they are in themselves, it is only to say that we cannot abstract them from their context in human action if they are to be interpreted aright and enjoyed to the full.

Art, creation and re-creation

It could be objected that the stress we have laid above on being faithful to creation's order entails a 'copy' or 'reproductive' theory of art—according to which art is at its best when it attempts to reproduce, point for point, some state of affairs entirely external to the artist. Yet this need not follow. Much depends on whether we are prepared to relinquish theories of the relation between person and world which turn on an absolute distinction between a naked 'object' and some disengaged, utterly independent 'mind'. In the arts, I have been contending, much more fruitful are models which suggest interaction through practical engagement. Consequently, we shall certainly say that artistic creativity demands respect and courtesy for what is given to hand and mind, but we cannot leave the matter there. New connections and novel meanings need to be established through enlarging and elaborating on whatever reality is encountered. Composers, for example, do more than discover and honour their material; they combine sounds in novel ways, explore fresh melodic lines, juxtapose rhythms and harmonies to create new musical meanings.

We might also cautiously speak of a 'redemptive' calling of the artist. The very fact that artists frequently describe their work in terms of a struggle with their chosen material can bespeak an encounter with the tragic, chaotic and destructive dimension of created existence, and a desire to re-order and re-create that which is subject to corruption. This, of course, can apply not only to the particular medium the artist uses, but to the other realities he or she encounters—for example, the brutalities of war, the fear of death, the suffering of the innocent. Sadly, much so-called 'Christian' art has turned a blind eye to such realities and degenerated into a superficial *Kitsch*, something encouraged all too often by art theories which insist that any hint of disorder in art is a mark of discredit. But, it is into the very heart of the darkness of evil—represented by Gethsemane and Calvary—that God himself has penetrated. Only by this route was redemption possible. There can be no attempt to diminish the horror of the tragic, by reducing it to appearance or subsuming it into a monistic and beautiful whole. The artist who passes lightly over the disorder of our world is in danger both of self-deception and of becoming utterly irrelevant.

Nevertheless, redemption achieves not only the exposure of evil, and the presence of God in the darkness, but also a transformation, a renewal of that which is distorted, in such a way that we are given a promise of the ultimate transformation and consummation of all things. This is the Gospel of Calvary and Easter. Christian theories of art which begin with the incarnation and end with the cross are seen to be woefully inadequate. Whatever else 'Christian art' is, it will be art which takes for its final reference-point the raising of the crucified Son of God from the dead. Such art will inevitably resound with an inner joy, even though it may only be a joy won through despair. Such art will be 'realistic' in the profoundest sense of that word, for, as Hardy and Ford remind us, 'The resurrection of the crucified Jesus Christ is [the] logic at the heart of Christianity . . . If this is basic reality then all existence can be thought through in the light of it. True realism will take account of this first, and live from it.'[38] Furthermore, insofar as art does takes its final cue from the resurrection, there will be in it an anticipation of the ultimate goal of creation, a provisional manifestation of a future glory beyond compare. Do we not see something of this quality in Rembrandt's 'Christ Healing the Sick' or El Greco's glowing representation of Christ in Gethsemane ('The Agony in the Garden')? As examples of this art in our own day, we might cite Olivier Messiaen's 'L'Ascension', Duke Ellington's 'Come Sunday', the early works of Graham Sutherland, and the luminous portraits of Georges Rouault.

To speak of the redemptive possibilities of art is, of course, hazardous. We could easily infer that Christ's work is no more than an aesthetic re-ordering of creation (when it is clearly much more than that).

Nevertheless, the renewal of creation in Christ clearly has an aesthetic dimension to it, and there would seem no good reason to deny that we can share in this dimension of God's activity through artistic creativity. More seriously, to claim that art can be redemptive might well detract from the supremacy of the salvation wrought in Christ. To counter this, we need to recall that the incarnation, crucifixion and resurrection of Christ provide not simply a detached *pattern* for the artist, a timeless 'form' to imitate, but actually *constitute* God's unique liberation *of* creation *within* creation. If this is so, the task of the artist is not to complement or add to the work of Christ but to share in its outworking: in trinitarian terms, to share by the Spirit with Christ in the work of the Father in bringing all things to their intended end.

The autonomy of art

Clearly, the drift of our argument to this point challenges the kind of excessive claims for the autonomy of art which we noted above. Art can, in fact, illuminate (or obscure) reality in ways that can be assessed and appraised, and it can do so without converting into something other than art. Art is capable of disturbing and unsettling us, illuminating our daily lives, changing our perception of the world, and provoking us into different courses of action. So Robin Skelton in his book *Poetic Truth* claims that poetry is quite able to convey 'to the sensitive reader a remarkably precise picture of the situation of man with regard to his apprehensions of time, history, evolution, language, and the world "outside" him'.[39] Or again, in his recent study of theology and literature, T.R. Wright sternly criticizes the fashionable retreat from talk about reference in some strands of modern criticism. He comments: 'it may bring methodological purity to literary criticism to say that it is concerned solely with the process of reading literature and not with the "meaning" of literary works themselves. But it is an impotent purity that undermines the importance of literature as a means of expressing the "truth" about the real world.'[40] Of course, quite *how* works of art 'refer' is a massive, complex and highly elusive matter. Attacks on crude theories of artistic referral (and on propagandist art) are often justified. But *that* a work of art can direct our attention to states of affairs beyond itself (and beyond the consciousness of the artist), and that it can reflect (with varying degrees of potency) values which transcend cultural preference, without thereby losing its distinctiveness as art, seems, from experience, undeniable.

Art and knowledge

It is unlikely that we shall admit this, however, if we cling to an account of human knowing which prohibits art from being counted as genuine knowledge at all. To return to Kant, it is to his credit that he shunned the Romantics' extravagant claim that the key to all knowledge lies with the arts. He also saw that aesthetic awareness—whether occasioned by a great painting or a beautiful sunset—cannot be explained away or reduced to some other type of experience. Nevertheless, the way in which he posits such a deep gulf between knowledge and aesthetic perception creates, I believe, more problems than it solves. Frank Lentricchia observes that Kant's

> intention of isolating the distinctive character of the aesthetic experience was admirable, but his analysis resulted in mere isolation. By barring that experience from the phenomenal world while allowing art's fictional world entertainment value, he became the philosophical father of an enervating aesthetics which ultimately subverts what it would celebrate.[41]

Regrettably, much modern epistemology has been far too narrow to do justice to the depth and power of aesthetic experience, not least our experience of the arts. It is oppressively restrictive to say that we know something only when we have a completely clear and indubitable conceptual grasp of it, and equally misleading to claim that art affords no cognitive contact with any reality beyond an individual's immediate experience. The autonomy of art will best be safeguarded, I believe, not by wrenching it apart from knowledge, nor by equating it with conceptual or moral knowledge, but by seeing it as a distinctive, particular but quite genuine means of knowing the world.

The artist in relationship

It is a repeated refrain in much Christian writing of recent years that people are what they are only by virtue of what they give and receive from each other. Against the Cartesian–Kantian tradition, with its conception of the person as essentially autonomous, it is rightly claimed that human persons must always be seen as persons-in-relation. At the heart of the Christian faith lies the truth that we find our true being only in relationship, supremely in relations of self-giving love. Paradoxically, it is only as we exist for and with others that our particularity and distinctiveness are preserved. And this is so because God himself is not a single monadic being, but is triune, existing as a free communion of distinct persons in relationship, eternally giving and receiving in love. The marvel of the Gospel is that we who pursue the quest for fulfilment through autonomous self-direction can discover our authentic humanity as persons-in-relationship by sharing in the eternal and perfect relationships of love within the Godhead.

The ramifications of this for the arts are immense. Here I can only mention a few. First, we will need to ask whether individualistic concepts of the person have obscured for too long the rather obvious truth that art is a vehicle of communication between people. Of course, artists may say that they make things 'only for themselves' or 'only because they have to'. A poet can write verse for no other reader, a composer can write a symphony for no other ear, and so on. But in the history of art, these are exceptions. Instead of seeing an artwork as an 'irrefutable object' or a 'gift from the self to the self' (Vitz's phrase), we would do rather better to regard it as a medium of personal exchange, in George Steiner's suggestive phrase, a 'trial of encounter'.[42]

Second, it follows that issues about an artist's obligation to society simply cannot be side-stepped (nor, by implication, can issues of constraint and censorship). There will need to be a sensitivity on the part of the artist to the shared values and assumptions of his or her social setting (in so far as there *are* shared values and assumptions). An artist's very vocabulary depends on a community of interest, on established precedents and particular conventions of appraisal. These, no less than the language, the marble, the paint, are part of the artist's raw material; to be used, tamed, sublimated, perhaps even rejected, but never thoughtlessly defied.

Third, we will be suspicious of speaking of originality as the supreme artistic virtue, and seek to rehabilitate a sense of the importance of tradition. Of course, important financial factors need to be faced here. Lack of funds may lead some artists to aim for instant satisfaction (and thus gain immediate popular support), but others are led into an obsession with innovation, matched in the art-critics by a celebration of new techniques, media and materials simply because they are new. However, an infatuation with originality not only makes us immune to anything in the past which might criticize and challenge us; it is ultimately self-defeating. For originality without tradition stagnates just as quickly as tradition without originality. Back in 1919, T. S. Eliot explored this theme with piercing insight in his essay, 'Tradition and the Individual Talent'. He notes the tendency to 'insist, when we praise a poet, upon those aspects of his work in which he least resembles anyone else. In these aspects or parts of his work we pretend to find what is individual, what is the peculiar essence of the man.'[43] Yet, Eliot continues, 'we shall often find that not only the best, but the most individual parts of his work may be those in which the dead poets, his ancestors, assert their immortality most vigorously'. Eliot argues for a strenuous engagement with tradition, for an 'historical sense' in the writer which involves 'a perception, not only of the pastness of the past, but of its presence'. It is this 'historical sense' which 'makes a writer most acutely conscious of his place in time, of his own contemporaneity'.[44] The implications of this for the interpreter of art are considerable, and have been taken up by many since Eliot. Interpretation need not be an attempt to transcend tradition but rather an engagement with it; we need not stand outside our own context but seek to understand the past in the present; and this encounter with the past need not be simply a way in which we understand the past, but also a means of self-discovery as our own deeply-held assumptions are modified, revised, and perhaps even surrendered.

Fourth, it is clear that the arts will flower best in the context of what Richard Bernstein calls a 'dialogical community', in which conversation, undistorted communication, and communal judgement inform our lives in the world.[45] Here the Christian artist can and should recall that he is first and foremost a member of a community which has access to resources which impart to it a genuinely 'dialogical' character. The Church is summoned to be a provisional embodiment within this finite world of a type of human existence which mirrors, and shares in, the life of the triune God, a place where we are given 'the freedom to act socially' (Fuller). It may well be that if the Church is to play a significant part in the renewal of art in the years to come, this will come about not through highly trained 'performers'—which can so easily plough into a new individualism—but through the emergence of new forms of corporate art, in which the unique relationships generated and sustained by the Holy Spirit are allowed to affect the very character of artistic creativity itself.

IV

The Trinity and art

It should be clear by now that the underlying theological grammar of this part of the chapter is trinitarian and incarnational, that is, it assumes that God is Father, Son and Holy Spirit, and that the Son of God has come amongst us as a man in Jesus Christ in order to draw us into the life and mission of the triune God. The doctrine of the Trinity, far from being an ecclesiastical antique to be periodically pulled out, scrutinized and then returned to storage, in fact becomes quite pivotal. For it tells us that reality as such, not least human reality, is *relational*. According to the Christian faith, no one can be made whole except by being restored to the wholeness of that being-in-relatedness for which God made us and the world, and which is the image of that being-in-relatedness of God himself. The Gospel is about discovering our identity in relationships which respect our distinctiveness and uniqueness. It is about being related through the Spirit to Jesus and his Father, to other persons, and to the non-human order created and redeemed in Christ.

The approach to art which we have begun to sketch above is intended to reflect this relational character of human existence. The richest sources of artistic creativity, I have been urging, are to be found not so much in the recesses of the artist's own soul, as in a dynamic interaction with the created world, society, fellow artists both past and present, and (for the Christian) with fellow believers and the Father who fashioned all things out of nothing through his Son. Moreover, to see the created world as the product of a trinitarian God who is love in his innermost being will remind us that non-human creation is there not as an inflexible machine, but as an environment given to us out of love, one which is appropriate for the development of free human persons, and therefore one which the artist should enjoy, respect and develop to the full.

Inspiration?

To conclude, and to bring out further the trinitarian dimensions of what we have been saying, let me turn to the work of the Holy Spirit. The concept of artistic inspiration is hardly a popular one today in aesthetic theory, and of course it has often been horribly abused, both inside and outside the Church. Against nearly every trend in modern aesthetics, I would like to make the audacious suggestion that it can and should be rehabilitated, in a way which will emphasize further the relational character of the arts. The key concept to grasp here is *responsiveness*. It is the task of the Spirit, I would submit, to make possible in the artist that free, purposeful interaction with one another, the physical world and the Creator, of which we have spoken above. The Holy Spirit is the Spirit of dynamic interplay, of that mutual giving and receiving which is integral to the artist's work. To be inspired, accordingly, is first and foremost to be responsive. As John Taylor points out in his celebrated book *The Go-Between God*, we commonly speak about the Spirit as the source of power. 'But in fact he enables us not by making us supernaturally strong but opening our eyes. The Holy Spirit is that power which opens eyes that are closed, hearts that are unaware and minds that shrink from too much reality.'[46] We can speak in this way, I believe if we take our cue from the most important work of the Holy Spirit shown to us, namely his activity in the person of Jesus Christ. There is a vigorous tradition in theology, with strong biblical support, which lays great stress on the Spirit's role in the whole life, death and resurrection of Christ. We can describe it in this way: in Christ, through the operation of the Spirit, our self-centred humanity (which the Son of God assumed from us) has been opened out—to the Father, to others and to our created environment. It has been liberated from sin, which is to say it has been enabled to relate appropriately and properly to all that lies beyond it. In Christ, by the Spirit, our personhood has been reconstituted in its true relatedness: it has been made *responsive*. It is now the work of the Spirit in us to bring about (albeit provisionally) what he has already accomplished in the Son.

In this light, artistic inspiration will not be regarded as a wholly passive affair, as traditional theories often tend to suggest. The artist is not simply a tool in the hands of some irresistible force, nor is he one who effortlessly receives divinely authenticated visions from above and then simply lets them flow out through a medium. (Very few artists speak about what they do in these terms. Mozart may have been an exception, but he is an exception in more ways than one!) Rather, it is probably better to speak about the Spirit initiating, enabling and sustaining a process of interaction between artist and subject, artistic medium, fellow artists, community, or whatever. This, we hardly need say, is an immensely costly business, not least because of our ingrained egocentricity with which the Spirit has to battle. Even artists who have been most conscious of being 'inspired' know only too well that they rarely escape struggle, the sweat of physical and mental exertion. Creativity is hard work. Inspiration does not do away with the need for strenuous, painstaking and often frustrating effort. Quite the contrary, it is in just this kind of toil that the Spirit is probably most active.

In this model, moreover, inspiration will not be seen as violating artistic freedom but actualizing it. 'Where the Spirit of the Lord is, there is freedom' (2 Cor 3.17). The ancient theory of inspiration as a divine 'take over' propelling us into a super-human ecstasy, is thoroughly misleading, for this would mean the end of our freedom. We would become less human, less ourselves. The Spirit is the One who draws alongside us, respecting our distinctness, making us not less human but more human, not less free but more free. His work in us is to open us up to things as they really are, yet without disrupting our nature as limited, finite and contingent creatures. I have already spoken about freedom as a matter of being rightly related to what is not of our own making, to what is 'other' than ourselves. Therein lies our authentic 'ecstasy' (*ek-stasis*), our being-drawn-out-of-ourselves.

Finally, all this lends extra weight to our comments above about the ability of art to pre-figure the final consummation of creation. Insofar as this happens, it will be as a result of the activity of the Holy Spirit. In the New Testament, the Spirit is the one who brings us a foretaste here and now of the new age, the age anticipated in the resurrection of Christ. Art which truly bears the imprint of the Spirit—inspired art—will thus not so much hark back to an imagined paradise which has been lost, as depict within space and time, imaginatively and provisionally but nonetheless substantially, the final transfiguration of the cosmos. What kind of art might emerge today if the Church had the courage to believe that this was a possibility? More pointedly, what might our part be in enabling such art to materialize?

Notes

1 P. W. Atkins, 'Art as science', *The Daily Telegraph* (18 August 1990), p. viii.

2 See above, pp. 40ff.

3 Peter Fuller, *Aesthetics after Modernism* (New York: Writers and Readers Publishing Cooperative, 1983), p. 19.

4 I. Kant, *Critique of Judgement*, trans. J. H. Bernard, 2nd edn (New York and London: Hafner, 1968), p. 38.

5 See below, pp. 87ff.

6 I. Kant, *Critique of Pure Reason*, trans. N. Kemp Smith (London: Macmillan, 1929), p. 127.

7 Roger Lundin, 'Our hermeneutical inheritance' in Roger Lundin, Anthony C. Thiselton and Clarence Walhout (eds), *The Responsibility of Hermeneutics* (Grand Rapids, MI: Eerdmans, 1985), p. 13.

8 Nicholas Wolterstorff, *Art in Action* (Grand Rapids, MI: Eerdmans, 1980), p. 10.

9 Clive Bell, *Art* (New York: Capricorn Books, 1958).

10 Clement Greenberg, *The Collected Essays and Criticism* 1: *Perceptions and Judgements, 1939–1944* (Chicago and London: Chicago University Press, 1968), p. 8.

11 As quoted in Fuller, op. cit., p. 32. My italics.

12 S. Gablik, *Has Modernism Failed?* (London: Thames and Hudson, 1984), p. 56.

13 See above, p. 45.

14 Richard Bernstein, *Beyond Objectivism and Relativism: Science, Hermeneutics, and Praxis* (Oxford: Blackwell, 1983), p. 20.

15 Lundin, op. cit., pp. 6ff.

16 Paul Vitz, *Psychology as Religion: The Cult of Self-Worship* (Grand Rapids, MI: Eerdmans, 1977), p. 61.

17 Janet Daley, 'Making an art of subversion', *The Times* (23 August 1989), p. 10.

18 Peter Fuller, *Beyond the Crisis in Art* (London: Writers and Readers Publishing Cooperative, 1980), pp. 45f. My italics.

19 As quoted in Charles Jencks, *What Is Post-Modernism?* (London: Academy Editions, 1986), p. 36.

20 Robert Hewison, *Future Tense: New Art for the Nineties* (London: Methuen, 1990).

21 Jencks, op. cit., p. 7.

22 Hewison, op. cit., p. 63.

23 Dick Hebdige, *Hiding in the Light: Images and Things* (London: Routledge, 1988), p. 210.

24 For a lucid introduction to deconstructionism and its predecessors, cf. Christopher Norris, *Deconstruction: Theory and Practice* (London and New York: Methuen, 1982).

25 J. R. R. Christie and Fred Orton, 'Writing on a text of the life' [sic], *Art History* 11.4 (December 1988), p. 556.

26 Lundin, op. cit., p. 14.

27 Julia Kristeva, 'Postmodernism?' in H. R. Garvin (ed.), *Romanticism, Modernism, Postmodernism* (Toronto and London: Associated University Presses, 1980), p. 136.

28 Hewison, op. cit., p. 79.

29 Lesslie Newbigin, *Foolishness to the Greeks* (Grand Rapids, MI: Eerdmans/London: SPCK, 1986), p. 90.

30 Igor Stravinsky, *Poetics of Music in the Form of Six Lessons*, trans. Arthur Knodel and Ingolf Dahl (Cambridge, MA: Harvard University Press, 1947), p. 51.

31 Oliver O'Donovan, *Resurrection and Moral Order* (Leicester: IVP/Grand Rapids, MI: Eerdmans, 1986), pp. 25f.

32 Dorothy L. Sayers, *The Mind of the Maker* (London: Methuen, 1941), p. 53.

33 Stravinsky, op. cit., pp. 64f.

34 Peter Fuller, *Theoria: Art, and the Absence of Grace* (London: Chatto and Windus, 1988), p. 234.

35 See below, pp. 90–1.

36 Wolterstorff, op. cit., p. 5. In the same circle of ideas lies Hans-Georg Gadamer's stress on the active, 'performative' aspect of the arts: he too is highly critical of any attempt to abstract art from its social and historical context, and rightly associates the growth of the modern museum with the kind of disinterested 'aesthetic consciousness' propounded by Kant. See *Truth and Method* (New York: Seabury Press, 1975), p. 78.

37 J. S. Begbie, *Voicing Creation's Praise* (Edinburgh: T. & T. Clark, 1991), pp. 207, 225f.

38 D. Hardy and D. P. Ford, *Jubilate: Theology in Praise* (London: Darton, Longman and Todd, 1984), p. 73. My italics.

39 Robin Skelton, *Poetic Truth* (London: Heinemann, 1978), p. 127.

40 T. R. Wright, *Theology and Literature* (Oxford: Blackwell, 1988), p. 32.

41 Frank Lentricchia, *After the New Criticism* (Chicago: University of Chicago Press, 1980), p. 41.

42 George Steiner, *Real Presences* (London: Faber and Faber, 1989), p. 137.

43 T. S. Eliot, *Selected Essays* (London: Faber and Faber, 1932), p. 14.

44 Ibid.

45 Bernstein, op. cit., pp. 223ff.

46 John V. Taylor, *The Go-Between God* (London: SCM, 1972), p. 19.

Knowledge and culture:
towards an epistemology of the concrete

COLIN GUNTON

The character of modern culture

The pluralism of modern culture, of which so much is made in so many places, is a myth, in the popular and pejorative sense of that word, at least so far as the West is concerned. On the surface there is diversity and variety in modern life, but beneath the surface there is a pressure for homogeneity which in effect nullifies them.[1] Kierkegaard was probably the first to notice and describe the levelling tendencies of modern life. Both in his life and in his writing his emphasis on individuals and historical particulars—derived from his belief in the particular event of the Incarnation—was in conscious resistance to this levelling trend. In our days his prophecies have for the most part been fulfilled. The agents of the levelling and homogenization of culture are the mass media and those whom they serve, the agencies of mass production. A significant symbol of the process is the frequent claim of those very agencies, in tacit acknowledgement or perhaps attempted concealment of these tendencies, to 'personalize' their products so as to try to persuade the consumer that the very individual particularities which are being undermined are in fact being catered for. In point of fact the individual is only of interest to them as a consumer.

Kierkegaard accused the Church of his day of acquiescence in, if not active conspiracy with, this process of levelling with its consequent loss of particularity. The root of the problem was for him to be found in the philosophy of Hegel, according to which the historical particulars became subsumed under the generalizing abstractions of reason. Developments both in epistemology—the theory of how we know things—and in society —how we live together—went hand in hand. Particularity was lost in abstraction, the individual person in the mass society. This side of Hegel's thought derived from the Enlightenment, and before that from the patterns of Greek rationalism which the Enlightenment developed in its own lop-sided way. Today it could be argued that the tendency has come to full flower. The rampant individualism which is so often and rightly

84

deplored conceals a deeper and parallel process in which the impression of pluralism is merely superficial, the mask worn by the suppression of individuality.

These remarks on our culture, although they are somewhat sweeping, are, I believe, not far from the truth about its general social tendencies. Bound up with these are a number of beliefs—often unrecognized and unquestioned presuppositions—about what it is to know. Some of these are dealt with in Chapter 2 by Mary Midgley, who brings out the effect such assumptions have on the way we live. The particular task of this chapter, however, is to address the underlying epistemological dimensions, and to uncover our assumptions and presuppositions about how we know people and things. It is, of course, the weakness of the academic mind to overstress the intellectual determinants of society, as if all our troubles stem from philosophical mistakes. But, without making such a claim, it can be held that the way in which we claim knowledge is an important element of our social and cultural development, and that it is especially important for the heirs of a movement which claimed to live by reason alone. Fortunately, we are now becoming aware of this baneful legacy which Enlightenment epistemology has bequeathed to our culture. I shall in this chapter attempt for the most part to describe the present situation without appealing to the various commentators who have charted the way, but I must begin with a reference to the direct links drawn between epistemology and culture by one of them.

To Michael Polanyi we owe not only the drawing of links between Enlightenment assumptions about knowledge and the growth of totalitarian ideology, but also the beginning of the fundamental shift in our conceptions that is required in order to escape this connection.[2] Polanyi developed a *relational* rather than an *objectivizing* conception of the knower and the known; that is to say, he stressed that our relationship to a person or thing is primary to our knowing them. Rational, conceptual knowledge arises out of the knowledge by acquaintance that characterizes our human situation in the universe. Because we are acquainted with our universe as its inhabitants, and because we are in a concrete relation to it, we can begin to develop, by the use of our intellectual and other faculties, some account of our knowledge. Even the more rational and abstract forms of knowledge are no exceptions to the concrete mode of our everyday interaction with reality. Rather, they are continuous with them because they arise from within a concrete relation. The crucial concept is one of indwelling. We do not contemplate reality from the outside, from a godlike distance—'objectivism'—but we indwell the world as part of it. All knowledge arises out of and is a function of relation.

Professor T. F. Torrance has suggested that the metaphor of indwelling takes its origin from its use in St John's gospel, where the Son indwells the Father, believers indwell Christ, and the Spirit indwells them. If that is so, then we have already before us one example of the historical impact of the Gospel on our culture. This in turn gives rise to another interesting speculation. It is often suggested that the development of modern science was made possible by the Christian doctrine of creation. That would be an even more remarkable instance of the impact of the Gospel on culture. It would suggest that the foundations of even those disciplines which are apparently most 'secular' are more theological than is often supposed. But where would such a thesis take us? We may have found instances of the historical effects of the Gospel on the development of modern culture. But, having done their work, might they not now be redundant? Our concern in this chapter is not with tracing historical causality, however interesting that might be, but with the question whether the Gospel now has any contribution to make to epistemology, that it, to our theory or science of knowledge, its grounds and its assumptions.

Pluralism and reductionism in the philosophy of religion

We have already suggested that modern culture, while laying claim to pluralism, tends to level down particularities and to homogenize varieties of human experience. The same tendency can be found among those who theorize about religion and religious knowledge, and this is so important that it needs to be illustrated at some length. We shall do this by reference to the writings of John Hick, who is one of its clearest and most distinguished expositors.

Hick's theory of religion is, like other theories of pluralism, in many respects the precise opposite.[3] It is, perhaps, best understood as a version of the Enlightenment theory that there is one religion of reason underlying all religions, in the light of which they can be evaluated and purified. One mark of Hick's approach is its denial or effective nullifying of particularity. Most of the things he writes about Christianity involve a reductionist reading of it which weakens or emasculates its offensive features, in particular the doctrine of the atonement. Here is an example of the homogenization of religion which does its utmost to reduce the different faiths to a kind of lowest common denominator.

Such general points against Hick's thesis have been made often enough. What concerns us here is the epistemological theory which underlies his enterprise. It is, as he says, a form of Kantianism (pp. 240ff.). Kant's theory of knowledge, like the theory of knowledge which Hick wishes to develop with reference to religious experience, is one which attributes a common structure to all forms of human knowing. It resembles that of Plato in that it holds that the concepts generated by human thought correspond to the way the world is. But Kant, despite his almost complete confidence in the capacity of Newtonian science to explain its own sector of reality, is far more agnostic than Plato about the possibility of knowing the world as it really is. The world in itself is unknowable, but in some way it brings about an impact on the sense organs of the knowing person, whose mind then orders these appearances into an intelligible form by means of what Kant holds to be a universal and unchanging conceptual structure. The mind, that is to say, supplies the concepts without which experience could not be ordered rationally. The concepts are the same for every rational mind, and they constitute our sole means of imposing order on the manifold phenomena which present themselves to our experience. There is only one way of knowing the world, and it consists in the mind's imposing of conceptual order on otherwise unknown reality.

Kant's philosophy is deeply sceptical in its fundamental tendency, for it holds not that we can know the world in which we live, but that our minds can in a limited way order the surface appearances of a world that is essentially other and unknown. It is a theory of knowledge which is grounded not in the relation in which we stand to that which we claim to know, but in treating it as a thing, a mechanical object from which we are inevitably distanced. It ultimately reduces all knowledge to a single pattern. It is well known that Kant revered Newton, perhaps understandably in view of the new worlds opened up by his physics, but the outcome would be a reductionism that would force all forms of knowledge into a single mould. If a claim does not fit the pattern of mechanistic physics, such a view would seem to require that it has no right to be made. The recent obituaries of A.J. Ayer have reminded us of the ideology which underlies the dogma that ethics, aesthetics and theology are essentially meaningless because they do not conform to a dogmatic and *a priori* criterion of what can and cannot be true about the world as it is. We have to say that Kant's theory of knowledge is wrong. John Hick, who borrows heavily from Kant, made the carefully qualified claim that 'Kant's broad theme, recognising the mind's own positive contribution to the character of the perceived environment, has been massively confirmed as an empirical thesis by modern work in cognitive and social psychology and in the sociology of knowledge'.[4] But the heart of the thesis, as outlined above and as adapted by Hick, is in fact under attack in very many areas of philosophy, including ethics,[5] the philosophy of science, and much post-Wittgensteinian philosophy.[6]

Hick borrows heavily from Kant in his theory of religious knowledge, in answer to the question 'How do we know God?' It is centred on Kant's distinction 'between the Real *an sich* (in itself) and the Real as variously experienced-and-thought by different human communities' (p. 236).[7] As a result it is only superficially pluralist: at root it is reductionist. It concentrates on the informational content rather than on the relation of a person to the world or to God. According to Hick, we experience the Real as the Kantian experiences the world, 'by informational input from external reality being interpreted by the mind in terms of its own categorial scheme. . .' (p. 243). Again, like Kant's theory of knowledge, it is essentially paradoxical, because it claims both that the information comes from the Real and also that it gives no actual knowledge of it. It even brings together those forms of religion in which the Real is thought of as personal with those in which it is impersonal. By suggesting that the two different concepts are complementary, Hick rules out the possibility of even raising what is one of the central questions which human beings can ask about the nature of the world, whether it is the product of personal creation or impersonal process. It is reduced to a question not about reality but about the way in which the human person experiences the world. The real is experienced in contradictory ways, but nonetheless it is the Real that we are experiencing. Hick draws the logical conclusion: 'we cannot, as we have seen, say that the Real *an sich* has the characteristics displayed by its manifestations . . . But it is nevertheless the noumenal ground of these characteristics' (p. 247). That is to say, we know that the phenomena, the things which we perceive, have a basis in some underlying reality, but we cannot draw conclusions about the character of that reality. On such a basis it is hard to see how it can be known that there is an underlying reality, if there can *ex hypothesi* be no knowledge of the real.

On this view, such knowledge of God as we have makes him an object of knowledge whom we can contemplate rather than the Being with whom we can interact and to whom we can relate. Our words describe *from outside* a transcendent, essentially unknowable reality. Faith, far from an expression of personal trust, becomes an almost entirely rationalist and objectivist conception. 'Faith', writes Hick, in the Semitic traditions where it has its primary home, 'generally meant propositional belief that is unwarranted, or only partially warranted, by evidence' (p. 158). Such a definition is Enlightenment in tone, with its demand for evidence, ignoring recent arguments that what counts as evidence is largely determined by the topic being examined. This view of faith is matched by the overall character of the thesis, which is very similar to the Enlightenment view that there is one true religion, the religion of reason, in the light of which all the particularities of different religions are finally irrelevant, except as versions of the one central truth. Indeed, Hick's theory of religion could be called the Enlightenment collapsed into idealism.

Pluralism, monism and the imagination

We have examined Hick's theory of religious knowledge in some depth, not for polemical reasons, but because it is when we examine the way in which Hick reaches his position that we can begin to discern the possible alternatives. Crucial here is the fact that in epistemology everything depends on where the markers are set. A small shift of orientation or expression often produces a change of ultimately wide significance—what in Chaos Theory has come to be known as the butterfly effect, according to which small differences of initial conditions can produce massive variations overall. In the same way, much depends on Hick's beginning with a view of perception as 'experiencing as', as he moves towards his own theory of religion. We do not perceive a tree, but we experience an object as a tree. In cases such as trees, there is virtually no freedom at all whether we experience them in this way or not. While we may sometimes make mistakes, generally it is the case that ordinary perception is a straightforward matter (pp. 140ff.).

The next step, however, is to hold that religious experiencing is a case of 'experiencing as' in which there is far more freedom in the way in which we experience the Real:

> In the form of critical realism that I am advocating in the epistemology of religion the element of interpretation plays an even larger part than it does in sense perception—thereby preserving our cognitive freedom in relation to the much greater and more demanding value of the reality in question (p. 175).[8]

What happens is that a theory of perception in which some (though comparatively little) weight is placed on the contribution of the subject, slips into a thoroughly idealist theory of religious knowing, in which the subject contributes virtually all the content of knowledge. The slip into idealism is made by stressing the part played by the mind first in experience in general, and then in the interpretation of religious experience. In experiencing a tree as a tree, the mind contributes but little. In religion, the subjective contribution becomes the greater, with the result that virtually no cognitive content is conceded to religious teaching; only that all religions point in some unspecified way to the single *unknown* Real underlying the different interpretations. (It is hard to see how this can be properly be called 'critical realism' when it is held that nothing can be known about the Real.)

One may concede the Kantian thesis that the mind contributes the concepts with the help of which experience is interpreted, and yet by a shift of the way in which initial conditions are understood one may end up with a very different theory of knowledge. Here I return to the enormous differences made by a slight shift in initial conditions. That is to say, it is possible to make considerable concessions to a Kantian view of things, and yet in a different context emerge with a radically different epistemology. Perhaps the best illustration of this is to be found in Einstein's belief that scientific concepts 'are free inventions of the human intellect',[9] apparently echoing the view of Hick cited above. There are, however, differences between Einstein's position and Kant's which make the outcome totally different, so that Einstein believed that our concepts in some way describe the world *as it is*, while Kant held that they describe the world as it is *presented to the mind*. One of these differences consists in the fact that, on Einstein's view, unlike that of Kant, these concepts 'cannot be justified either by the nature of the intellect or in any other fashion *a priori*'; nor can they 'inductively be gained from sense experience'.[10] There is no means of justifying the choice of one set of concepts rather than another, either on grounds of logic or from the experience of the senses. They are *free* creations, not part of the structure of the mind nor rationally read off the world. I am not intending to use Einstein here as a universal authority. I cite him merely to give one instance of a successful modern epistemology which fits into none of the patterns, whether so-called rationalist and empiricist, or the Kantian 'middle way', recommended by Enlightenment thinkers. Nonetheless, Einstein's theory of knowledge is like Kant's in conceding that concepts are supplied by the mind.

Another difference is to be found in the account that is given of how concepts come to be, and how they are justified. Here a contrast between the approaches of Plato and Kant is instructive. Plato's theory is that the concepts were known in eternity, outside the temporal process, and that the task of philosophy is to recall them by a process of recollection. Kant held that they were timelessly written into the human mind. Neither of them has a place for the mind's freedom in developing concepts. Plato and Kant are alike in seeking philosophical certainty from unchanging structures and concepts. That is precisely their failure. I would like to suggest that the error of both these enterprises is to isolate the merely intellectual contribution to human rationality from a broader conception of the relation of a person to reality as rooted in time and space. What they neglect in particular is the contribution of the imagination to epistemology.

Imagination is one of those words which we readily use, but which defies simple definition. Etymologically, for what it is worth, it has to do with the creation of images. It is most obviously at work when the mind produces images of the world. This function is so obvious that it is fatally easy to fall into a view of language as directly imaging or picturing the world in some direct way. Even this has its value in reminding us that imagination represents the material and, so to speak, embodied character of our relations with the world. It shows that all our thinking begins from our concrete acquaintance with the material world in which we are set and of which we are a part. There is no discarnate rationality. This contrasts with the aim at pure intellectuality that led from Plato to Kant and beyond him to modern reductionism. There is no disembodied knowledge, because our ability to form concepts emerges from our bodily relation to the world.

This side of the argument is best illustrated by the part played by metaphor in the advance of knowledge. It is now widely accepted that almost all intellectual advance takes place by means of metaphor. New knowledge comes into being as new ways of speaking—new uses of old language—are shaped by the interaction of mind and reality. This is not the place to develop a detailed account of current thinking about metaphor, although there is now a considerable literature to show that metaphor is not mere ornament, but an indispensable means of articulating the shape of reality—of 'cutting the world at its joints', to use Richard Boyd's expression.[11] For our purposes it is important to note that metaphors—the product of the free and spontaneous imagination—image not by imaging, or rather by imaging indirectly. They are the means of interpreting one part of the world by another, a sign that the words refer and describe without direct imaging, but by imaginatively transcending the imaging power of language.

That is not to say, however, that imagination's function is limited to what obviously appear to be images or their derivatives. The most abstruse mathematical systems are in some way or other the product of the imagination. That is part of the point of Einstein's appeal to freedom. In producing its ideas, the mind moves beyond its previous achievements by a creative leap. There is, of course, a remaining link with the material world, as in Riemann's development in the nineteenth century of a geometry of curved spaces; but pure mathematics is what it is by virtue of its abstraction from the particular characteristics of material being. When we speak of the use of the imagination in pure mathematics, philosophical speculation or musical composition, we are referring to the creativity of the human intellect which produces, sometimes spontaneously and sometimes with great labour, works that could not have been predicted in advance. Coleridge held that in this respect the imagination mirrors the creator's work after him. It is here that we need to bear in mind the concept of inspiration and of the place of freedom given by the Holy Spirit in all human creativity (better described by J.R.R. Tolkien's word 'sub-creation'). Here too we return to Einstein's point that concepts are free creations in the sense that they are readable neither from the human mind nor directly from reality. *And yet in some way or other free creations are discovered to reflect the structures of being*, as is shown by the way that Riemannian geometry, independently developed, provided a mathematical vehicle for Einstein's physics. That is the sense in which all knowledge is the gift of the creator Spirit.

The conclusion of this section of the argument is, accordingly, that the human rational imagination bears witness to essential truths about the mystery of being. What it suggests is that neither the Platonist nor the Kantian approach begins to come to terms with the mystery and openness of being. The imagination is witness to the fact that human knowing is at the same time bound to the earth, and within that boundedness it is able to transcend it. Platonist and Kantian as well as empiricist epistemologies attempt to evade or escape that boundedness by futile attempts at pure rationality or at delimiting the sphere within which, and only within which, there is safe and certain knowledge.[12] They are doomed attempts to achieve the infallibility which only God possesses, and to deny the central place of the free Spirit of God in all human discovery. To say this is not to object in principle to the enterprise represented by such epistemological theories, because we are bound to generalize and to attempt to say what are the universal features of our human condition. That is of the essence of our human rationality. What is mistaken about rationalisms of all kinds is the degree to which they deny the material basis, particularity, freedom and fallibility of all our human systems of science and thought.

Epistemology and the priority of the personal

In this section I propose to argue that, far from requiring us to go cap-in-hand to modern cultural forms for assistance, Christian theology is in a strong position to offer a model of rationality which will throw light on many of the problems which our culture faces. (We have already seen how it can be claimed that it has in fact contributed to the shape Western culture has taken.) To do so, we shall appeal to the particular in a way which is directly opposed to the idealist basis of Professor Hick's form of rationalism. The reason for this is that, despite its frequent failure to make the most of its potentialities, Christian thought has the resources to transcend the current alternation between the 'coincidence of opposites' represented by objectivism and idealism, and individualism and collectivism.

Christian theology is grounded in history, and this provides the basis for an epistemology which integrates rather than alienates the particular and the general, and the imaginative/concrete and the rational. Charles Norris Cochrane noted this in his study of the relation of Christianity and classical thought. Christian theology, by its integration of spirit and matter, provided the basis for science which a decadent classicism had failed to achieve.[13] As Hegel was later to realize, the basis for such an integration is to be found in Christology. God and man were brought together in a particular historical event, and here lies the basis of an epistemological synthesis of the particular—the historical—and the universal, God. Hegel's project was the renewal of modern culture on the basis of the Gospel; a precursor of the concern underlying this volume to relate the Gospel and modern culture. According to Hegel, the particular was to be at once maintained and elevated to a higher, universal, level in a philosophical synthesis; the Christian Gospel to transform Western culture. As we have seen, Kierkegaard with good reason found the programme to fail. Instead of elevating the particular, the synthesis abolished it, and the reason for this lay in the attempted removal of precisely those features requiring imaginative representation which made the particular what it was. A theological assessment of what happened would say that Christology is swallowed up in a kind of rationalist pneumatology. Father, Son and Holy Spirit do not maintain their reality as persons, but the Father and the Son are little more than stages on the way to the final self-realization of the rational Spirit.

Here we return to the point at which this chapter began. The problem of modern culture is its abolition of the particular, and especially of the particular person. Accordingly, the question our critique of Hegel forces us to ask is as follows: Where can be found an epistemology—a general theory of knowing—which maintains the reality of the particular from which it takes its starting point and which does not end in the abolition of the particular? What is required is an epistemology which, by avoiding the abolition of the particular, integrates into itself human personality, with its unique worth and dignity. It is the person who is destroyed by collectivism (the abolition of personal particularity) and by individualism (with its denial that personal existence subsists in concrete relation to others). Hegel saw that the right place to begin was Christology, for it is there that we find the presence of both the particular and the universal. But how are we to avoid the pitfalls into which he fell? The answer is to base our approach on a different theology of the Trinity. Hegel's Trinity, as I have already suggested, is essentially modalistic in direction, in that the three persons of his Trinity do not have ultimate reality, but are in some sense modes of divine being, as though they were epiphenomena of an underlying divinity. In that respect Hegel is a true representative of the Western tradition, which since the time of Augustine has found it difficult to avoid modalism in some form or other.

The Gospel's unique contribution to epistemology is best illustrated by means of an instance of creative and imaginative rationality, which is still essentially grounded in the concrete and the particular. Once again, it is convenient to make our approach by means of a contrary view with which our own can be contrasted. Hick in several places expresses his debt to Enlightenment individualism:

> The Real *an sich* cannot be said to be personal. For this would presuppose that the Real is eternally in relation to other persons. Whilst this is of course conceivable, it constitutes a pure *ad hoc* speculation rather than the most economical interpretation of the available data. For these include the facts (a) that the only persons of whom we know, namely humans, have existed . . . for about fifty thousand years, and therefore cannot provide for an eternal dialogue partner for the Real . . . (p. 264).

Such an assertion not only begs a most central and interesting theological question, but enables us to engage with another modern tendency in theology which may appear to be even more challenging than that represented by Professor Hick. I shall approach both at the same time.

The first question concerns whether it is right to assume (as Professor Hick does in the quotation above) that the only persons we know are human persons. Is not the Christian Gospel based on the belief that we do know persons other than human, for we have been brought into relation with the Father through the Son and in the Spirit? We know therefore the divine persons of the Father, Son and Holy Spirit. But, it may be objected, does not this constitute an illegitimate move from human to divine persons, from the finite to the infinite? What is the nature of the analogy that is being used? Here we must reply that, if it is believed that we speak of the personality of God only because we have experienced human personality, which we then project on to the deity, there is indeed a foothold for the kind of argument made by Professor Hick above. In view of the fact that some religions have a personal deity while others do not, it could be said that the attribution to deity of personality may appear to be based on less than a consensus. In the light of the history of religion, we must for this reason remain agnostic about whether God is personal, and therefore whether we know any persons other than the human.

To understand such a view, however, we have to realize that there underlies it an ideology of fairly recent provenance (though anticipated in antiquity) associated with thinkers such as Feuerbach, Marx and Freud, that language about God in general derives from the projection upon the universe of magnified human qualities. On such a theory, analogy is always a process of reading upwards from below. Recently, however, there has been a widespread questioning of such a conception of theological analogy, with criticisms taking two forms. Pannenberg has argued that, as a matter of history, far from its being true that the language of persons is projected from finite to infinite, the very opposite is the case. According to him, the concept of the person derives from a religious experience of reality.[14] Human beings attribute personality to themselves because they first of all recognize it in their deities.

A different case, but with the same conclusion, is argued from the nature of language. In an important paper, Roger White has claimed that a venerable tradition of philosophers and theologians has argued for the priority in linguistic usage of the theological. Four such diverse thinkers as Plato, Aquinas, Barth and Wittgenstein all hold different versions of the same thesis that the standard meaning of a word is theological and that its finite equivalent is derivative from that. If you want to know what a word means, you must first attend to its transcendental usage, and move from there to its use for finite realities.[15] Analogy works from above downwards. If, accordingly, these two considerations are placed together and applied to the concept of the person, it can be suggested that it is wrong to limit our knowledge of the personal to humans. We are able to use the concept of the person about human beings because we know something of the nature of a personal God.

In the case of Christian theology, it can further be argued that a particular theology of the person has as a matter of fact been derived from thought about the Gospel. According to Christian tradition, our personal relation with God which brings us reconciliation to the Creator through his 'two hands'—the Son and the Spirit—forms the basis for the particular Christian understanding of God which is distinct from its alternatives; and indeed it made its way in the teeth of a pluralism very much like that commended by Professor Hick. Suppose, however, that instead of his phrase 'pure *ad hoc* speculation' we prefer something like 'imaginative and creative speculation on the basis of the Christian life of worship and action', we could hold quite to the contrary not only that God is personal but that such a belief provides the basis of a distinct and, in our culture, desperately needed theology of the human person.

Before, however, we outline a possible concrete epistemology that derives from such an affirmation, a further tendency to which we have already alluded must be faced. For there are positions being taken far more radical than those we have examined, in which the whole discussion of epistemology becomes an irrelevance, because the whole quest is mistaken. Involved in many so-called 'postmodern' discussions of the nature of theology—and indeed of other disciplines and practices—is the contention that the sheer plurality of human cultural phenomena compels the conclusion that the task of any intellectual unification is an impossible one. Thus Don Cupitt has claimed that 'postmodernity is a flux of images and fictions' so that 'truth is human, socially produced, historically developed, plural and changing'.[16] The implication is that, far from being faced with a choice between opposing epistemologies, we are wasting our time talking about epistemology at all.

One way of approaching such a position is by seeking its intellectual provenance, and in what I say here I would claim some support from Dr Begbie in the preceding chapter. In the light of what we have seen above, clearly Cupitt's position bears some relation to that of Professor Hick, who holds that the Real is essentially unknowable. If the real cannot be known, it is better to dispense with any conception of an objective real. Cupitt dispenses with two features of Kant's position (accepted by Hick) which maintained its essential realism and universality; that is to say, the belief in the existence of ultimate (if unknown) reality, and the assumption that there are universal features of human cognition. Postmodernism is the subjective side of Kantianism, beginning, as it does, with the structures of human experience, collapsed into an individualism which borders on solipsism. Here, it could be said, is one possible outcome of the realization that the Enlightenment's quest for human certainty is a chimera. Postmodernism refuses to accept that, because there can be no certainty, we should be content with what is now known as fallibilist epistemology, that is to say, the view that we have every right to claim to know, even though we are aware of the fact that we may be and often are mistaken. Instead, postmodernism takes the human, limited and historical nature of culture to be its disqualification as knowledge. But that begs the question of what might be involved in human knowing.

It is my belief that the kind of view represented by Cupitt carries the most appalling threats to civilized human existence. Taken to its logical extreme, it means that finally we are all enclosed in a kind of self-centred isolation, a form of autistic solipsism, in which there can be no real communication between people and their world, because each individual is finally unrelated to anything else. It is a nightmare vision, reflecting a breakdown of confidence in the reliability of nature, which is still at the heart of the assumptions of Western science, despite the shaking of some old confidences. Worse still, it is failure of confidence in that community of human existence on which the possibility of ethical discussion and action is grounded. It is one extreme outcome of the recommendation made by both Descartes and Kant (and by many between them) who hold that we should turn inwards, to the experience, thought and existential nature of the individual, if we are to discover how things really are. The contribution of postmodernism is to have spelled out the logic and to have revealed the intellectual and moral decadence of the modernist tradition.

As that remark is meant to hint, the claims made by Cupitt obscure the fact that his interpretation of the direction of modern culture is by no means uncontested. (One of the odder features of his position is that it claims a universal validity for a theory which argues that there can be no universal norms or criteria.) Peter Fuller, for example, has brilliantly exposed the sham of some recent art,[17] while much modern philosophy, far from accepting the conclusions of linguistic philosophers and its successors, is returning to something like a traditional vision of its task, as the writings (for example) of Alasdair MacIntyre and Stephen R.L. Clark illustrate. The fact is, as the writings of even the most strident postmodernist demonstrate, there can be no discussion or writing without assuming some community of human interest or some laws of logic, both of which beg to be explored with the help of epistemological theory. And, to return to the theme which has been in the background throughout this chapter, theories about how we can know are bound up with our knowledge, if it be knowledge, of who we are and what is the nature of the world in which we live. If we do not discuss epistemology and develop a consciously held theory of what it is to know, we shall assume one and smuggle a hidden metaphysic into our theories which may even themselves deny metaphysics. It is better to come into the open with our claims for meaning and truth. And so I close with what is in brief outline the kind of epistemology that is possible on the basis of the fundamental Christian claim that through the Son and in the Spirit we are brought into relation with God the Father, creator and redeemer of all.

To begin at the beginning, we could say that the basis of our epistemology is a concrete relation, a kind of knowledge by acquaintance. In place of the information-processing model, we have quite the opposite: a claim that primarily in worship, but in other relations as well, the Christian community is brought to the Father by the Spirit through the Son; or, similarly, but with a slight difference of emphasis, through the Son and in the Spirit. That, we might say, is the essential reality-claim made by the words we typically use in worship. Without necessarily wishing to deny the claims of other communities that what they do is the worship of God, the Christian claim is something quite particular. Believing the world to have been created and redeemed by God the Father, through the Son and in the Spirit, the Church responds with the particular mode of action and life which she believes to be appropriate to her belief.

On such a basis, we could say that, just as science articulates rationally, and in particular mathematically, the dimensions of the material world which we indwell, so theology is the rational articulation of the character of God, and of human reality and the world characterized by a particular relation—the indwelling of Christ through the agency of the Spirit. The doctrine of God is at the centre of such an articulation: it is what makes the Christian claim take the shape that it does. On such a basis it is indeed speculative, but then so are the theories of evolution and relativity, being equally products of the rational imagination. That is to say, certain universal claims about God follow from the particular relation in which worshippers find themselves, and they are made by means of the use of the disciplined rational imagination. It is disciplined because it must not contradict the relationship on which it is based; but it is imaginative, because in the freedom of the Spirit it develops those concepts—such as 'person', 'relation', 'communion'—which enable those universal claims to be made on the basis of which the rationality and truth of Christian claims may be judged.

What are the universal claims that theology makes as the result of imaginative speculation on the basis of the worship relationship? The affirmation is that God is what he is, not as an unknown and *possibly* personal Reality, but that he is personal to the very heart of his being. Faith seeks understanding, and comes to learn that to be God is to be the communion of divine persons who are what they are by virtue of their relationship to the other persons. Father, Son and Spirit, in constituting the being of God by their mutual and free relatedness, confer particularity and we might even say, so long as we avoid the pitfall of individualism, confer individuality upon one another. That is a unique and fertile understanding, for both Church and culture, of what it is to be God.[18] In it, there is no final conflict between the particular and the universal, the one and the many.[19] The social implications of such a doctrine are both evident and far ranging, a real contribution of the Gospel to our culture. There should be no final choice between individualism and collectivism, because both derive from a common failure to respect both particular persons and their nature as beings-in-relation. The epistemological implications are less obvious, but since they are the main object of this chapter, they must be spelled out briefly.

The chief thing to be said is that here we have an epistemology in which claims for knowledge derive from the concrete relation in which a person exists with reference to whom and what he knows. It is Platonist in the sense that ~~that~~ it holds to the priority of the rational as that which is given: rationality is not something which we create, but something there for us to find. This is particularly important as a corrective to post-Enlightenment rationalities with their drive to dominate and control, and to postmodern irrationalisms with their refusal to face the question. Rather, knowledge has first to be received. That is the point which Polanyi has attempted to make in claiming that all knowledge is a form of faith seeking understanding, faith here referring to a way of being in relation to God, other people, or the world. The approach, however, is also Kantian, in the sense that it holds to the centrality of the active mind, albeit in a secondary and derivative sense. To the priority of grace (that which is given) there corresponds the Spirit-given freedom to respond (the active mind). But it is neither Platonist nor Kantian in its refusal to attempt any escape from the material world in which all our rationality is embedded. We cannot climb out of our bodies into some purely conceptual reason. Our human condition is inescapably material, particular, fallible and finite; and knowledge which seeks to evade this ceases to be human knowledge and so is not knowledge at all. That is the negative note we must sound in face of all continuing attempts, derived from both Greek and Enlightenment rationalism, to be like God. The positive note, the contribution the Gospel can give to culture, is the articulation of the promise inherent in our createdness: that creation embodies the rationality given to it by its maker and redeemer, whose Spirit liberates the human mind to discover what is, and what is to be.

Notes

1 'The contemporary debates within modern political systems are almost exclusively between conservative liberals, liberal liberals and radical liberals': Alasdair MacIntyre, *Whose Justice, Which Rationality?* (London: Duckworth, 1988), p. 392.

2 The basis of Polanyi's development is in the use of tactual rather than visual metaphors for the development of a theory of our relation to the world. By this means, he avoids

the suggestions of distance implicit in understanding of perception as a form of sight, rather than touching or hearing. See my *Enlightenment and Alienation: An Essay towards a Trinitarian Theology* (London: Marshall, Morgan and Scott, 1985), especially ch. III. Polanyi's classic is *Personal Knowledge: Towards a Post-Critical Philosophy* (London: Routledge and Kegan Paul, 1962).

3 John Hick, *An Interpretation of Religion: Human Responses to the Transcendent* (London: Macmillan, 1989). Further references to this work will be in parentheses in the text.

4 Hick, p. 240. It is noteworthy that the two disciplines mentioned are concerned with subjective rather than objective reality. Had Professor Hick looked for evidence from other sciences, he might have found them less supportive.

5 Alasdair MacIntyre, *After Virtue: A Study in Moral Theory* (London: Duckworth, 1981).

6 Richard Bernstein, *Beyond Objectivism and Relativism: Science, Hermeneutics and Praxis* (Philadelphia: University of Pennsylvania Press, 1985); R. W. Newell, *Objectivity, Empiricism and Truth* (London: Routledge and Kegan Paul, 1986).

7 Hick's use of the concept of the Real begs a number of questions. For example, by supposing that the object of religious devotion is rightly so called, it appears to rule out a doctrine of creation, like that of classical Christian theology, which holds there are two beings or realms of being *equally* describable as the real, both the Creator and his creation.

8 That in itself is an epistemological assumption of breathtaking proportions. How many religious believers, except perhaps those in thrall to Enlightenment categories, really believe that their belief is the result of some kind of semi-autonomous choice?

9 Albert Einstein, *The World As I See It*, trans. Alan Harris (London: The Bodley Head, 1935), p. 134.

10 Cited by T. F. Torrance, *Transformation and Convergence in the Frame of Knowledge* (Belfast: Christian Journals, 1984), p. 79.

11 Richard Boyd, 'Metaphor and theory change. What is "metaphor" a metaphor for?' In A. Ortony (ed.), *Metaphor and Thought* (Cambridge: Cambridge University Press, 1979), pp. 356–408. This paragraph summarizes ch. 2 of my *The Actuality of Atonement: A Study of Metaphor, Rationality and the Christian Tradition* (Edinburgh: T. & T. Clark, 1988), pp. 27–52. See also Janet Martin Soskice, *Metaphor and Religious Language* (Oxford: Oxford University Press, 1985).

12 Such insights as these underlie the increasing frequency of attacks on what has come to be known as foundationalism. Broadly, this is the belief that any assertion or set of assertions wishing to qualify to be knowledge must conform to particular intellectual criteria specified in advance: to some system of basic principles or concepts, or to some supposed structure of concepts inherent in the human mind or the human response to reality. The empiricist and rationalist strands of Enlightenment epistemology, whose reconciliation Kant claimed to have achieved, are rival enterprises in foundationalism. The facts that there has never been agreement in what the foundations are, and that sheer unpredictability and even anarchy (Feyerabend)—its inescapable dependence upon imagination—are to be found in the advance of science, rule out any uniform method. There have also been in recent years numerous philosophical attacks, in my view convincing, on foundationalism. Hick's attempt to derive rationally an essence of religion is, of course, deeply foundationalist. See, for example, pp. 213f.

The attack on foundationalism has in places led to the rejection of epistemology not only in its classical—Enlightened—form, but in any form. Because, it appears, the only criteria of truth in a system are internal to that system (anything else involving the imposition from outside of criteria being by definition foundationalist and therefore Procrustean), it has appeared to some that all that remains is an appeal to pragmatic criteria or, indeed, that anything goes and that all claims for truth are equally 'valid'. (It is interesting that such a conclusion could lead back to a kind of Hickian 'pluralism', once again showing that slight variations in initial conditions make enormous differences in the outcome of an epistemology.) It was precisely the apparent uncontrolledness of imagination—its temptations to mythologizing?—that made it so suspect to the Age of Reason. If we are to see it as a means of gaining knowledge, it must be in some way linked with reason without succumbing to the kind of rationalizing tendencies which have been the bane of recent epistemological theory.

To deny foundationalism—the Procrustean imposition upon an area of thought of supposedly universal epistemological criteria—is, however, not necessarily to deny the possibility of any epistemology, nor is it to be restricted to *merely* internal criteria of rationality and truth. Internal criteria are, indeed, important, because until we know what claims for truth a system has, we are unable to specify what kind of evidence is appropriately to be sought in defence of those claims. The internal coherence of a system and pragmatic testing of its implications are also likely in many cases to be relevant. Thus while Christianity is in some respects irreducibly paradoxical—and it may indeed be the case that because of the limits of human fallibility and sin *any* attempted overall view of reality will, if it is of any interest at all, be irreducibly paradoxical—it would be difficult to maintain if it could be shown to be unmitigatedly contradictory, without any general coherence, while alternative visions of reality commended themselves as coherent.

But it must here be emphasized that an anti-foundationalist position does not require appeal solely to internal criteria, only the refusal to countenance externally imposed limits that are inappropriate to the kind of claims that it makes. If we look at the way in which disputes about meaning and truth are solved in the real world—and it is here surely significant that there is now a large body of evidence to suggest that it is Enlightenment foundationalism that has made it impossible even to discuss rationally the differences between people (Alasdair MacIntyre)—we shall see that a very wide range of criteria operate. In the sciences, for example, as we are often reminded, a theory is often felt to be supported by the simplicity and beauty of its equations—an appeal to aesthetic criteria in stark contradiction of mainstream Enlightenment epistemology. In Christian theology it is impossible to propound a widely acceptable doctrine without at least some reference to scripture and tradition, even though, as we well know, there are deep differences about the character and status of those authorities. To those semi-internal criteria are added many more that operate at different levels and in different ways. Among them are many that involve interaction with other areas of thought that use similar or overlapping conceptualities: philosophy, the natural and social sciences, and so on. The point is that to deny foundationalism is not necessarily to claim that all systems of thought and belief are closed systems, incapable of interaction with others. Christianity has always been part of its surrounding culture, although at the same time a distinctive presence within it. The question for us is not whether it is related to the culture(s) in which it is set, but how.

13 Charles Norris Cochrane, *Christianity and Classical Culture: A Study of Thought and Action from Augustus to Augustine* (Oxford: Clarendon Press, 1944).

14 Wolfhart Pannenberg, *Basic Questions in Theology* 2, Trans. G. H. Kehm (London: SCM Press, 1971), p. 230.

15 Roger White, 'Notes on analogical predication and speaking about God' in B. L. Hebblethwaite and S. R. Sutherland (eds), *The Philosophical Frontiers of*

Christian Theology: Essays Presented to D. M. MacKinnon (Cambridge: University Press, 1982).

16 Don Cupitt, *Creation out of Nothing?* (London: SCM Press, 1990), pp. 77, 45.

17 Peter Fuller, *Theoria: Art and the Absence of Grace* (London: Chatto and Windus, 1988).

18 In saying this, I am adopting a particular version of the Church's doctrine of the Trinity. It is very much that taken in the recent report of the British Council of Churches Study Commission, *The Forgotten Trinity* (London: British Council of Churches, 1989). I have defended the conception and spelled out some of its possibilities in *The Promise of Trinitarian Theology* (Edinburgh: T. & T. Clark, 1991).

19 J.D. Zizioulas, *Being as Communion: Studies in Personhood and the Church* (London: Darton, Longman and Todd, 1985).

Contemporary culture and the role of economics

JANE COLLIER

Introduction

The most dominant of our cultural 'paradigms'—or intellectual frame-works of thought—is given to us by the discipline of economics. If cultures are ways of living articulated in language, rituals and institutions, then our modern culture *is* 'economic' culture. The language of economics is the language through which the world is understood, the language by which human and social problems are defined and by which solutions to those problems are expressed. Our lives are dominated by the rituals of 'getting and spending'. Political options translate into economic decisions; political decisions are implemented by economic institutions.

Economics is not simply an ivory-tower activity undertaken by academics in universities; its propositions interact with the real-world economy in a manner which is both informed and supported by the status accorded to the 'economic' in our culture. The dominance of the economic is captured in the notion of 'economism' which, according to the *Oxford English Dictionary*, 'imposes the primacy of economic causes or factors as the main source of cultural meanings and values'. Economism pervades our everyday lives, and the discipline of economics is the intellectual framework which generates and articulates that cultural nexus of meanings and evaluations.

Cultural critique of all kinds is a necessary part of the search for truth. Economics is challenged in our society by people of all persuasions who are concerned about the depersonalization, the spiritual impoverishment and the environmental destruction which we have wrought in our search for economic progress. The Christian critique shares those concerns, but it stems from an inspiration and a vision which we call 'Gospel'. This vision, unfolded in the scriptures, is one of God in relationship with humanity—initially in a covenantal relationship with a people, but subsequently in a relationship of fatherhood with the Son in whom He becomes incarnate. In this way God the Creator becomes Father to all who share humanity with Jesus, and we in turn become called to 'image' the likeness of the Father which we see in Jesus. We are to 'give to God what is God's' (Matt 22.21), to 'be perfect as our heavenly Father is perfect' (Matt 5.48), and that perfection is to express itself in our relationship with our brothers and sisters in Christ, known and unknown to us, as well as in our concern for a world which has been entrusted to us as 'stewards'.

The Christian vision, the Gospel, is thus not just a vision of a God, but also of what we as men and women are and have to be in God's Kingdom. It thus gives us not only a theology, but also an anthropology and a cosmology. Furthermore, our relationship as sons and daughters of God binds us together in the human grouping we call 'Church', so that we look to the Gospel to discern the elements of an ecclesiology. The Church in the world is the sign that the Kingdom grows in the midst of everyday life, that 'sacred' and 'secular' are inextricable. God is one with our humanity, and the world is 'charged with the grandeur of God' (Gerald Manley Hopkins). The Council of Chalcedon, which in AD 451 affirmed the simultaneous divinity and humanity of Christ, gives us a model which is normative for our understanding of the relationship between Gospel and culture; to believe, therefore, that there is a dichotomy between religion and any other aspect of our lives is effectively a Christological heresy. There is no part of our existence, no aspect, whether cultural, historical, social, political, communal or familial which is not called, through conversion, to become the stuff of which the Kingdom of God is being fashioned.

A call to conversion

What follows is an attempt to articulate that call to conversion in the sphere of human relationships concerned with what is 'economic'. The call to conversion is addressed to all who share the Christian concern for the welfare of the human person. The Gospel proclaims the news to persons and communities of a salvation which is not just *future* but also *present*; it affirms their worth, their dignity, and their right to fulfil their potential as part of a new creation. The 'person in community' is thus the Christian 'unit of analysis', and all economic realities must be discussed in these terms. It is always tempting to discuss the world in terms of 'isms'— capitalism, economism, consumerism, and so on. We talk frequently of 'structures', systems, principles, often to the point where we are reminded of Paul's cosmology of 'principalities and powers'. But this approach has its limitations as well as its uses. The problem is that it encourages us to see these 'isms' as living entities or mysterious forces capable of governing the world, and thus to attribute events and states of affairs to the workings of blind fate or impersonal forces. If we think like this we are in danger of forgetting the fact that what happens in the world is in nearly every case the result of human action, and that the responsibility for what happens is always a personal responsibility, whether the particular consequence is intended or not.

This perspective governs the choice of focus in what follows. This chapter attempts to look at the way in which human action creates what is 'economic' in our culture. It begins by evaluating the work of economists as formulators of economic knowledge. This is necessarily a critical exercise, not only because theoretical economics is divorced from real world considerations and problems, but because economics has so far failed to take seriously the need to develop new thought forms and a new language appropriate to the changing nature of the economic problem. This train of thought leads to an analysis of the relationship between economics and everyday action. What we do is dependent on how we think, on our beliefs, values and judgements. All of these derive their particular characteristics from the cultural context in which we live. I therefore discuss the extent to which our actions as economic and social agents are influenced by one particular cultural strand—i.e. by the presuppositions and values enshrined in the thought forms generated by economics as a discipline, and by the way in which these influences are imposed in social and organizational contexts. The final sections examine the outcomes in terms of human welfare, and identify the 'conversion' of perspective and action which is required of all of us.

Economics and economists

We begin with the community of economists and the academic enterprise in which they are engaged. This enterprise generates the thought forms which underpin the 'culture of economism'. The ruling paradigm in economics is that of the neo-classical school, a paradigm which remains relatively unchallenged by alternatives such as Marxian, radical or institutional economics. The neo-classical framework of thought has as its primary concern the optimum allocation of scarce resources, and analyses this in 'formal', or largely mathematical terms. Neo-classical economics not only satisfies the need within the discipline for intellectual consistency, but it also serves to fulfil the function of an ideology in social terms, of a belief system in political terms, and of a puzzle-system in intellectual terms. Most important of all, it enables economists—and others—to see economics as 'scientific' (and therefore epistemologically and culturally respectable) because neo-classical economics resembles physics, the ideal science, in structural and conceptual terms.

In a society where science had become the only legitimate form of knowledge it was not surprising that the aspiration of nineteenth-century economics was to be accepted into the community of science. Economists had attended the annual meetings of the British Association for the Advancement of Science each year since 1833, but were only fully accepted into the Association when they abandoned classical 'political economy', with its interest in the creation and distribution of wealth, in favour of neo-classical economic science, which defined welfare purely in terms of getting the most out of available resources. This was a shift with profound implications not just for the future of the discipline, but for humankind as a whole, because it committed economics to an interpretation of human benefit based on the premise that 'more is better', and to the view that the cause of human happiness or welfare is best served by the achievement of economic growth.

But 'scientific' respectability was bought at a price. An economic 'science' needs theory, but it was not possible to build rigid theoretical frameworks to explain a real world which is subject to constant change. So economic theory was formulated as a collection of 'axioms'—i.e. statements about the world which are generally accepted. Axioms, says Frank Hahn, are 'claims about the world so widely agreed as to make further argument unnecessary'.[1] A basic axiom of neo-classical economics is that economic agents are rational in the sense that they know what they want and how to choose it from the possible alternatives. Axiomatic economics sees 'truth' as being contained in and generated by such axioms. Ludwig von Mises,[2] for instance, argued that 'social and economic theory is not derived from experience—it is prior to experience . . . no kind of experience can ever force us to discard or modify a priori theorems'. The axioms may not be 'realistic' in the sense that they accord with experience, but their use can be justified by arguing that the real world is less than perfect and therefore does not measure up to the perfect world of economic theory. Even then axiomatic statements are no more than statements; they explain nothing by themselves. In order that they could be used as theory to explain and predict they had to be 'idealised and strengthened'[3] by the addition of assumptions such as perfect knowledge, correct expectations, and maximization under certainty. These assumptions allow the economist to build theoretical structures from which predictions can be generated, and to express them in elegant mathematical models, but they bear no relation to reality. The theorist justifies their use by saying that it does not matter whether or not assumptions are realistic, because assumptions are no more than convenient fictions with which to construct predictive theories. However, the outcome of this procedure is that neither the form of economic theories nor the assumptions on which they are based accord with reality.

'Formalism'—i.e. the necessity to cast all explanation into a form which can be handled mathematically—is not the only problem faced by the discipline. Science must be empirical if it is to provide any understanding of the real world. Economics has a problem of 'access to reality' in the sense of 'isomorphism', or correspondence, between the structures of the world—i.e. its own empirical reality—and the linguistic/mathematical structures of the discipline. 'Experience' of this reality for economics comes through statistical data which are centrally collected according to a prior classification system whose basis requires a great deal of simplification and homogenization. It is thus not necessarily suitable for analytic use; the pouring of data into conceptual categories is often an *ad hoc* procedure.[4] Data collection is in any case subject to problems of error, of misrepresentation, of non-reporting,[5] and insofar as it is produced by survey techniques rather than by observation, it is influenced by the fact that people have very little awareness of what affects their own behaviour. Above all, data can be politically manipulated. The basis of calculation for UK unemployment figures has been changed a number of times in recent years. The rate of inflation is dependent on what is included in the Retail Price Index. Poverty no longer exists as an economic 'reality' in the UK because since 1988 poverty statistics are no longer collected; there can therefore be no discussion of policy initiatives to fight poverty.

There is also the problem of relating the statistical data to ordinary-language economic concepts. We have a difficulty in demarcating and establishing definite individuality, separating one entity from another, the whole from the sum of its parts. When does a car become a car? Furthermore, classes and aggregates are inexact. If we count the unemployed as those who are without work for fourteen days, is the person who has been without work for thirteen days employed? 'Loose concepts' is the term coined to mirror this problem of the indefiniteness of individuals and the inexactness of classes. A real example of 'loose concepts' is the money supply. Definitions of the money supply proliferate, their content changes constantly with the exigencies of policy expediency. Any measurement of the relation of money to Gross Domestic Product, or to any other aggregate, is therefore no more than notional.

Statistical data are thus a very imperfect mirror of economic reality, not only because of the practical problems connected with their collection, but also because of the very weak link between concept and data. Data as such have no 'meaning'; it is not possible to establish any economic 'fact' unless one has a prior set of concepts by which to interpret it and contextualize it. A money transaction conveys no information to the observer unless he or she has notions of purchasing power, price, sale, barter and acceptability within which to interpret it. A figure for the capital/output ratio in any given industry says nothing unless we also know the extent of spare capacity in that industry. What all this implies is that the empiricist view that the meaning of economic concepts is to be found in their empirical counterparts is untenable. The economic 'facts' which data collection provides us with are not the 'objective facts' required by the canons of scientific respectability. It is possible to argue that this is an indication of

> the immature state of social inquiry, which may be measured by the extent to which the operations of fact-finding and of setting up theoretical ends are carried out independently of one another, with the consequence that factual propositions on the one hand and conceptual or theoretical structures on the other are regarded each as final and complete in itself.[6]

But this is a view which not only fails to take account of the complexity of the 'quantum-leap' required to bridge the gap between theory and reality, but is also dismissive of the need to do so. Cogent analysis of economic problems and effective policy solutions both depend on a resolution of this problem.

I have argued that economics has a problem of handling reality, both because its theoretical structures are built on unrealistic assumptions, and because there is a 'crisis of abstraction' which creates unbridgeable gaps between the theory and the reality it is supposed to mirror. Realism is therefore unattainable even in the most 'naïve' sense of the word.[7] Economists might argue that this is not important if formalism ensures the scientific status of economics. But scientific knowledge requires verification, or at the very least falsification, and economic theories cannot be tested, because the premises governing the data from the real world do not match the assumptions embodied in the theoretical structures. Furthermore, although it is possible to generate testable hypotheses from the theory such as 'if we cut wages inflation will decline', a confirmation of the hypothesis does not validate the theory, it only tells us that in that instance the hypothesis was true. If the hypothesis turns out to be false, 'scientific' methodology would dictate that the theory should be modified, but this does not happen. It is difficult to conceive of a principle of demarcation between science and non-science without testability, and the argument that mathematical rigour is an adequate substitute for testability is unconvincing. Neo-classical theory must therefore be seen as a mathematical rather than a scientific research programme. This perhaps explains why economics, unlike most of the other disciplines, is perceived as having made little contribution to human happiness, in spite of the fact that it has a great deal to say about defining the concept of human welfare.

All of this raises the question of the way in which economists interpret their own position. In recent years economists have undergone a period of collective examination of conscience, triggered by the perceived lack of credibility experienced by the profession as a whole, and by the failure of the discipline to improve the sum total of human welfare, or to predict, explain or suggest solutions for the economic problems of the day. The lack of identity and the paralysis which has resulted from this have left the discipline wide open to manipulation for overtly ideological purposes. Mainstream economics originated in, and has now reverted to, a laissez-faire individualist ideology, which rests on a belief in the efficiency and therefore the desirability of market allocation of resources, and a conviction that the state should retreat from all aspects of economic life. Research priorities are decided not by what society necessarily wants or needs, but by the need to legitimate political decisions, so that in the last decade there has thus been a 'shift from what economists imprecisely know to what ideologists are determined to justify'.[8]

It is generally accepted that there is no such thing as ideology-free economics, but there is a certain academic independence of thought which encourages the pursuit of research or knowledge for its own sake. Why, then, have economists not resisted these pressures? One answer is that academic progression and advancement depends on research, and research needs money. Also, it is easier to allow habit to substitute for truth, to tackle puzzles rather than real-world problems, to preserve the power of the old over the young. The response of the profession to ideological manipulation can be explained not by corruption or conspiracy or oppression, but simply by the existence of a 'déformation professionelle' which stems from the fact that economists have been trained to believe that it is possible to do 'value-free' economics.[9] This belief is grounded in the programme of logical positivism—a philosophy which maintains that evaluative statements are meaningless in knowledge terms. Economists who subscribe either explicitly or implicitly to this viewpoint are less likely to be aware of the values hidden by the work they do, and more likely to be insensitive to the ideological agenda behind research initiatives.

It is worth reflecting on the role that positivism has played in the development of economics. Because of a particular semantical confusion, logical positivism as a philosophical position has become enshrined in the discipline as the distinction between 'positive' and 'normative' economics, rather than as a set of norms for demarcating the scientific from the non-scientific. The confusion arose because the distinction between 'positive' and 'normative' was originally drawn by J. N. Keynes (John Maynard's mathematician father) to distinguish 'economic uniformities, economic ideals and economic precepts'[10]—in other words, to distinguish the 'science' of political economy from the ethics and the art of political economy, respectively. 'Positive economics' thus originally referred to the descriptive empirical side of the subject which would be used as a basis for the more evaluative exercise of saying something about the problems of political economy. It was the aspiration of economics to 'scientific' status which led to the acceptance of the canons of philosophical positivism and to a consequent confusion between 'positive' in the sense of non-normative (J. N. Keynes's view), and 'positive' in the sense of observable and testable (the view of philosophical positivism).[11] Schumpeter sees this confusion as misleading:

> The word 'positive' as used in this connection [discussing J. N. Keynes] has nothing whatever to do with philosophical positivism. This is the first of many warnings about the dangers of confusion that arise from the use, for entirely different things, of the same word used by writers who themselves confuse the things.[12]

In terms of positivist thinking economics should not concern itself with the normative—i.e. human welfare—if it is to be validly scientific—a position which neither J. N. Keynes nor any of the classical political economists would have accepted. The whole meaning of 'positive' economics has thus shifted:

> from being the opposite of normative it has moved—because the normative is non-observable and non-testable—to being the opposite of non-observable. The logical positivist or radical empiricist will not recognise that there is a range of meaning involved; normative equals metaphysical equals non-observable equals non-testable equals meaningless.[13]

The consequence of this is to equate the normative with the meaningless and thus to establish freedom from values as an essential characteristic of scientific respectability in economics, in spite of the fact that in philosophical terms the distinction between fact and value in general is no longer accepted as legitimate. In this way the discipline perpetuates the belief that economics has not and must not have anything to say on the question of values. Objectivity and value-freedom thus become synonymous, and implicit values can easily be made explicit for ideological purposes.

Economics and human action

I have argued that economics suffers from a formalism and a 'crisis of abstraction' which makes it difficult for it to address real world problems and issues, and that its failure as a 'science' in the instrumental sense, together with its adherence to an outdated conception of 'value-free' science, renders it vulnerable to ideological manipulation. Why then, it may be asked, does economics have such a profound influence on our world—more specifically, if economics does not function as a successful science, what are the channels of its influence? The simple answer is that the thought forms which are implicit in the type of reasoning done in economics lie at the basis of personal understanding and judgement, and hence condition action. We can distinguish three ways in which this is the case. In the first place, the presuppositions which form our 'world-view' are provided by a culture in which economic concerns tend to dominate all areas of life. Secondly, economics provides us with particular interpretations of intrinsic cultural values; and finally, our actions are structured and constrained by the norms of the social and organizational contexts in which we live.

What we do is determined by how we think: knowing, in other words, is basic to action. Our decisions are grounded in our experience, in the way in which we interpret and understand that experience, and in the judgements we form in consequence. The process of coming to know is dependent on the way in which we 'see' the world, and that in turn is structured for us by our cultural context. Our experience is interpreted in the light of our presuppositions, our understanding of the world is formed by our theories and culturally given models of reality, and our processes of judgement are influenced by cultural ideas of truth and culturally established methods of verification.

(a) Presuppositions

All our thinking takes place within an overarching framework of metaphysical presuppositions which we can designate as a world-view, a world-picture, or, more properly, a cosmology, since it comprises fundamental ideas about the structure and function of 'world'. The particular world-view which we hold, restrictive though it may be, plays a central role in a culture where the demise of religious belief has left us with a psychological void, where rationality precludes reliance on myth, and where 'the challenge of the increasing fragmentation, specialisation and babylonisation of knowledge systems and languages'[14] creates an ever greater necessity to make sense of the world. The parameters of our world-view are the presuppositions of a scientific culture. However, they are also given to us by the 'culture of economism', because the framework of thought is embedded in the discipline of economics itself. The presuppositions, models of reality, and ways of establishing rational conclusions which most influence our thinking tend to reflect images of the economic world, the way it is structured and the way it functions, and they both determine and are derivative of the way theory is formulated.

Our scientific culture structures our views on the structure and substance of the world, as well as on its underlying causality. We subscribe to a belief in the objectivity of science, and to a faith in its power to achieve the progress of humanity. Economics, as a segment of our scientific culture, has its own set of metaphysical beliefs. In *structural* terms the world-image of neo-classical economics is that of a giant machine. Newtonian physics provided Adam Smith with his model of an economy where the decisions of a myriad of self-seeking individuals combined to create order and harmony—i.e. equilibrium between the forces of demand and supply in interconnected markets—and thus stable prices. He attributed the possibility of such order and harmony to the fact that the economic system was architected by a 'divine being', an 'invisible hand', whose intervention would ensure that the economy replicated the workings of the physical world. Smith's real aim was to legitimate the workings of the free markets of his day by proving that the mechanics of the market are rooted in the 'natural' human motivations of self-interest, competitive striving, and ambition. But this is no truer today than it was in Smith's time. Polanyi,[15] for instance, points to the fact that all the evidence we have from other cultures prove that the motivations which form the basis of economic activity are culturally determined rather than in any sense 'natural', so that the behaviour of economic agents is determined by the way in which the economic system is embedded in social relations rather than by personal motivation as such.

Nor is it possible to accept that the unfettered workings of the market mechanism are necessarily beneficial. They may be efficient in the sense that they determine what is produced and to whom it is distributed without the necessity for planning, but they are not equitable. The whole idea of 'laissez-faire' neglected the fact that with a market context some people are more able to act in such a way as to ensure their own interests than others. Low standards of living result in a lack of ability to work and thus a lack of income to fulfil basic human needs. When needs are not satisfied, people are less able to compete because of poor health, poor education, poor information and an inability to understand the complexities of the system. The ideology of free enterprise assumes that the stronger will break out of this vicious circle and claw their way upwards—a kind of social Darwinism. But this assumption neglects the fact that free markets are never free. They are controlled by power blocs—large companies, trade unions, media influences, pressure groups. The result is that any order which does exist in markets exists in such a way as to allow the strong to benefit at the expense of the weak; no better example of this exists than relationships between First and Third World countries on international trading markets. Smith's assumption that a 'natural' order implied a 'just' order was therefore simply incorrect.

The image of the market economy as a self-regulating mechanism is a powerful one; it continues to function both as belief and as theory. The specification of this mechanistic cosmology in terms of an economic model requires assumptions of no time, no space (so that all market participants have perfect information), no social interaction, and some kind of gigantic auctioneering process to ensure that markets 'clear'. And yet it is the belief which forms the basis for current political thinking and policy not only in the West, but increasingly now in Eastern Europe—a view which

> rests on the fundamental belief that a market economy has self-regulating properties of astonishing refinement—properties which if formally laid out make the performance of an automatic pilot in an aeroplane or the guided mechanisms of an intercontinental missile look like child's play.[16]

More important, perhaps, is the fact that our retention of the image of the machine carries with it the assumptions on which it is based— assumptions which reduce the notion of human action to a predetermined stimulus/response behaviour pattern, where the stimulus is the price signal and the response is in terms of demand or supply of goods or work. It ignores all institutional and class relationships, neglects the issues of power and conflict in society, and depersonalizes relationships.

In *functional* terms the presupposition of a mechanistic economic universe rests on individualism as a vision of society. Individualism thus becomes part of the dominant ideology of capitalism. In economics this translates into 'methodological individualism'—a principle which not only accepts the truism that the world is made up of individuals, but also maintains that the facts of the world can only be explained in terms of facts about individuals. This is a positivist understanding of the world, which sees individuals as real, but social phenomena as constructs of the mind and therefore meaningless in empirical terms. (Mrs Thatcher is on record as saying that there is no such thing as society.) The consequence of this for economics is a form of reductionism, whereby aggregative propositions are derived simplistically from individual propositions and empirical laws are derived from the aggregation. Economists are thus enabled to retain the idea of free will and at the same time to have a rationalistic explanation of economic equilibrium.

The characteristics of individualism are *self-interest* and *rationality*. The assumption of rationality has two aspects. We assume that the rational thing for agents to do is to maximize their utility, or satisfaction, given their preferences ('epistemic rationality'). We also assume that the rational thing for them to do is to buy or sell in the way that they do ('practical rationality'). The concept of utility is thus endowed with what Joan Robinson calls 'impregnable circularity': 'utility is the quality in commodities that makes individuals want to buy them, and the fact that individuals want to buy them shows they have utility'.[17] The situation is deterministic, in that both the ends from which the economic agent has to choose and the selection criteria are given, and the means relative to each are known. Rational economic man is thus no more than a robot, and cannot be said to be an actor in any human sense. As a thinking person, an 'intentional self', he is purely passive. Winter comments[18] on how strange it is that in an age where the natural sciences gave such powers of autonomy and control to the human race, the 'social science' of economics should see it as enslaved by personal wants and market forces. By denying any basis in behaviour governed by choice to economic theory and neoclassical theory in particular, economics ensures its own inability to be 'scientific' in terms of prediction and control.

(b) Values

I have argued that the experience, understanding and processes of judgement which ground our understanding are based on the presuppositions which shape our cosmology. But action is based not just on judgements of fact, but also on judgements of value. The values which ground our judgements as to what is 'worthwhile' are culturally given, and an important segment of that cultural influence for us is constituted by the economic dimension of our social existence. The valuations embodied in economic thought and practice tend to be the ones which we apply to evaluation in general. In a cultural sense, these values have been retained and perpetuated because they are enshrined in ways in which we think about the economy, and thus tend to pervade our evaluational processes in general. The language we use to talk about economic matters assists in the formation of evaluations. In particular, the intrinsic social values of welfare, justice and freedom are given a particular interpretation in the economic context, and insofar as this interpretation prevails we are led to adopt a particular set of instrumental values which are alien to those central to the message of the Gospel.

Notions, concepts and meanings of 'good' all arise in the interaction between cultural thought forms and their articulation on the one hand, and lived experience within that culture on the other. We tend to overlook this, to believe that our own sources of value in our culture are absolute and 'given' while at the same time perceiving the taboos and norms of other cultures as culturally determined. The fact that we are unaware of the cultural origin of our own values means that we tend to regard discussion of values as merely one aspect of ideological discussion in general. This belief serves to legitimize the cultural values which condition and mould our ways of evaluating, since they can never be validly questioned.

The process of value formation is not static. Processes of valuing change as political ideologies change: Thatcherism, for example, turned the optional values of initiative, competition, hard work and enterprise into specifically instrumental ones. Furthermore, different institutions within society also play their part in value formation. We can look, for instance, at the ways in which business corporations act as shapers of values. Their products assist in shaping the material environment, providing the images on which we base our valuations, our assessment of what is beautiful or ugly. They shape our symbolic environment by providing verbal, visual and auditory forms of articulation for those values. The sophistication of advertising ensures that our symbols of power are provided by the products of the car industry, that cosmetics symbolize beauty, that the care of a mother is symbolized by detergent. Production processes define what is thought of as work in our society, how work is evaluated, and what work is deemed to be worthwhile. And finally, corporatism provides society with the value of novelty, the evaluation that product and process innovation is good in itself, even though, for instance, it may create unemployment or develop and market inappropriate or injurious products, as in the case of Nestlé's babymilk products in developing countries.

How, then, are values chosen? Aristotle's answer to the question 'How do we know the good?' is that the good appears to each man in a form answering to his character.[19] But choice is difficult: general cultural values are given the sanction of acceptability, but individual values often conflict with these. The upshot can be either a process of interior moral struggle, which can only be resolved by making conscious options or—more likely, perhaps—by a side-stepping of the problem. One way of doing this is to choose a focus for evaluation, and consign conflicting planes of evaluation to the background. In our culture, the conflict is often resolved by accepting the one-dimensional scale of values provided by utilitarian forms of thought. Utilitarianism is one-dimensional in that it conceives of only one definition of value, so that there is no value conflict. It is restrictivist in the sense that it assumes that everyone has the same status as valuing agents. It also negates the context of the development of moral sensibility. It fails to take account of the fact that there is both a quantitative difference between people in terms of the degree to which they are sensitive to values, and a qualitative difference in terms of the fact that they have different value perspectives or 'spectacles'.

We now turn to more specific issues. If we accept that values are culturally given and interpreted, that they arise in the interaction between society's needs and the ideological formulations which result, we are led to focus on the way in which the major one of these needs—i.e. the economic—creates a nexus of values within society. We have, however, to distinguish the levels on which this operates. There is firstly the question of the values embodied in the 'doing' of economics. The economists who generate knowledge systems which generate cultural change are themselves part of the culture; they inherit the value premises embodied in economics, but they also bring to their endeavours their own particular set of values.

Judgements made by economists are both methodological and normative, for 'doing economics' itself involves value-based choice. Economists demonstrate their own particular bias in their choice of problem for research, in the selection of hypothesis by which to test their ideas, in the choice of data to fit the hypothesis, in the interpretation of results, and in the language by which all this is described. Description itself involves selection. Sen[20] reminds us of the ways in which description can be good in the sense of appropriate, without being a good (in the sense of truthful), description of what is being described. Usefulness and realism are not the same thing; we can describe a selective educational system as efficient without saying anything about its divisiveness, or unemployment as rising without indicating how it is distributed within households or by region. Value-laden description is an inherent part of this process.

At a deeper level, economists demonstrate their own bias by the degree to which they can comfortably subscribe to the research 'paradigm' within which they operate. The programme of formalism attempts to distinguish 'positive' from 'normative' economics in the sense that facts are held to be value-free, but it also attempts to establish the factual as normative.

Evidence of the prevalence of women in low-pay trades, for instance, can provide a warrant for the employment of women in those trades: it is seen as 'normal'. This is an example of the way in which what 'is the case' becomes what 'ought to be the case', simply because 'this is the way it has always been'. This has the effect of discouraging challenges to the status quo. Furthermore, it is frequently the case that factual and empirical conclusions are constructed in support of a particular political programme. For instance, Minford[21] uses the argument that people do not seek low-paid jobs as grounds for the political recommendation that social security benefits ought to be cut so that people are forced to take such jobs. Sen's comment is that 'the implicit assumption seems to be that if everyone agrees on a value judgement then it is not a value judgement at all, but is perfectly "objective" '.[22]

Welfare, justice and freedom
We now look at the way in which the prevalence of the 'culture of economism' leads to specific cultural interpretations of the intrinsic social values of welfare, justice and freedom, and the way in which these interpretations designate as particular instrumental values selfishness, efficiency, rationality, merit and competition. Human welfare defined in an economic sense means the satisfaction of basic needs—for shelter, food, warmth and security—in such a way that people are freed from anxiety about themselves and their families. But this is not how economic welfare is normally interpreted. On an overall level, welfare, imperfectly measured as the Gross Domestic Product of an economy, is interpreted as 'more is better', and maximized when the available resources produce as much as possible. It is assumed by economics that this will maximize the 'utilities', or satisfaction, of everyone concerned, in spite of the fact that nothing is said about the distribution of the wealth available. There are profound problems associated with this interpretation of economic welfare. The major problem for the purposes of this argument is that it enshrines in our cultural mind-set the view that selfishness is 'normal', or 'human nature', or 'necessary for survival'. Satisfaction of wants takes precedence over fulfilment of needs, not just on a personal level, but also on a social level. Homelessness and hunger coexist in our society with a personal affluence which is taken completely for granted.

Justice, too, is a value to which all cultures subscribe, but which different cultures define differently. In our culture justice is not distributive justice in the sense of 'justice-as-equality'. Economics enshrines a view of justice as commutative—i.e. it is based on the procedures for distribution rather than on the consequences of that distribution. Entitlement to what is produced stems from property rights in labour or capital and factors of production. Work and effort generate productivity, which is meritorious and deserving of reward. Profits are the legitimate return to capital, and thus deserved. The notion of effort-as-merit, and of deserving as the basis of reward, are cornerstones of our cultural interpretation of justice-as-fairness. How is it then possible for us to hear the message of the Kingdom contained in the parables of the servant's reward (Lk 17.7–10), the unjust steward (Lk 16.1–7), the wicked husbandmen (Mk 12.1–12, Matt 21.33–46, Lk 20.9–19), and the vineyard workers (Matt 20.1–13)? In the parable of the servant's reward even the good are not rewarded, in those of the unjust steward and the wicked husbandmen bad servants do better out of being bad than they would have done if they had been good, and in the parable of the vineyard workers, the story which grates so uncomfortably on the ears of modern capitalist hearers, not only do the good and hardworking not get what they think they deserve, but the lay-abouts get what they have not earned. God, in other words, is 'not fair'. There is a profound conflict between our valuation of the importance of merit for justice and our understanding of a Gospel based on the gratuity of God's gifts.

Freedom, the third basic cultural value, is interpreted by us as freedom to choose, often in a market context. There is no other part of the capitalist economic system which is so deeply imbued with ideology as the notion of the market. It embodies not only Newtonian conceptions of order and harmony, but also Darwinistic notions of human progress and development. Choice in markets involves competition. Competitive striving is seen culturally as essential not only to market functioning, but as central to the process of human growth and as a spur to personal and social development. The idea of the market is then absolutized, reified and applied to other disciplines and areas of social life. What is fundamentally a social institution becomes a kind of universal human situation with almost biological connotations. We are thus encouraged to make the factual/normative shift in our thinking, from a position where the market exists to one where it is legitimized; from a position where it is legitimized as a social institution to one where the human attitudes necessary to function in it and to make it function are held to be good because they make the market work. This in turn gives a particular connotation to the socio-political value of freedom, and causes it to be interpreted in a particular way.

Market functioning relies on the prevalence of certain attitudes which are then themselves held as instrumental values. Selfishness and avarice are exalted to the rank of virtues, competition—which is really strife—

becomes praiseworthy. There is a cultural assumption that it is 'natural' to be competitive, and that what is natural is right. The market values competitiveness because it is competition which weeds out the inefficient and drives prices lower. But this assumes that people are equally able to compete. The argument that competition brings efficiency always assumes that power is equal in the market, that people are not being squeezed out or prevented from competing on the same basis as others. People may be given equal rights in a market system, but they differ in their ability to use those rights. In parts of the market—for instance, in the labour market—there is clearly an inequality of power when it comes to wage bargaining. Ability to compete for goods depends on income; some are strong enough to compete for jobs and wages, some are not. In the case of non-price competition it is companies with the most money to spend on advertising who can compete most efficiently. Monopoly and the consequent exercise of power are the inevitable outcome; competition therefore holds the seeds of its own destruction. This in itself has profound implications for the belief in free markets as the optimum economic system.

It is not only inequalities of power which can lead to competition on unequal terms. The allocative consequences of market functioning must also be called into question, because the dynamics of the market mechanism itself can result in an widening of inequalities. This is particularly the case in an international context. Market responses in trading terms vary in their sensitivity to price changes. Third World countries selling primary products on world markets face a no-win situation. If they increase their production in order to make more money, world prices will fall because world responsiveness (or elasticity of demand) to commodity price changes is low, and incomes of primary producers will therefore fall. The rate of growth of world demand for primary products is slow enough to ensure that there is a continual downward pressure on the relative incomes of primary producers. The prices of manufactured goods, on the other hand, are not determined by the free play of markets, but by costs of production, and these are continually rising because of world inflation. The gap between rich and poor, North and South, therefore widens because markets work to the advantage of the North.

The foregoing has argued that economics provides culturally prevalent interpretations of basic social values. The other side of the coin is the way in which the everyday language we use to discuss what is economic is itself evaluative. In the first instance, the concepts we use may give us little grip on the lived realities of economic life, but they serve to shape the way in which we think about that reality. The concepts we use are chosen to fit the overall image which mechanistic theoretical approaches present. Equilibrium, stability, elasticity, expansion, inflation and contraction are all words in the everyday vocabulary of economists and journalists. They are all borrowed from mechanics and thus, although they have particular technical meanings in economics, they carry with them connotations of economic process as mechanistic and deterministic rather than as the outcome of human action. The importance of this lies in the way our thought processes are influenced and our experience shaped.

Economic concepts support overall images, they also help to bend our perception of our own everyday participation in economic life. Work, for instance, is something which in general terms is often—perhaps usually— experienced by people as life-enhancing. But neo-classical economics considers work to be a 'disutility'. People require to be compensated by higher pay for working harder or longer hours. A job, on the other hand, is something which has no neo-classical connotations. A job—i.e. permission to work—is something which we consider desirable, but work itself is considered undesirable. The value of work done is assessed on the basis of its market value—i.e. value as equated with price. The work of a construction engineer is considered 'better' or more worthwhile than that of a dustman or a canteen worker or even a nurse—not just subjectively, but even in terms of social valuation. It is, however, usually true that our society tends to value jobs which result in concrete products more highly than those which involve repetitive service to other people. Our whole experience of the world of work is thus moulded by a 'received' viewpoint.

The concepts which we use also limit the ways in which we can think about what are becoming ever more urgent issues. Changing social, cultural and technological conditions present economists with the necessity to analyse problems of ecology, of long-term unemployment, of pollution. We have, for instance, no way of distinguishing conceptually between a resource which is renewable and one which is not. The only way we can discuss pollution is in terms of social costs, or 'externalities'— i.e. via a technique which seeks to quantify the costs arising from the particular situation, but which is totally inadequate to cope with the longer-term aspects of these problems.

There are other ways in which the concepts we use encourage a reductionistic view of economic existence. Because all our evaluations are market-based we are unable to use our concepts to include wider dimensions of any given issue. We think about efficiency—a concept which is always defined in an allocative or technical sense—in a way which makes us unable to evaluate meaningfully the relative efficiency of nuclear power and solar energy; if we think that nuclear power is more efficient simply because it can produce more energy, do we make allowances in the evaluation procedure for potential long-term hazards and for costs of giving subsidies? We measure potential industrial success in terms of productivity, but to what extent can we validly use an overall index of industrial productivity as an indicator of the state of the economy when there are people unemployed and therefore not productive? How can we use profitability as a concept with positive connotations when profits are bought at the expense of incalculable social costs?

It is also the case that the way in which language is used in economics affects the way in which we use language in ordinary speech. The tendency to reduce everything to a matter of quantities leads to depersonalization; the economy is viewed as being made up not of people and what they do, individually and institutionally, but of aggregates such as unemployment, labour, consumer demand, saving, expenditure and so on. The other face of this is the tendency, which has crept into ordinary-language use, to personalize the institution. We talk of unemployment rather than of people who are unemployed, but we discuss the way in which the economy can become 'leaner, slimmer, fitter' as a result of government policy. Companies are healthy, or competitive, marketing policy is aggressive, sales or profits 'forge ahead'. Ordinary language tends to ascribe personal—and usually masculine—attributes and attitudes to institutions, while at the same time discussing people as a non-personal aggregate.

This kind of language use is ideological in that it mirrors the evaluative basis of thought. The kind of symbolism mirrored in language derives its nature from the social context, in particular, from the system of production. But the language of economics can be used in a more overtly ideological fashion: witness the way in which current usage works to convey an idea of the sacred, to sacralize the secular. Politicians talk about 'pontificating on economics',[23] about the Church being 'cheapened' by its involvement in social and economic affairs. Much of the monetarist rhetoric, as Seabrook says, has been drawn from 'incursions into the territory of the spirit', a plunder of religious terminology and imagery. We talk about the Japanese 'economic miracle', we 'prevail' against striking workers, 'rejoice' at the victory in the Falklands. Wealth is 'created', the economy is subject to 'laws' which have the force of moral sanction: woe betide those who hinder the workings of the market. Capitalism is no longer seen as a bringer of insufficiency and hunger, but as a provider of all good things; salvation comes through abundance, and is made possible by money. The symbolism of economics has become quasi-religious, a conflation of values with value, which 'plunders the symbolism of Christianity to dignify its ideology'.[24] Precisely because the culture of economism is a quasi-religion, with a pretence of encompassing the totality of life and of bringing happiness and fulfilment, we find ourselves obliged from a Christian point of view to denounce it as a dehumanizing idolatry, which worships profit made by the strong at the expense of the weak, and is deaf to the word of a God who hears the cries of the poor.

(c) Structures

Presuppositions and values, which derive at least in part from the economic dimension of our existence, form the basis of our actions. But our actions, and the decisions on which they are based, happen in a social context, within the structures which society creates and within which we all belong. These structures are largely economic. They can be formally organizational, such as companies or banks, and they can also be less formal social groupings—clubs, work groups, family structures—but they can also be simply ways of doing things or conducting relations between agents which are laid down by the rules governing such relationships (as, for instance, in the case of trading relationships, or ways of celebrating marriages). Structures, whether formal or otherwise, are produced and reproduced by their participants as they conform to and act according to the rules and practices governing those structures. Social structures, in other words, are no more than lived social practices. Those who participate in and thus replicate social structures are continually monitoring the consequences of action in a social context, and the outcomes of this monitoring process become the conditions which generate future action.

We spend our lives within a network of interlocking structures, and each one of us belongs to a variety of social groupings. Structures both enable and constrain our action. They enable action, because organized groups are more efficient at getting things done than individuals. In social terms we could not survive unless we collaborated with others. But there are a number of ways in which structures operate to constrain the possibilities of personal action. We can categorize these possibilities into two groups, depending on whether we are outside or inside particular structures.

The lives and actions of those outside the structures in question are constrained by the realities of power exercised by those structures. The workings of competitive markets lead inevitably to the dominance of the strongest, and to the concentration of power in the hands of the few. We can see this happening politically and economically, nationally and internationally, in the sphere of ideas and information transmission, and not least in the Church. Power is also exercised against others through bureaucracy—in other words, by people working within structures. Injustices can be incidental, deliberate, or unperceived because they are institutionalized in the rules and procedures by which structures operate. If we want to think concretely about this particular issue we have only to think of the workings of the Social Security system, and to reflect on the many instances and anomalies of treatment of claimants reported in the press and in sociological studies.

However, it is a category mistake to assume that injustice happens without human agency. Everything done by and in the name of structures translates into human action and hence into human responsibility. We do not invent the rules, but it is we who live them and perpetuate their existence. We may be powerless to relieve the oppression which we or others experience because of something we can do nothing about—property rights, or the workings of commodity markets, or the allocation of government expenditure. But most of us help to perpetuate structures which in some way or another constrain the lives of others, and many of these structures are economic.

It can be argued, however, that we have little choice in this matter; because for those who live and work inside structures, action is also constrained. Organizations assign roles to their members, and expect that those roles will be fulfilled in ways specified. Groups within organizations exert pressure to conform, and the success of such pressure is a function of the degree of power exercised on the one hand and our own vulnerability on the other. Group pressure to conform succeeds not just because of our acquiescence, but also because of the fact that it modifies our own beliefs, values and attitudes.[25] Also, there are dynamic processes at work which operate on group decision-taking and its attitudinal basis in such a way as to distort the judgemental processes of group members and trigger the phenomenon of 'groupthink'. In these instances individual judgemental processes are entirely suborned by what is going on in the group, and organizational processes condition individual action.

The consequences of economism

There is always an interaction between thought and world, between culture and the paradigms which structure and govern its functioning. These interactions create the characteristics and parameters of the historical situation within which the Gospel is lived; they provide, in other words, the challenge of 'inculturation'. The particular mind-set which I have dubbed 'economism' has consequences on every level of existence, and consequences which apply not only to our culture, but above all to other cultures which have proved less ready and less able to cope with the brutalities of industrial market capitalism.

On a world level, economic development has involved the demise of cultures. We only have to look at Africa to see the end product of a process which began some two hundred years ago, and has been painfully completed over the last two decades. Strangely enough, although we are incapable of seeing what the advent of industrialization did to our culture we can see very clearly what it has involved in the cultures where it has been imposed as 'development'. The word 'develop' had an earlier meaning which implied 'disclose', or 'unfold'; only in the mid-nineteenth century did it come to mean progression from a lower to a higher or more complex form of existence. In the last four decades it has acquired a pejorative meaning for those countries seen as 'underdeveloped' by advanced economies.

Attempts to bring development to these cultures have created a poverty never previously known. Their economies have moved from a position of austere sufficiency to a position of life-threatening deprivation. They experience a 'scarcity (which is) the self-fulfilling assumption of modern economic culture'.[26] For us, development has meant riches in comparative terms, but a prosperity which has been characterized as 'the joyless economy'.[27] We are constantly faced with our inability to satisfy our continually created needs. Our environment is plundered and despoiled in the pursuit of the growth for which we strive. We experience an insecurity which derives from the threat to our environment and our planet. Wealth and welfare are divorced; the costs of wealth creation in human, social and ecological terms must be set against the benefits of the race for growth.

On a personal level, 'economism' has created a meaninglessness in our lives because it has limited our choices and our freedom. Our creativity and our imagination are increasingly subject to the exigencies of organized production. For millions the quality of our leisure is structured by the limitations of urban living and the congestion of our countryside, and dictated by the persuasiveness of the media and television. Above all, we are in danger of losing the ability to take time for ourselves, time to listen to others, time to enjoy the company of our friends, time to 'stand and stare'.

Conversion

This chapter has outlined the ways in which the theory and praxis of economics places a particular set of cultural barriers in the way of the

Gospel message. The argument has concentrated on identifying these barriers, and has to some extent neglected the explicit contrast between the 'culture of economism' and the values of the Gospel. Nevertheless, the contrast becomes stark when we remember that that the Kingdom which Jesus came to preach is a Kingdom of justice which embraces all who experience poverty, whether material or spiritual. It is a Kingdom of love which reaches out to the weak, the powerless and the needy. It is a Kingdom of peace which demands altruism, compassion and self-sacrifice. And finally, it is a Kingdom which reverses all our preconceptions, all our values, and all our aspirations. How easy do we find it to accept that those who work one hour should be paid the same as those who have worked all day (Mt 20.1–13)?

The Gospel calls cultures, and all aspects of cultures, to conversion. In the light of this, what is required? We can divide the process into two stages.

(a) The effectiveness with which the Gospel is preached depends on the mission and witness of the believing community in our culture. The Church is the community of persons which keeps the Gospel alive as an inspiration in daily living. In order to transmit that inspiration to others it needs to be sensitive to cultural needs for healing and wholeness, and to the needs of persons for faith and hope in their lives. It must also remember that whereas on the one hand it is a pilgrim Church, it is also a human institution which itself stands in need of conversion. If it is to be effective as a sign of the presence of God in the world the institutional Church must engineer its own structures of critique, by which it can identify the failures of inculturation within our own 'culture of economism'.

The Church also needs to be creative, and to take advantage of the same channels of transmission by which cultural ideologies are transmitted. Faith must speak not only *to* culture, but also *through* the use of cultural forms of every kind. It must speak not only through the obvious forms of ritual, myth and symbol, but also through other media which can communicate its content—language and the printed word, art, film, television. But faith also has to use thought forms proper to the different disciplines, and the understanding which they achieve, to interpret the historical situation as God sees it. Theology in particular must take serious account of the power and force of contributions from other disciplines if it is to have anything to say to audiences outside 'Church' and 'academy'.

The dialogue between theology and other disciplines is not only necessary for interpretative purposes. There is an essential role for a prophetic voice to be exercised in our society by those who hear the word of God and reflect on it. The prophetic voice is not merely a critical voice, it is also the voice which gives hope and encouragement to those who pray the God's Kingdom may be established 'in our lifetime and in our days . . . even speedily and at a near time' (Kaddish). People need to see and hear 'signs of the Kingdom' in their own culture and their own language. The prophetic voice can convey the hope of this Kingdom because such hope is both the basis from which theology springs and the outcome of the search for understanding which it represents.

(b) The call to conversion is addressed to all, believers and non-believers alike. It is addressed to economists, and articulated firstly as a requirement that they reassess the value of what they do in the light of the contribution it makes to human welfare, and secondly that they seek new ways of 'doing economics'. We have all at one time or another been persuaded to believe, to value and to practise what is deemed culturally acceptable. Our cultural symbols, myths, rituals, forms of social inter-action and discourse all embody presuppositions and values which appear so self-evident as to be unassailable. As economists—and also practitioners of other disciplines—we are, on the one hand, caught in a climate of opinion where doubt has been expressed about the wisdom and relevance of what we do—witness the many references to critical material in this chapter. On the other hand, we exist in a situation, as we saw earlier, where our livelihood, our research and in the end our thought is ideologically pressured and politically manipulated. It is all too easy to flow with the tide. We may do so for purely instrumental reasons, we may not even realize the extent to which we succumb to effective conditioning. What is needed is an 'intellectual conversion', by which the economist 'appropriates' himself or herself as someone capable of knowing, judging and criticizing the way in which knowledge is produced. Such a critique will involve questioning the relevance of science-as-knowledge within the discipline of economics, rejecting empiricism and positivism, and challenging ideologies. It will generate a practical concern for the fate and quality of social life; this requires on the one hand a commitment to a critical realism which believes that 'world' is more complex than the sum total of what can be perceived, and on the other hand a questioning of growth as the basic 'organizing principle' of the discipline.

Conversion is not only intellectual, it is also moral. The Gospel challenges all who live as 'economic agents' to a moral self-transcendence and moral autonomy which opens their eyes to the gulf between the values of the Gospel and the values of 'economism'. Moral conversion entails the rejection of the primacy of self-interest. It involves a reinterpretation of welfare in terms of the needs of people and the quality of life rather than in terms of the quantity of goods. It involves a commitment to the achievement of social justice as a prior requirement for peace within families, communities, cities, and at a world level. It develops a vision of freedom as freedom to live in such a way that the experience of God's redemption can become a personal reality. Above all, it involves the realization that we do not succeed, and that there are never any absolutes. In fact, the whole enterprise of 'inculturation' has to be relativized in the light of a Gospel which has a habit of casting changing lights on the human situation in order to illumine the darkness and the ambiguity. No analysis can be the last word: it is offered, therefore, as no more than a sign of a hope which seeks understanding in a confused and confusing human situation.

Notes

1 Frank Hahn, *In Praise of Economic Theory: the Jevons Memorial Lecture* (London: University College, 1985), p. 5.

2 Ludwig von Mises, *Human Action* (London: Hodge, 1949), p. 190.

3 Hahn, op. cit., p. 7.

4 Alfred Eichner, *Why Economics Is Not Yet a Science* (London: Macmillan Press, 1984), Introduction.

5 Martin Hollis and Edward Nell, *Rational Economic Man: A Philosophical Critique of Neo-Classical Economics* (Cambridge: Cambridge University Press, 1985), p. 81.

6 John Dewey, *Essays in Experimental Logic* (Chicago: University of Chicago Press, 1983), p. 507.

7 Cf. for example the first essay in Roy Baskar, *Scientific Realism and Human Emancipation* (London: Verso, 1986).

8 Phyllis Deane (ed.), *The Frontiers of Economic Research* (London: Macmillan, 1990), ch. 1.

9 Argued in Richard Lipsey, *An Introduction to Positive Economics* 5th edn (London: Weidenfeld and Nicolson, 1979), Introduction.

10 Quoted in Fritz Machlup, *Methodology and Economics and Other Social Sciences* (New York: Academic Press, 1978), p. 490.

11 Cf. for example Jack Wiseman, *Beyond Positive Economics* (London: Macmillan, 1983).

12 J.A. Schumpeter, *History of Economic Analysis* (London: Allen and Unwin, 1954), p. 8, note.

13 Machlup, op. cit., p. 438. Cf. also Alan Coddington, *Canadian Journal of Economics* (1972) 1, pp. 1–15.

14 Gerald Radnitsky, *Contemporary Schools of Metascience* I and II (Göteborg: Academiforlag, 1970), p. 90.

15 Karl Polanyi, *The Great Transformation* (London: Gollancz, 1945).

16 Robert Neild, 'The case for the reconstruction of economics', *Business Economics* (winter 1982), p. 5.

17 Joan Robinson, *Economic Philosophy* (Harmondsworth: Penguin, 1964), p. 10.

18 Gibson Winter, *Elements for a Social Ethics* (New York: Macmillan, 1986), ch. I.

19 Aristotle, *Nicomachean Ethics* in *Basic Works*, ed. R. McKeon (New York, 1964).

20 Amartya Sen, 'Description as choice' in *Choice, Welfare and Measurement* (Oxford: Blackwell, 1982).

21 Patrick Minford, *Unemployment: Cause and Cure* (Oxford: Robertson, 1981).

22 Amartya Sen, *Collective Choice and Social Welfare* (San Francisco: Holden Day, 1970), p. 57.

23 Jeremy Seabrook, 'Face to faith', *The Guardian* (26 November 1984).

24 Ibid.

25 Jane Collier, *The Culture of Economism: An Exploration of Barriers to Faith-as-Praxis* (Frankfurt: Lang, 1990), pp. 266–81.

26 A.L. de Romana, 'The autonomous society', *Interculture* 22.3 and 4 (fall 1989).

27 Tibor Scitovsky, *The Joyless Economy* (Oxford: Oxford University Press, 1977).

Education and the Gospel

BRENDA WATSON

Why we have schools

Mark Twain is reputed to have complained that his education was interrupted by his schooling. Whatever may have been the case for him, we shall be considering here how far this may be true for our society and what might be a Christian response to both education and schooling. In fact today we find no less than five different approaches to schooling, each of which deserves a short examination:

(1) The liberal concept of education

Schooling can focus on personal development, encouraging the young to develop their capacity for reflectiveness and to take responsibility for their own unique fulfilment as persons in their own right. Autonomy and responsibility are closely linked in this approach to education. 'Words like freedom, growth, autonomy, co-operation, democracy, negotiation and justice . . . are the traditional values which have informed the world of education since the 1960s.'[1]

(2) The utilitarian model for schooling

Schooling can train the young for specific work roles or for some other use of time and talent in their adult life. This approach does not have to be seen as making educators 'just puppets of the economy or the state'.[2] Rather, it is an attempt to break down the artificial barriers between the school and the wider world, especially the presumed inferiority of practical and organizational abilities. Irritation is felt by the protagonists of this approach at the irrelevance of so much present schooling, and at the placing in jeopardy of a country's future vitality and prosperity as it falls behind its international competitors. 'In the 1990s there is another set of values coming to occupy the "high ground" in education. These are the values pertaining to the world of business and industry.'[3]

(3) The so-called academic approach

Schooling can promote access to knowledge, teaching children the necessary skills and thus enabling them to become students and perhaps scholars. By 'academic' is meant 'ability in logico-deductive reasoning and propositional knowledge, abilities which have stood at the heart of Western philosophy, science and technology for over 300 years'.[4] Care has to be taken that this kind of 'academic schooling' does not lead to isolationism, pride or second-hand thinking. At the heart of this model is what has been called 'the discipline of encounter with otherness'.[5] This academic approach, properly understood, prepares students for the world of work; an example of this is that graduates in the classics are employed across the whole spectrum of the industrial and commercial market place.

(4) The ideological approach to education

This is a view of education which sees it as appropriate to use schools to indoctrinate young people in particular ideological positions, whether cultural, political or religious.

> This typifies a mode of thinking . . . which has sometimes been associated with the church—as in the period of the Inquisition—and which has flourished more recently in Marxist states and in Nazi Germany . . . Its validation derives from an ideology that must never be questioned . . . an assumption of infallibility, or at least of revealed truth, motivates its enquiries . . . it is intolerant and dismissive towards criticism, and its style is chosen not for its ability to encourage the pursuit of truth, but for rhetorical effect.[6]

This approach is inconsistent with the liberal and academic approaches to education, in which pupils are encouraged to think for themselves. It is also inappropriate for the utilitarian approach, for today's world—which is always tomorrow's world—requires people who are not programmed but prepared to be flexible and creative. It is incontestable that ideological indoctrination has at times crept into the classroom. It may 'brainwash' the young into particular attitudes towards race, or sexism: it may consist of political or religious indoctrination. It has to be admitted that at times in the past the Church has been guilty of this kind of teaching.

The question of indoctrination is difficult. The word is sometimes used simply as another word for teaching. Indoctrination, however, in a pejorative sense, is educationally inadmissible. It does not concern the content of teaching, for any content becomes indoctrinatory if it is taught in a manner which, intentionally or not, precludes people thinking about it freely. Any teacher in the classroom who uses his or her powers of persuasion to make pupils adopt particular beliefs and values in a way which undermines their capacity to reflect upon these matters is guilty of such indoctrination. The presence of indoctrination can be detected in its effects, 'closed minds and restricted sympathies', in Professor Mitchell's splendid phrase.[7]

Indoctrination in this sense is more pervasive than we generally realize because it happens most effectively through omission: pupils cannot think about what is never presented to them. It is largely in this way that indoctrination into a secularist approach to life takes place in Western societies.

(5) Moral and cultural approach to education

This is a view of education concerned with the wider perspectives of social outcomes and ethical dilemmas. Some would wish to focus on inducting children into the moral and cultural heritage of Western society or of a particular immigrant culture; others wish to move significantly beyond this into multi-culturalism and global awareness, and link this with environmentalism. A green movement of considerable importance has found its way into educational circles.

The moral and cultural approach to education sees the purpose of schooling not so much in the promotion of autonomy, utility or learning for its own sake as in the nurturing of pupils into patterns of understanding and behaviour which either have shown themselves to be sustainable over centuries, or are urgently called for in today's world. This approach tends to set high store on experience, participation and imagination, and is often concerned about the spiritual development of pupils. We have already noted that influencing the young is inherent in any model of education. Such influence should not inhibit the pupils' ability to think and to decide for themselves. They should be free to question these ideals and practices and values, and even to reject them, but only after they have entered into them and know what it is that they are questioning and, if need be, rejecting. Genuine space and encouragement needs to be given, beginning when children are quite young.

The Gospel and the need for balance

A good education requires a proper balance of all these approaches except for the ideological, which is incompatible with the others. Such a basis for education has a sound theological foundation. We are not mere individuals: we are all born into a tradition, and we can only grow into maturity as persons through communion with others. Such an understanding is at the heart of the Gospel. At the same time, each individual is made in the image of God. The gift of reason, although it is to be found in its rudiments within the animal kingdom, is, in its articulated and conscious form, a special characteristic of humanity whereby we resemble God and are made in his image. Education therefore must encourage the power of reasoning. Another unique characteristic of humanity is our power of reasoned choice, our ability to decide for ourselves, and this is another aspect of the image of God in which we are all made. A liberal education encourages us to make responsible use of this freedom. Humanity is born to work. Christians also see work as God-given. According to Genesis, work is part of the human condition which we inherit from our past. It is therefore an important aspect of schooling that we have sufficient training to enable us to earn our living when we are of age to do so. The wider aspect of the utilitarian approach to education is also thoroughly Christian in orientation, in that the Gospel contains many indications that practical matters are important and that the stewardship of resources and talents is required. Concern about efficiency, and for the well-being of as large a number of people as possible, are ways in which *agapē*, Christian love, can be exercised.

A combination of these four approaches respects the inalienable uniqueness and worth of every child, the importance of knowledge and understanding, the need for people to stand on their own feet in the world, and the awareness of the communal nature of both human life and the search for truth. On the other hand, the ideological approach to education is inconsistent with the Christian faith (even though Christians may have used it in the past). It must be rejected, because it does not respect the image of God in which we are all made, and it inhibits our freedom of choice and our power of intellectual discrimination.

The prevalence of relativism

Education, at least in Britain, tends to lack the necessary integration of the liberal, the academic, the utilitarian and the moral and cultural approaches to education which are needed for good schooling. In particular, moral and cultural education is in chaos. Most educationalists have lost their nerve. They feel that they can do no more than clarify positions. As Professor Pring has put it:

> Part of the present moral and social climate is a distrust of authority, especially in the realm of values. Without an agreed tradition of values it is not easy to see how one can promote with confidence one particular set of values rather than another.[8]

The implication here is that only authority and consensus can give adequate grounds for values, and as our pluralist society is significantly lacking in both, each individual must choose these for himself or herself. The problem which is increasingly being perceived by those at the chalk-face of education is that such privately-held values affect public decision-making, and that children pick up like litmus paper the values by which adults in their world live. Moreover, the discerning teacher knows that, however much particular interpretations of the moral law may have been challenged, words like 'ought', despite every endeavour to banish them, are still lurking in the background. They are constantly reappearing in disconcerting forms, challenging former certainties, as for example the values of tolerance and openness in the light of perceived injustices such as racism and sexism. The feminist movement in schools furnishes a good example of the way in which values can be affected:

> Bad language and sexual innuendo are no longer the preserve of boys, it seems . . . By entering the male subculture sexually, girls have turned their backs on some important and timeless values . . . These include love, of course, as indeed a complex of emotions associated with the female gender and based primarily upon the search for a pair bond. Western society has to some extent been built upon these. It is interesting to speculate what the sociological and psychological spinoffs will be, once these value constituents are no longer there.[9]

Religious considerations and acceptance of absolutes seem to be automatically ignored and assumed to be irrelevant. This kind of relativism is not only found in the present practice of education, but it has also been at work for at least thirty years in educational research.[10]

Muslims have seen such relativism as an attempt to brainwash Muslim children:

> If the curriculum, the methods of teaching and the school ethos are based on the philosophy of changing values that are dependent on external social change and not on the philosophy of the absolutes in human nature which provide the unchanging universal norms of truth, justice, righteousness, freedom, pity, mercy, honesty, compassion and charity, Muslim children will suffer from the conflict that people suffered in England in the 19th century and the sense of loss, uncertainty, and insecurity that is prevalent in the 20th century.[11]

With such relativism in human values and ethics, our schools today lack an essential component which is necessary for a growing young person to achieve a sound education. Nor is it difficult for Christians to see that 'education in Britain reflects the non-cultural values and objectives of European secularism'.[12]

What schools are actually conveying

We turn from examining the purposes of education and its underlying assumptions to consider what is actually being done in practice.

At one level, the purposes which people have in mind for schooling are only too effectively communicated to children and to youngsters. The real problem is not how to get them learning, but what they learn. A child starting school has already mastered an incredible array of both content and skills, almost all of it entirely self-taught. The capacity for learning does not evaporate when the child enters school. The child picks up most effectively the hidden messages of the total environment of the school, the quality of relationships in it, the character of the teachers and so forth, and no teaching can prevent this learning. This is just as true of adolescents, who are extremely sensitive to atmosphere and innuendo.

If the messages received are confused, then the child or student struggles to adapt, like the ten-year-old from a difficult background who boasted about his prowess at football, and who replied, when he was asked whether he was in the school team, 'I'm too good for that'. This kind of pretence both reflects and reinforces a lack of proper self-affirmation, especially when the most important messages received, whether intended or not, include competitiveness and achieving standards set by other people.

There is, perhaps, so much talk today about the importance of personal development because of the perceived lack of it in so many pupils and students. The system carries a huge number of casualties. Many educationalists see schools for whatever reason as producing failures, and yet giving no help at all on how to cope with failure.

From one point of view this is not surprising. It is an experiment unique in the world's history to try to educate (as opposed merely to train, nurture, or indoctrinate) all children in a society. Nevertheless, no educationalist can fail to be concerned at the present situation. If children learn so easily, why does there appear to be so great a difficulty in encouraging motivation to learn when in school? Whatever view of the purpose of schooling is held, the task of achieving it is experienced in our schools as laborious and precarious. Even utilitarians and would-be indoctrinators have difficulties here. Teachers who take seriously liberal, academic and moral/cultural goals not only have to work very hard but at great nervous cost. Why has there to be so much emphasis on keeping discipline, on giving entertaining lessons and presentations, and on the use of competition and examinations in order to get pupils to work? This is related to the general indiscipline and instability of so many children's home backgrounds, and to the effect of the mass media on children, as well as to the artificiality of herding people of the same age together for compulsory learning. Effective and easy learning requires freedom and spontaneity. It has to be adapted to the unique needs and interests of every person, and this cannot happen in today's busy and mostly very large schools.

It is not surprising therefore that the intention of liberal educators is only very patchily achieved. Despite accepted theory about the importance of autonomy, in practice most students receive very little help. Here is a paragraph from the final report of the National Extension College on a project:

> The majority of 6th form students have had no previous experience of individualised learning . . . As a consequence, almost none of them have the skills necessary to organise their study for themselves.[13]

This is a massive indictment of the education system's failure to educate. Even when the intention is there, the reality is very different.

This failure to help children and students to arrive at the point where they can be self-educating, and can show genuine autonomy instead of dependence on teachers, is not usually the fault of the teachers, although many do seriously underestimate children's capacities. Despite the goodwill of most members of the teaching staff, more pressing requirements tend to take priority. Deadlines have to be met, targets reached, 'essential' subjects attended to, examinations and reports prepared, meetings attended, and responses made to a constant stream of initiatives. Schools are very far indeed from being the places of leisure which the derivation of the word (*scholē* in Greek), as well as the nature of the task which they should be performing, alike suggest that they should be.

In the light of this, it is hardly surprising that consumerism and pragmatism are the major lessons which pupils actually learn, even though this more often happens by default rather than by official pronouncements. Schools of all types, primary and secondary, state and church, urban and rural, constantly need to resist the grip of a rigorous utilitarian approach whereby only that which is of immediate relevance or obvious long-term usefulness can be assured of any priority in the distribution of time, resources, staffing, status and encouragement.

At a lower level—apart from the odd inspirational session—most schools convey a moral humanism, usually thought of as traffic rules for enabling society to remain civilized. There is rarely much sustained attempt to meet the latent scepticism of the young which is in evidence at quite an early age. A primary school teacher recently told me how clearly the seven- and eight-year-olds in her school see through the hypocrisy of teachers with their simple 'We must be kind to people who help us' approach. Little wonder that by the time such children have reached their teens the half-hearted attempts of the adult world to moralize are not appreciated.

Moderate hedonism, individualism and insistence on open-mindedness were among the key aspects that emerged in some research conducted in 1977 on young people's beliefs. 'A strong dislike of having other people's beliefs pushed on you' was particularly noted.[14] Their own beliefs seemed superficial, consumerist and pragmatic, tinged with some fascination with the occult. They put their faith in facts and a simplistic scientism, and they saw no point in trying to reflect on a consistent and well-founded philosophy of life. Religion took up no part of their world. I suspect that the fourteen years since this research was undertaken have not altered the beliefs of most youngsters significantly. Here is a comment, out of scores of possible ones, from a youngster in a Roman Catholic Sixth Form College:

> If people asked me if I went to church my curt reply would be, 'What do you think I am—some sort of religious freak?' They would snigger at that reply but laugh even more if I said 'Yes'. Well, let's face it, people think that if you are between 13 and 18 and you still go to mass it's either because (a) you are made to go, (b) there is something wrong with you, or (c) you want to be a nun or a priest.[15]

The cynicism and absence of a religious dimension is sometimes accompanied by a feeling of despair, especially when associated with bleak prospects of personal status and success. Mark Roques in his book *Curriculum Unmasked* considers that a view of life as meaningless is conveyed to many. He argues that 'the spirit of the 1980s and the dominant spirit of our schools is much more pessimistic than pragmatic'.[16]

Nevertheless, there is to be discerned a far greater awareness among some children and young people of global and conservationist issues, and with it a sense of responsibility akin to stewardship. There is also an encouraging increase in multi-cultural understanding in certain areas. It is impossible to generalize, but it does seem that there is greater openness and tolerance as well as concern for justice amongst many young people, and that the credit for much of this should go to their school experiences. This improvement in attitudes is, I think, also reflected in a much better image of religious education amongst some. The need for improvement here however has been, and, still is, very great indeed.

The role of religious education

The priorities of schools can clearly be seen in connection with what has happened to religious education.

When the culture of a society is as pronouncedly secular as ours, it is even more important that children seriously deprived in this area in their home environment are helped to reach the level of awareness of which they are capable. To use current educational jargon, they are 'entitled' to this. Official documents, such as the Crowther Report of 1959, the Newsom Report of 1963 and the Plowden Report of 1967, have acknowledged this, and most recently the Education Reform Act of 1988. Yet the role of religious education in schools has been consistently marginalized. In the Education Reform Act it is mentioned as 'basic', but not accorded even the status of a 'foundation' subject, which means that in real terms it is likely to continue to have to struggle for survival.

This is borne out by the statistics disclosed in a booklet produced by the Religious Education Council and based on recent DES findings. These cover staffing provision in primary and secondary schools, staff qualifications, average time allowance for teaching the subject, and opportunities for in-service training. Figures for RE are given alongside those for the other subjects required by the National Curriculum. It makes disturbing reading: a picture emerges of extremely poor provision by comparison with most other subjects. The leaflet opens with a 'Health Warning'!

> It is our fear that the scale of the problem is worsening. Without direct intervention to recruit and retrain more RE teachers, the expectations for RE and collective worship as specified in the Education Reform Act will be exposed as an empty delusion.[17]

The situation is worse than that however, because the quality of neither teaching nor content was considered. I will briefly draw attention to three issues.

(1) *The traditional problem of the equation of RE with moral and social education*. A glance at Agreed Syllabuses drawn up in the last two decades will confirm the woolliness of thinking here in assuming that religious education that was largely 'implicit' was discharging the educational responsibility of helping children to understand religion.

(2) *Extreme reluctance to introduce theology into primary school RE*. This has characterized the last thirty years since Goldman applied Piaget's psychological research to RE. Talk about God has been effectively banished from primary schools as being necessarily abstract and thus beyond

pupils' capabilities. The validity of the research has since been seriously questioned, but this has not yet percolated down to the classroom.[18]

(3) *The 'phenomenological' approach.* Since the 1970s this approach has brought the study of religions other than Christianity into the classroom, but necessarily largely in a form suitable for a de-religionized majority[19] and in such a way as to limit controversy. Complaints by Muslims, Hindus, Sikhs and other religious groups have underlined how from their point of view RE lessons have been secularist and unhelpful. Themes such as festivals and rites of passage, grasped eagerly by schools desperate to include multi-faith work in a way which might be interesting and make sense to their pupils without upsetting religious believers or offending secular consciences, normally receive predominantly sociological treatment, or consist of largely factual information with little discussion of the fundamental beliefs behind the ritual. Mark Roques considers that the impression about Christianity put across in schools is often that 'Christianity is merely a cult performance that we exploit at birth, marriage and death'.[20]

The slide into moral education, sociological education and relativism within religious education renders the latter's plight far worse than the DES tables suggest. Nor can relief be gained from the fact that religious assemblies for worship have been legally required. Research by Bernadette O'Keeffe, working from King's College, London, and published in 1986, has revealed that 'the majority of county schools have lost all contact with collective worship which seeks to express a divine–human relationship', and that 'as a school activity worship is considered inappropriate in view of the diverse religious and non-religious backgrounds of teachers and pupils'. O'Keeffe concludes:

> In responding to the religious pluralism of pupils, church and county schools, for the most part, separate faith from culture, and in doing so they fragment the essential wholeness or unity of human life.[21]

The interface between education and Christianity

I would like to begin discussion of this with a quotation from fourteenth-century England which may remind readers of the enormity of the task with which education is concerned:

> What is more, even Grammar, the basis of all education, baffles the brains of the younger generation today. For if you take note, there is not a single modern schoolboy who can compose verses or write a decent letter. I doubt

too whether one in a hundred can read a Latin author, or decipher a word of any foreign language.—And no wonder, for at every level of our educational system you'll find Humbug in charge, and his colleague Flattery tagging along behind him. And as for dons and Divinity lecturers—the men who are supposed to master all branches of learning, and be ready to debate every question and answer every argument—I am ashamed to say that if you were to examine them tomorrow in the Arts and Sciences, they would all be ploughed![22]

Even in an age when schooling was restricted to a tiny minority of the population, and when it was almost wholly in the hands of the Church, the results were disappointing. In the eyes of one of the most perceptive observers of any age, William Langland, author of *Piers Plowman*, outward commitment to Christianity did not ensure integrity, selflessness and sound learning.

Education is bound to be precarious. Freedom has to be given and preserved, both to teachers and to taught; human nature at its best and its worst—which includes its capacity for indolence, rigidity and egoism—has to be addressed; and the inalienable uniqueness of each person—who is nevertheless organically linked to all others through family, friends and society—ensures the inevitable particularity and uncertainty of the outcome. To learn effectively means to attend, as Simone Weil noted in her brilliant essay on the meaning of school studies in her book *Waiting on God*.[23] This in itself is an extraordinarily difficult thing to do. The educators' role is so to structure the environment and inspire by choice of content and method that pupils find themselves wanting to learn and therefore able to overcome, within themselves and without, all obstacles to attentiveness without which learning is impossible.

Awareness of the complexity of the task may save us from a simplistic analysis of current trends and likely solutions. If the whole of the educational service—structure, management, teaching—were truly impregnated with Gospel principles, then the likelihood of a more genuinely educated society would be greater, but it would still not be *ensured*. Even Jesus, the educator *par excellence*, could only inspire those who allowed themselves to be inspired by him. It is not surprising therefore that his followers through the centuries—so often more in name than actuality—have had a huge failure rate.

In our British society, Christians have had considerable advantages. Education was almost wholly under the control of the Churches until Forster's Education Act of 1870 set up board schools independent of any religious organization. The first training colleges were all under Christian auspices, and even as late as 1970 almost a third of all teachers trained in Britain passed through colleges run by Christian denominations.

The secularization which is so marked a feature of today's educational system has arisen out of a situation which was originally called Christian. New factors are responsible for many of the forms in which secularization manifests itself, but incapacity to educate people in such a way that they can meet these challenges without succumbing to the latest fashions in beliefs and values suggests that something far more fundamental needs to be uncovered.

The challenge of the Gospel

There is no question that the Gospel poses a deep challenge to much of what goes on in the educational world, as regards both theory and practice. It asks searching questions about the assumptions and priorities actually adhered to.

It brings to schooling the perspective of eternity—everything is seen in a fresh light if perceived *sub specie aeternitatis*, as St Augustine put it. The Christian affirmations of the reality of God, the incarnational presence of the Divine within the structure of the world and of history, and the primacy of the spiritual dimension to life, still today, as in the Thessalonica of St Paul's day, have the power to 'turn the world upside down'. Qualities of love, forgiveness and holiness, springing from a genuine and sustained following of Christ, have a creative impact wherever they occur. They can lift the school experience into something profoundly meaningful.

Retreat before secularism should be halted. Christians need to find a confidence to stand firm on gospel principles. They need to take note of the words of Lord Jakobovits in the House of Lords on 3 May 1988:

> From schools that had confidence in their Christianity I learned an answering pride in my Jewishness and I discovered that those who best appreciate other faiths are those who treasure their own.

But this confidence should not hint of aggressiveness or smugness. Christians must acknowledge they do not come with clean hands to the dialogue with educationalists.

One quotation may suffice to remind readers of one of the key reasons for the movement away from religion—the sectarian bitterness and dogmatism of Christians themselves. Let Lord Brougham speak, who was one of the pioneers of education for the whole population. Because of the venomous strife in the 1830s between Christians, he reluctantly voted for a purely secular educational system. In exasperation he noted:

> Between the claims of contending factions in Church or in State, the legislature stands paralysed, and puts not forth its hand to save the people placed by

providence under its care, lest offence be given to some by the knots of theologians who bewilder its ears with their noise, as they have bewildered their own brains with their controversies.[24]

Although most Christians today would wish to dissociate themselves from any such sectarianism, the effects are still with us. Furthermore a reluctance to affirm others can still be found, as in the lack of generosity accorded to children of other religions in many Church schools which, according to Bernadette O'Keeffe,

> fail to treat seriously those religious dimensions for non-Christian children which they believe to be educationally important for Christian children.[25]

A change of heart is called for. Christians may need to recognize in the incoming tide of secularism the penal waters beneath which the Church needs to be submerged in order to be purified of the narrowness and bigotry, the mistaken priorities, and the various kinds of idolatry to which it has from time to time given way, thus betraying the Gospel in the eyes of the majority of our contemporaries in the Western world.

Appreciating the unfortunate validity of much of this secularist criticism, Christians may be in a better position to evaluate secularism itself. They should be saved from any easy dismissal of it as altogether idolatrous and evil. They should be able to discern many precious insights which have perhaps been better grasped and preserved within secular channels than often in religious ones. Adrian Hastings, professor of theology at Leeds University, has spoken of academic life genuinely lived as 'arguably more successful in producing courtesy, truthfulness, gentleness, amiability, a sense of justice than Christianity itself'.[26]

This does not mean that the Gospel is not supremely important; it does mean that saying one is a Christian does not guarantee goodness, for religions, including Christianity, can become the enemy of the good. It also means that there is a secularity which is noble, uplifting, concerned with high spiritual qualities and able to communicate these effectively. The excellence of so much of Mark Roques's book is marred by what one reviewer called the over-simplification of just two contrasting world-views, the biblical and the 'idolatrous'. Marius Felderhof asks, 'Can our pluralist culture be dismissed under the one heading of "idolatrous" world-view?'[27]

Christians must fight the shortcomings and negative aspects of the contemporary world, but they must also gladly affirm its insights. In fact, within the secular world Christians have many allies. There is no dichotomy between education properly understood and Christian faith.

Nothing of the educational ideal outlined on p. 132 is incompatible with the Gospel.

Revelation reveals what is; education seeks to know what is. Robots cannot receive revelation; education cannot be content with what is not, with error, blindness, or misunderstanding. Enlightenment is a word which could properly belong to both revelation and education.

Education only fails to be in line with the Gospel when it fails to be true to itself, that is, when it becomes exclusive, erecting barriers against other ways of knowing.

The centrality of epistemology

How we may be said rightly to know is a crucial question for Christians to deal with in today's world. The impact of the various -isms such as positivism and relativism referred to elsewhere in this book and powerfully at work in schools, means that if truth-claims are not made central, justice cannot possibly be done to the Gospel. As Lesslie Newbigin puts it:

> The church exists as witness to certain beliefs about what is the case, about facts, not values. This view is excluded from the realm of public truth as taught to children in public schools.[28]

Proclamation, however, is not enough, for this will be seen—to some extent rightly—as a form of positivism which substitutes for the authoritarian status of science an equally authoritarian view of scripture or Church or of private experience.

The problem is what counts as 'facts': these cannot be what the Church says, because the Church could be wrong and can and does say different things which are sometimes contradictory. Similarly, the appeal to revelation is necessarily an appeal to what I or we consider to be trustworthy.

Christians must wrestle with these questions and encourage pupils and students to do the same. Lesslie Newbigin considers that:

> there are signs of an attempt to do this, but they are as yet small. Christians cannot evade this tough intellectual task if they are not to become irrelevant to the real world.[29]

The greater openness which is beginning to be discernible with regard to science, and the increased awareness amongst teachers that education is not and cannot be at any point value-free, means that relativism is now becoming a greater enemy in education than positivism.

Once again Christians must be careful, because relativism creeps in so easily to the teaching of religion. Whenever Christianity or any other religion is presented as a way in which different people see life and belief, relativism will almost certainly, in our current climate of opinion, be communicated. The only way to avoid it is to deal directly with truth questions, and to invite people to reflect and consider evidence.

A major reason why many Christian teachers avoid doing this is because of their concern not to indoctrinate. Much Christian education in the past has been guilty of trying to force belief onto youngsters, assuming that they do or should believe. Christians need to take special care therefore to avoid any pejorative innuendoes in the way they present Christian truth-claims.[30] This does not mean failing to say anything at all, which merely allows a different form of indoctrination to take place. It means expressing Christian beliefs in a way that invites honest and genuine reflection without assuming what the outcome might be. Such openness of approach, promoting dialogue instead of passivity, is perfectly in tune with the teaching methods of Jesus himself.[31]

This point is particularly important today in light of the requirements of the 1988 Education Reform Act for 'predominantly Christian' religious education and school assemblies. This emphasis can easily give the impression of Christian imperialism to those outside the Churches, who, in educational circles, constitute the majority. Yet imperialism has nothing whatever to do with authentic Christianity. Where it appears it is always a cancerous growth. Christians should acknowledge it as such and help pupils and students to appreciate these distinctions. The purpose of the legislation was not in fact to belittle other religions, but to ensure that something of the predominantly Christian cultural heritage in this country should not be neglected. Unfortunately, the way in which the Act was pushed through has encouraged for many a further polarization of the 'Christianity versus multi-faith' issue. Sensitivity, empathy and honesty are required to mitigate the effects of this false polarity.

Conclusions

How can our educational principles and practice be brought more into line with the values of the Gospel? I end this chapter with four main conclusions:

(1) The primacy of education in beliefs and values

This should be undertaken by all schools as a means, firstly, of helping pupils reflect on what is communicated to them both in school and out, and, secondly, of encouraging them to find their own authentic commitment. This should be seen as part of a lifelong search for truth in which the insights of others are taken seriously. Criteria for discernment concerning beliefs and values need to be shared with pupils, beginning in the primary schools. Such criteria include those mentioned by Hugh Montefiore in the Introduction to this book (pp. 9–10) and also by other contributors (pp. 31ff., 54ff., 69ff., 97ff., 125, 156ff., 180ff.).

(2) Ensuring space for religious education in depth

Religious education is of major importance, and needs to be accorded proper status, and resourced and staffed appropriately. Furthermore, major research is needed on how to help children to a real understanding of the concepts involved, especially the concept of God. Theology must be brought into the classroom in ways which are meaningful even to young children, so that they can learn to engage in the reflection upon it of which they are capable. Recent research has shown that their capacity is far greater than most adults allow for, provided no jargon is used, and concepts are related to what is in the range of the child's experience.

A moving example of the strength and authenticity of a young child's faith is given by Jack Priestley, who recalls hearing Robert Coles, professor of psychiatry at Harvard, explaining what he owed in his career to Ruby:

> She was black and she wanted to go to school to learn to read and write. Her attendance at an all-white school led to a boycott of schools in New Orleans. While others investigated how the rednecks, as they were called, who lined her route to school every day could scream and shout abuse and issue threats of violence and murder to one little 6-year-old girl, Coles himself watched Ruby. He knew she must crack under the strain. She didn't. To his amazement she not only endured, but he found that she prayed for the rednecks the prayer, 'Father forgive, they don't know what they are doing'.[32]

(3) A concern for nuts and bolts

The question of priorities is fundamental. There is a great deal of goodwill on which to draw. Most teachers do wish to promote genuine education, imagination, space for reflectiveness, and many other aspects of spiritual development, but the distractions of school life and the expectations of parents, governors, and future employers force them into a pragmatic attitude which becomes habitual. The idealism of teachers in training rapidly becomes diluted within modern schools.

The following ways forward may appear exceedingly radical, but I see them as essential.

(a) *There is a need to press for an integrated approach to learning which transcends the subject divisions.* The National Curriculum Council does not lay down that the subjects must be pursued in separate timetabled lessons—there is room for manoeuvre and considerable freedom in schools, as many schools have shown.

Whole-school policies and the abandonment of rigid timetabling permit much more flexibility and emphasis on both teacher and pupil involvement. The way the timetable is set up should help teachers to be aware that no learning happens in isolation, that what they teach in science or English or any other subject affects learning in every other area of the curriculum through its reinforcement of certain assumptions, attitudes and outcomes.

(b) *The need for teachers to be primarily person-centred, not subject-orientated*. Enlightened infant schools have long understood how education can be person-centred. This approach needs to be extended to the whole of schooling. If schools are too large, structures must be found to make for tiny schools within the large. Teachers should see themselves as not so much purveyors of specialist knowledge as educators. This calls for a change in teacher attitudes, but one which many, perhaps most, would be willing to make if encouraged by the system.

(c) *The need to harness modern technology to pupil-based learning, as regards both content and pace*. The potential benefits for education of technology are enormous and wide-ranging. It can relieve the conscientious teacher of an almost intolerable burden of providing information, packaging it in interesting and manageable portions for children, and delivering it. The amount of preparation needed in order to do justice to the material and to the pupils has operated against that inspirational freshness and willingness to reflect which is so vital for effective education. Furthermore, widespread and proper use of computers eliminates the need for the uniformity of the class lesson approach. The implications of this are staggering if they are once considered.

(d) *The importance of 'meeting' in education*. The teacher's role should become one of keeping a watchful eye on the progress of individuals, encouraging them and suggesting targets for them. Time to listen to them, to converse with them, and to have meaningful and genuine discussion groups, together with various forms of communal activities and sharing between pupils, will promote real education, as well as affording greater satisfaction and enjoyment to teachers.

David Aspin, professor of education at King's College, London, concludes a chapter on the many problems of multi-cultural education thus:

'All there is finally is people talking to each other'.[33] The Gospel too is about meeting.

These points should apply to all schools. But could not Church schools, or some of them, lead the way and pioneer a courageous experiment with a truly holistic approach to education?

(4) The importance of Christian self-education

If Christians are to influence the educational process, help children in their thinking, and support teachers appropriately, the self-education of all Christians is vital. This is not just because education can and must happen in the home and in the church as well as in school, but because in a society which puts a high premium on education, Christians must be able to witness to their faith without causing unnecessary offence, or rendering any thicker the smokescreen which stands between so many people and the Gospel in a secular age.

The Churches should look to the self-education of all their members. Frances Young, in her inaugural lecture at the University of Birmingham on 5 May 1987, drew attention to the impressive nature of the early Church's intellectual rigour:

> the assurance of its quest for truth, the daring of its criticism and its conceptuality, and its determination to educate its members to a high level of awareness of the issues involved. The average minister today would blanch if he read some of the lectures given to the prospective Church members in the Fourth and Fifth centuries: tough reasoned argument is characteristic of them, for Christians had to understand their faith in a pluralistic world. Spirituality and rationality went hand in hand.[34]

Whether or not this is an idealized portrayal of the early Church, such education of all Christians was never more needed than now.

Notes

1 M. Tasker, *Values and Teacher Education*, paper produced for National Association for Values in Education and Training (May 1990).

2 D. Plunkett, *Secular and Spiritual Values* (Routledge, 1990), p. 117.

3 M. Tasker, op. cit.

4 K. Robinson, *Royal Society of Arts Journal* (July 1990), pp. 352f.

5 M. Reeves, 'Why history?' in R. Niblett (ed.), *The Sciences, the Humanities and the Technological Threat* (University of London Press, 1975), p. 124.

6 C. Cox and R. Tingle, 'The new barbarians', *The Salisbury Review* (October 1986).

7 B. Mitchell, 'Indoctrination' in *The Fourth R* (SPCK, 1970), p. 358.

8 R. Pring in J. Thacker, R. Pring and D. Evans (eds), *Personal, Social and Moral Education in a Changing World* (NFER-Nelson, 1987), p. 27.

9 C. Ulanovsky, *New Values* 3 (spring 1990).

10 J. Wilson, 'Relativism and consumerism in educational research', *Educational Research* 32.2 (NFER, 1990).

11 S. A. Ashraf in B. O'Keeffe (ed.), *Schools for Tomorrow* (Falmer, 1988), p. 71.

12 E. Hulmes in an unpublished discussion paper for 'The Gospel and Our Culture' discussion group on education.

13 *National Extension College Report: Flexible Learning Project in Small Fifth and Sixth Forms* (1985).

14 B. Martin and R. Pluck, *Young People's Beliefs* (Church of England Board of Education, 1977).

15 Booklet compiled by St Francis Xavier's Sixth Form College (1988), p. 12.

16 M. Roques, *Curriculum Unmasked—Towards a Christian Understanding of Education* (Christians in Education, 1989), p. 89.

17 *Religious Education: Supply of Teachers for the 1990s*, Religious Education Council pamphlet (1989).

18 R. Goldman, *Readiness for Religion* (1962) has had a very wide readership. Both Piaget and Goldman have since then been heavily and justly criticized, e.g. by O. Petrovich in her Oxford DPhil thesis (1989).

19 N. Slee has pointed out the inadequacies of a phenomenological approach, arguing the need for a *rapprochement* with the confessional approach to RE on the grounds that violence is otherwise done to the wholeness of experience: 'Conflict and reconciliation between competing models of religious education: some reflections on the British scene', *British Journal of Religious Education* (summer 1989), pp. 126–35.

20 M. Roques, op. cit., p. 88.

21 B. O'Keeffe, *Journal of Beliefs and Values* 10.2 (1989), p. 9. The research was published in *Faith, Culture and the Dual System: A Comparative Study of Church and County Schools* (Falmer, 1986).

22 Langland, *Piers the Ploughman* (Penguin Classics, 1989), p. 228.

23 S. Weil, *Waiting on God* (Fontana, 1959), pp. 66–75.

24 Lord Brougham in *Gladstone Tract* 24 (Hawarden: St Deiniol's Library, 1839), p. 47.

25 B. O'Keeffe, op. cit. (note 21), p. 9.

26 A. Hastings, *The Times Educational Supplement* (7 September 1990).

27 M. Felderhof, *The Gospel and Our Culture Newsletter* 4 (winter 1990), pp. 3–4.

28 L. Newbigin in *The Place of Christianity in Religious Education* (Action Group for the Encouragement of Religious Education, March 1989).

29 L. Newbigin in L. Francis and A. Thatcher (eds), *Christian Perspectives for Education* (Fowler Wright Books, 1990), p. 99.

30 Cf. B. Mitchell, op. cit., pp. 353–8.

31 Cf. D. Plunkett, op. cit., p. 135. A little-known book by D.S. Hubery provides a succinct summary of this: *The Teaching Methods of Jesus* (Chester House Publications, 1970).

32 J. Priestley in *Personal, Social and Moral Education in a Changing World*, p. 120.

33 D. Aspin in *Schools for Tomorrow*, p. 48.

34 F. Young, *The Critic and the Visionary* (University of Birmingham, 1987), p. 10.

Health, healing and modern medicine

JOHN YOUNG

In his book *Foolishness to the Greeks*, Lesslie Newbigin has reminded us that we are inevitably influenced by our culture and the cultures before our culture.[1] In particular, modern Western culture has been greatly influenced by the Enlightenment and by the subsequent advances of science. This scientific approach has influenced our theological attitudes. It has influenced even more the attitude of the person in the street. There is a mistaken common view that science has few limits. Basically, it only enables us to answer the question 'How?'.

Science has been described as 'knowledge ascertained by observation and experiment, critically tested, systematised and brought under general principles'.[2] Again, Newbigin has written: 'The real world disclosed by the work of science was one governed not by purpose but by the natural laws of cause and effect. Teleology has no place in physics or astronomy.'[3] It is certainly the view of very many in this scientific age that it is no good looking in the real world for evidence of purpose. The relentless search for cause and effect (or rather what has caused the effect) has led to far greater attention being paid to systems, sub-systems and micro-systems, and therefore to a loss of appreciation of a mechanism or organism understood as a whole. Understandably, this has led to increasing specialization, individualism and fragmentation.

Modern medicine has been dominated by this approach. We must thankfully admit that it has achieved some very good results. It has, however, emphasized the mechanistic approach with an increasing attention to the function of the parts, and a decreasing emphasis on the function of the whole. To counteract this mechanical understanding of disease there has been a reaction which has tended to belittle the achievements of science and to 'return to little things'.

The discovery that in some diseases there is a chemical malfunction of part of a system had led in the first place to the treatment of that disease by an appropriate agent which will correct it. As nearly everything which we eat or drink may have an unwanted side-effect, the appropriate agent may produce some unpleasantness. In the old days the nauseous taste of some cough medicines was rationalized as being good for us, on the principle that the worse a medicine tastes, the better it is for us. The side-effects of analgesics or of anti-inflammatory drugs are likewise questioned today, in the light of the old dictum 'First do no harm'. And so, to alleviate the iatrogenic ills such treatment may produce, some people look for alternative methods of alleviating disease. Many of these alternative therapies have not been critically tested or brought under general principles. As I understand it, many of them are not capable of being so tested. This has led scientific opinion to decry them as unscientific, while those who hold to alternative therapies criticize this attitude as a mechanistic and fragmented 'scientific' approach. Thus there has arisen a polarization and a distancing of those on both sides. We have to ask ourselves, however, whether the so-called scientific approach is truly scientific. The true scientist has to admit that, *in the light of present knowledge*, certain causes produce given effects. But such a scientist will often be found in the position of saying 'I do not know' or 'I cannot explain certain phenomena'; or may even have to reinterpret the facts in the light of new knowledge.

The doctor is concerned with alleviating suffering, and, if possible, with restoring function. To achieve this, the doctor treats the patient in order to effect a cure. Only very rarely do doctors speak of healing, e.g., the healing of wounds, ulcers or fractures. Cure is therefore the restoration of function; and it is achieved by the treatment given to the suffering patient.

In 1948 Aneurin Bevan introduced the National Health Service, of which we in Britain can rightly be very proud. The object of the service is to reduce suffering and, if possible, to restore function. It is open to all and free to all. For over forty years doctors and other health care professionals have been combating disease by researching into its cause and by doing their best to remove it. Most of us have benefited from this. At the same time it has tended to promote a common understanding of 'health' in terms of the absence of disease.

One of the areas in which this used to be apparent is the sphere of psychosomatic illness. At one time all disease was believed to be of physical origin. However, as time went by, it became clear that emotions could produce physical symptoms, and so some diseases were seen to have an emotional component. Now more and more diseases are understood to have such a component. Most doctors now accept this.

Nonetheless, the mechanistic approach to disease still prevails; and it has resulted in an extension of the theory of physical cause and effect. When a machine breaks down the mechanic diagnoses the fault, and removes or corrects the faulty part; and then the machine functions again. Similarly, when there is a failure in the physical body, society expects the doctor to diagnose the problem, remove or correct the faulty organ or system; and the body will then function normally again. Modern advertising helps to fortify this attitude: 'Do you feel one degree under? Take. . .'. The implication is that the bodily machine is functioning less well, and that a pill will put it right. This attitude can lead to the fear, or even to the denial, of the possibility of approaching death. Death, which is in fact the only certainty in life, is regarded as the ultimate failure of medicine; and as such it cannot be faced. Such a philosophy places great expectations on doctors. In an almost mystical way they are thought to possess superhuman powers. If they fail to achieve the expected result, then they are seen as failures, or, more probably, as negligent. And if they are negligent, then they are culpable, and may be sued at law.

This kind of attitude produces a defensive reaction in doctors; and defensive medicine is the result. This is particularly evident in the USA, where doctors are commonly sued at law. The patient is subjected to almost every conceivable investigation and possible treatment so that, if there is no successful cure, the doctor in retrospect will be seen to have done everything possible; and so a legal action will be averted.

Dr Michael Wilson, discussing health at a special committee convened to consider Christian healing in the light of hospice experience, pointed out that the idea of health 'differs from culture to culture and is an important value word which tells us upon what basis a society founds what we might call "the good life"'.[4] In Africa it is a family or inter-personal quality. For the Navaho Indians, health is a 'green' quality of life: they speak of 'beauty and blessing'.

One effect of our own culture on our ideas of health is to individualize the source of all health. Just as parts of the body are seen to malfunction, so individuals are seen to malfunction within society as a whole. One may suffer from infection, another from ulcers, a third may be accident prone, and a fourth fails to make satisfactory relationships. Our tendency has been to see each as individual malfunctions, unconnected with society as a whole. Our response has been simply to treat the individual and to push him or her back into the fray again.

An individual must in our culture have rights. These rights inhere in the individual. The effects may be harmful to other people, but they are tolerated because of the 'freedom' of the individual. To pursue their rights seems to be the aim of some members of our society. This amounts to a philosophy of 'looking after number one'. Its consequences may well be reflected in our criminal statistics and divorce rates, etc. It may account for the move towards magic, that is, the manipulation of external forces for our own benefit and the appeasement of the unknown dynamics of our age.

Such is the impact of our culture upon our attitudes to health and to healing. Before we consider the way in which the Gospel interacts with our culture in such matters, we need to look briefly at concepts of health and healing in the Old Testament (the Hebrew Scriptures) and also during the intertestamental period, and then to look at health and healing in the Gospels.

First, however, we need to admit that there are differing Christian viewpoints about creation. There are those who take a literal interpretation of the opening chapters of Genesis, seeing Adam as having been made perfect, tempted by sin, falling from a relationship with God and passing on this condition to mankind as a whole. In this way the present state of affairs is explained as a condition in which we are alienated from God and out of harmony with ourselves, with other people and with our environment. On the other hand, there are those who accept an evolutionary explanation of the creation but who still think that there was a historical occasion when man 'fell'; and that our present situation results from this fall. In both these views redemption is understood as the gift of grace bestowed on us by Jesus through his death and resurrection 'redeeming' us (buying us back) to God. But there is a third view, which affirms the evolutionary view of the origin of life. God is seen within the whole process of evolution. There never was a historical moment of 'The Fall'. Man is understood as repeatedly 'falling' and being restored into a new relationship through the grace of God at work in the life, witness, death and resurrection of Jesus, the true Adam. The Garden of Eden is at the end, not at the beginning.

What really matters to Christians is our relationship with God and the manifestation of this relationship in our lives; but the viewpoint which we adopt about creation may well influence our ideas of healing. In the first two viewpoints, salvation can be seen as a restoration to what was before. But according to the third viewpoint, salvation is seen rather in terms of growth into a new relationship with God.

In the Old Testament health relates to every aspect of corporate life, as well as to the life of the individual. Rebellion against God and disobedience lead to sickness; but repentance and forgiveness by God bring relief and cure and the restoration of broken relationships. YHWH (the Hebrew name of God which was too holy to be pronounced) is traditionally taken to mean 'I am who I am'; but it is translated by the Jewish philosopher Martin Buber to mean 'I am He who is present with you, going with you and directing your cause'. YHWH is not remote, detached, and impersonal, known only to intellectuals: he is God manifest in action, his dynamic character maintaining a claim on the loyalty of the individual and the allegiance of his people whose trust must be solely in him. It is obedience to this God which is salvation. Righteousness, according to which both the community and the individual are in a right relationship with God, is central to this Hebrew faith. This righteousness, therefore, must be manifest in relationships not only with God, but also with others, with the environment and with the self.

The concept of health is expressed by fullness, well-being and wholeness in all aspects of life, and, as Dr John Wilkinson writes, it is best summed up in the word *shalom*.[5] As Hugh Melinsky has written, 'The ideal' is 'that a man's spirit should be in harmony with the spirit of Yahweh'.[6] Departure from this results in sickness and death. 'The goal towards which God is working, i.e., the ultimate end of mission, is the establishment of *shalom*, and this involves the full potentialities of all creation and its ultimate reconciliation and unity in Christ.'[7] The essential for healing which leads to health, according to the Old Testament, lies in acknowledging the God of our fathers, the Lord of all.

The intertestamental period stretches from the last writing of the Old Testament to the first book of the New. It is very important for the understanding of the Gospel. At this time there was a great increase among the Jews of influences other than Yahweh. When the Jews went into captivity to Babylon, they were confronted with a religion different from that of the monotheistic Hebrew God. They found themselves in a world dominated by spirits who, it was believed, influenced human beings. These spirits were held to be responsible for many illnesses. Satan, who had originally been the Seducer, became the chief spirit of evil. In the intertestamental period there arose a belief that it was possible to have power over these spirits. There arose many superstitions in connection with the demons, as they came to be known. For example, protection could be obtained by amulets, and these could also effect cures. Over the years the Jews tended to personify Satan and his army of demons, and the concept of the two kingdoms of Yahweh and Satan arose. Although magic was officially forbidden, the Israelites used it unofficially as a preventative and an antidote, not least in the practice of exorcism.

It was during the end of the Old Testament period, and during the intertestamental period, that 'wisdom literature' grew up among the Jews. While this had links with similar literature in other cultures, the Jewish wisdom literature is unique because it incorporates the distinctively Jewish world view with Yahweh at its centre. There we find the physician recognized in Israel. In the Book of Ecclesiasticus (written in the second century) we read (38.1–8):

> Honour the physician with the honour due to him, according to your need of him, for the Lord created him; for healing comes from the most High and he will receive a gift from the King. The skill of the physician lifts up his head, and in the presence of great men he is admired. The Lord created medicines from the earth, and a sensible man will not despise them . . . By them he heals and takes away pain: the pharmacist makes of them a compound.

Here the physician's skill comes from God, and his medicines are gifts of the Creator. As Wolf has commented on this view of the doctor, 'He can arrive at the right diagnosis, can relieve pain and perhaps preserve life. But his gifts have their limitations and he does not always have them at his disposal.'[8] The wisdom literature is based on the covenant which God made with the Jewish people, which demands of them holiness. As Atkinson has written, 'This involves ordering each aspect of life into line with God's character. This ordering normally will include care for health, but health to serve the quest for holiness.'[9]

There also arose in New Testament times a band of holy men (*hasidim*) accredited with authority over evil, and with the power to heal even when they were not physically present. They lived in Galilee, and placed great emphasis on prayer.

The first recorded words of Jesus' ministry are 'The time is fulfilled, and the Kingdom of God is at hand; repent, and believe in the gospel' (Mk 1.15, RSV). The Gospel is the good news of the reign of God breaking into, transforming and renewing the world order of sin, decay and death. Jesus spoke of 'entering the Kingdom' which implied a sphere of influence and authority. This Kingdom comes near to those who meet him and accept him. The Kingdom is here, but not yet fully here, challenging us to re-think, to repent and turn to God. The inner change when we do this will affect our motivation and actions. God must be in the centre of life. Because evil is so rife, turning to God will involve healing. The healing of an individual is important if he or she is to fulfil God's will in the community. In turn, the healing of the community is important because the community is formed of individuals.

Without doubt Jesus treated and cured many people, as did some of his contemporaries. We may note certain points about Jesus' healing ministry.

1. Usually it is not possible to make a certain diagnosis of his cures on the basis of the evidence in the Gospels. The stories are recounted not as case histories, but to demonstrate the authority of Jesus and the patient's encounter with the Rule of God.

2. The Hebrew and Greek words used, in the original words in which the scriptures were written, deserve attention. The Hebrew *shalom* becomes the Greek *eirēnē*, translated into English as 'peace'.[10] Another word used in the cures is often translated into English as 'salvation' (but in its verbal form, sometimes as 'to make whole'). The Hebrew word here is used in the Old Testament to describe God's deliverance of his people from the slavery of Egypt. In the New Testament deliverance includes both salvation and healing, and it is in this context that *sōtēria* (and its cognates) is often used in Jesus' healings, as it is also used in a broader context in the Epistle to Titus (2.11): 'The grace of God has dawned upon the world with healing for all mankind'.

Some translations of the Bible have misled people here. They have confused cure with healing. Jesus, in fulfilling the Old Testament concept of cure, enlarged it by confronting people with God's kingly rule, so that they 'might have life and have it in all its fullness'. The Gospel, so far as it is concerned with healing, is thus seen to be in contrast to the prevailing culture in which it first appeared.

On the one hand, there was a need to reaffirm the traditional Jewish faith which required a personal relationship with the living God. This, despite the teaching of the canonical prophets, and the witness of the *hasidim* and others, seems often to have degenerated into an impersonal legalism. On the other hand, there was a declining belief in God the Lord of all creation, replaced by a dualism of the two kingdoms of God and Satan. The view that demons caused disease and misfortune led to a turning from God to superstition and magic.

Jesus by his preaching of the Gospel, and by what he was and did, challenged these two false conceptions of God. The Christian Gospel brought healing, but not always cure. Curing in the right atmosphere can lead to healing, and healing can produce cure, a return to the *status quo ante*: but they are different concepts.

Is the situation very different in our culture today? There is a declining belief in God. There is an increasing tendency to look at forces other than God, demonological or occult or whatever. God is no longer regarded by many as the sovereign Lord of all. At the same time our concept of health is largely that of the medical model. The advantages of this approach must not be denied; nor must they be abandoned. The tremendous advances made in our knowledge of physiology, anatomy, pathology, pharmacology, therapeutics, etc., have completely changed our view of treatment. Yet the very variety of these disciplines suggests fragmentation. A more holistic approach of a person in community is needed. As Dr Wilson has written:

In a Christian context we must largely put on one side the question of medicine, etc., and concentrate on issues of human right relatedness in our common life, issues of the environment, life style, employment, sound agriculture and enough money to purchase a good diet, etc.

We now recognize quite readily that most disease is psychosomatic: how long will it be before we recognize that disease must be seen in terms that are 'eco-pneumo-psycho-socio-matic'? If we are to relate the Gospel to healing in contemporary culture, those of us who belong to the medical profession will have to face a number of questions:

1. Healing requires taking a whole view of the patient. Traditionally the doctor has always been the responsible person for the treatment and care of his or her patient. With increasing technology, how long can this be maintained as a credible view? To what extent can the doctor now delegate some of his or her responsibility to members of other disciplines? This is certainly happening already, especially in psychiatry and geriatrics, and to some extent within general practice. But how much should we give up our present authority? Some doctors (for example, the Revd Dr Michael Wilson) have suggested that the basic care of the patients really belongs to the nursing profession, and that doctors should have only a consultative role.

2. How much are we prepared to share our skills with an unqualified practitioner? Are we to remain protected by the requirement of scientific proof before we allow (or encourage) our patients to seek help elsewhere? How much are we prepared to learn from them? Hugh Montefiore has written: 'In the first place, the Christian will want to co-operate with all genuine healing [does he mean curing?] as a means of co-operating with God and in accordance with the mind of Christ'.[11] Of course we need to be assured of the genuine good that can come from other therapies, but how much does 'professionalism' prevent us from a fair appraisal and co-operation?

3. How much are we influenced in our therapy by the unwarranted expectations of our culture? Our society, we have already noted, has been encouraged and conditioned to see health in terms of physical well-being, with established external agencies responsible for coping with disease, and a naïve expectation that the medical profession will remove disease and produce a cure. This attitude fails to take into account the totality of human nature as personal and rooted in community. Often it reflects failure to face up to the inevitability of death. Sometimes it reflects the guilt and/or unhappiness of relatives. Does the medical profession encourage these false attitudes towards disease?

4. Our materialistic culture has emphasized cure, the relief of symptoms and the eradication of the cause of disease. Instead of wholeness (which is one meaning of *shalom*), healing has come to refer to different therapies used to produce a cure. The Gospel declares that healing involves relationships with God, with other people, with ourselves and with our environment. Any attempt at healing and making people whole must include these relationships, as well as therapies needed for cure. It is not enough to treat people by giving them a pill, a bit of acupuncture, and perhaps recommending 'a bit of religion'. God is involved in everything, our relationships as well as our skills as doctors and our medicines and therapies. This is the truth behind 'whole person medicine'. It may be contrasted with so-called 'holistic therapies', which often merely tend to substitute alternative therapies for conventional allopathic treatment. We doctors must ask ourselves questions about our own relationships with our patients. Indeed, we even have to go further, and ask ourselves awkward questions about our own relationships with our families and friends. It may be a source of healing for our patients if we share with them our personal experiences in order to give them strength and encouragement. By so doing, we make ourselves vulnerable; but Christians will remember the words of St Paul: 'My power is made perfect in weakness' (2 Cor 12.9).

5. The Church must stand under judgement as well as the materialist world in which it is set. Originally the work of healing lay within the province of the Church. But for long there has been a neglect of the healing ministry within the Church which has only lately been rediscovered. One unfortunate feature of this revival is that there are present-day Christians who have a very naïve view of healing in terms of miraculous results from prayer and the laying-on of hands, without those changes in deeply personal relationships which we have seen to be a necessary part of true healing. Nonetheless the question must be asked: how much do we involve the Church in our work of healing? All health care professionals are included in the healing team, but does this also include the spiritual adviser that the patient requires? Do we ask the locally authorized people (clergy and laity) to enter into the ministry of healing? Do we suggest that there may be spiritual causes underlying some physical diseases and illnesses? Do we help people to link up with a worshipping, praying and loving community?

6. Newbigin has pointed out that different Christian traditions, perceiving Christ through the spectacles of their own culture, can help others to see how much the vision has been blurred or distorted. He has emphasized that this kind of mutual correction is at the very heart of the

ecumenical movement when it is true to itself.[12] I would like to ask how much we, with our scientific approach, are prepared to accept the views of other cultures on questions of healing and health. Surely, if we are truly scientific, we must not close our eyes to phenomena seen and experienced in ways different from our own in other cultures, just as people in other cultures must not close their eyes to the good things experienced in our own?

These six groups of questions show something of the confrontation between the Gospel and our culture so far as health and healing are concerned.

Notes

1 L. Newbigin, *Foolishness to the Greeks* (London, 1986), p. 4.

2 *Chambers English Dictionary* (Edinburgh and Cambridge, 1988), p. 1316.

3 L. Newbigin, op. cit., p. 24.

4 In a private communication, 1990. Cf. M. Wilson, *Health Is for People* (London, 1975), pp. 90f.

5 J. Wilkinson, *Health and the Church* (Edinburgh, 1984), p. 7.

6 M. A. H. Melinsky, *Healing Miracles* (London, 1968), p. 10.

7 J. G. Davies, *Worship and Mission* (London, 1966), p. 30.

8 H. W. Wolf, *Anthropology of the Old Testament* (London, 1974), p. 146.

9 D. Atkinson, 'Towards a theology of health', unpublished paper.

10 J. Macquarrie, *The Concept of Peace* (London, 1973), pp. 14f.

11 H. Montefiore, *Risen with Healing in His Wings* (Birmingham Diocesan Church House, 1973), p. 3.

12 L. Newbigin, op. cit., pp. 146f.

Mass media, British culture and Gospel values

JIM MCDONNELL

In modern Britain, the mass media express, circulate and popularize underlying cultural assumptions and attitudes. An adequate understanding of the relationship between the Gospel and our culture must give due attention to these mass cultural processes and products which permeate the business of everyday living.

Ideas, beliefs, assumptions and values are not circulated through the mass media like water in pipes. They are selected, shaped, organized, and evaluated by the media system which transmits them. The mass media are complex institutional structures as well as technologies. Media products are shaped by the demands of technology; by the ideological and personal presuppositions of those who regulate, own and work in the media; by the demands of the political and commercial system in which media organizations operate; and, to a greater or lesser extent, by the tastes and predilections of the consuming public.

Any discussion of the mass media has to distinguish between expectations that people have for the media, the assumptions they make about how the media operate and the actual experience of the media. Much of what passes for debate on the influence of the mass media, for example, is simply the clash of expectations and assumptions with little or no relation to the experience of the media in the lives of either media practitioners or audiences.

Media massage and media messages

Before we begin our discussion of the assumptions which we bring to the media, however, it is important to consider the influence of the media as media. We remember that Marshall McLuhan coined the phrase 'The Medium is the Message' but we tend to forget that he also wrote that 'The Medium is the Massage'.

McLuhan's insight was that the strongest influence of a mass medium, particularly television, lies in its capacity to convey the same message instantaneously to thousands or millions of people at the same time.

While people may be sharply aware of the content of television programmes or of newspaper stories, for example, they are rarely aware of how much time they actually spend in absorbing media messages. McLuhan's point is that we have allowed the mass media to 'massage' us into a state of unreflecting and undiscriminating cultural consumption.

Our relationship with the media helps to give form and order to our daily lives. For most people in British society the media are the taken-for-granted background to domestic, leisure and work activities. We awake to the sound of the alarm clock and the radio. Breakfast is accompanied by a quick glance at our favourite newspaper or the background of the breakfast radio or television programme. If we drive to work we may switch on the radio in the car or perhaps play our favourite cassettes. The train commuter is absorbed in the newspaper or in a paperback, often isolated further by the personal 'Walkman'. The person at home switches on the radio or television for company throughout the day, while in factories and offices portable radios of every description are providing a pleasant background to routine work. In the evening the family leisure time is dominated by television or by the video recorder. Young adults retire to the security of their rooms to listen to the radio or play their favourite rock music. In more and more households multiple radio and television sets allow each family member to satisfy their own interests and tastes in solitary splendour.

The volume of media messages and the number of media technologies mean that it is increasingly difficult for individuals to disengage from the media environment. We receive more messages from more sources than our forebears. We find it ever more difficult to process the unrelenting stream of information and sensation. Like background traffic noise, the media hum becomes assimilated into our consciousness to such an extent that we notice its presence only rarely. This continuous assault on our senses contributes to the growing sense of the fragmentary nature of everyday experience.

The constant flow of messages, good, bad and indifferent, entertaining, educating and informing, makes it difficult for us to pick out the significant and discard the irrelevant. We skip from newspaper to radio to television, from one news item to another, from one advertisement or programme to another, without expecting or demanding any obvious relationship between them. Our experiences are disconnected and chaotic, linked by no common thread. We just let the media tide wash over us.

This bombardment of messages is accompanied by a fragmentation of corporate experience as subcultures proliferate. The host of special interest magazines and newspapers on sale in any large newsagents underlines the point. The world presented in the pages of a newspaper like the *Sun*, for example, is not the world as expressed in the pages of the *Guardian*. This range and diversity of special interests is presented by the advocates of the free market as an extension of human freedom and choice. And so it is. But this extension of choice has a cost. As subcultures increase in number, and as more and more special interest groups create their own media outlets, it becomes increasingly difficult to reach a common under-standing as a society on basic values and assumptions. Very few people ever read both the *Sun* and the *Guardian*, for example; the cultural worlds are simply too far apart. The problem was addressed directly by Rabbi Jonathan Sacks in his second Reith lecture of 1990. He said, using a media metaphor, 'We no longer talk of virtues but of values, and values are tapes we play on the Walkman of the mind: any tune we choose so long as it does not disturb others'.[1]

The challenge facing all of us in a media society is twofold. Firstly, we have to learn how to cope with this flood of media experiences in a crea-tive way; secondly, we have to find ways to counterbalance the tendency for society to fragment into mutually unintelligible cultural worlds. For Christians these tasks should have a particular urgency. As Christians we believe that the values of the Gospel should permeate all sectors and levels of society. If that is to happen in a society and culture permeated by the mass media Christians have to be able to identify those elements in the media that are points of contact with Gospel values. But the world of the media is a fast-changing and ever expanding world, and we have to come to terms with the influence of the media on our culture *now*. The longer we refuse to take the media's cultural influence seriously, the more likely it is that the media environment will become less and less friendly to the values we cherish.

Basic assumptions about the media

It is as well to begin our discussion by examining some of the more common and deep-seated assumptions which we make about the media, both as individuals and as a society. These assumptions, some of which contradict each other, constitute the perceptual frame through which we order our understanding of the experience of the media. Upon these assumptions we build expectations about how the media ought to func-tion in society. The degree of acrimony which tends to infuse debate about the media can often be accounted for by the extent to which dif-ferent sets of assumptions are being invoked and different expectations are perceived to be frustrated or subverted by media practice.

As a society we make one basic assumption about the media which has, in some form, near-universal acceptance. It is a belief in the instrumental effects of the media upon the behaviour of individuals and groups. In other words, the messages conveyed by the mass media are thought of as essentially persuasive, inducing people to think and act in certain ways.

This belief is deep rooted in all our public discourse about the media and is revealed in the institutional arrangements we make to regulate the media. It appears, however, in a stronger or weaker form, depending upon one's view of the capacities of the media audience.

One widely held view is that the feelings, opinions and actions of the majority of human beings are essentially malleable and easily manipulated by those with a message to sell. This assumption underpins and justifies all those elaborate institutional and regulatory safeguards which we have constructed to circumscribe media power. The most obvious example is that of censorship, either moral or political. Censorship laws and regulations express a social concern that not all forms of media expression are desirable and, indeed, that some of them may be harmful to social harmony as a whole, or to particular groups such as children. The degree to which we rely on formal censorship is a good indication of how confident we are as a society in the informal and unspoken rules which guide the practice of those working in the media. There are times when there appears to be a sharp division between significant sections of society and media institutions and practitioners. At such times the demand for increased censorship and tighter regulation of media output is expressed more vigorously and loudly than usual. In recent years, such a public outcry was especially evident in regard to the proliferation of so-called video 'nasties': violent and pornographic video cassettes which were supposedly being avidly watched by huge numbers of children. Less dramatic, but often no less bitter debates arise every time a cinema film or a television programme is felt by a significant number of people to have challenged existing frontiers of good taste or decency.

This sensitive relationship between media content and public taste is constantly changing. At present we seem to be entering a period in which the public, or at least those who claim to represent the public, is less willing to give media producers a high degree of trust. The establishment of the Broadcasting Standards Council, for example, is a symbolic expression of a deep-rooted feeling that broadcasters have become too far detached from the current social consensus.

A more optimistic view of the media audience is that people are quite able to discriminate among the messages that reach them and are active shapers of their own meanings rather than passive acceptors of the meanings of others. This view less easily finds institutional expression than the more pessimistic belief in powerful media influence. The more sanguine belief is usually articulated as a set of views concerning the freedom of the individual to choose what he or she reads, listens to or watches. It is also expressed in terms of the responsibility of the individual to choose their media content wisely. The prevalence of this view tends to reflect the extent to which the media are felt to be in tune with prevailing public tastes and sentiments. Usually the stronger the belief in the power of media to influence behaviour, the more critical is the view of existing media and media institutions.

Overlaying these fundamental assumptions is a further ideological predisposition regarding the extent to which the cultural or commercial aspects of the media are deemed of most importance. Where the mass media are seen primarily as industries offering a range of consumer products, the ideology invoked is that of the market. Media audiences are characterized as rational consumers choosing among a range of products to satisfy their own tastes and needs. Where mass media are seen primarily as cultural products, the ideological stance tends to be one that demands limitations on the working of the market in the interests of some greater public good, such as the quality and diversity of programmes. The market, in this view, is an imperfect mechanism for registering and satisfying audience needs and tastes, as the audience needs to be educated and challenged as well as satisfied.

This complex of diverse assumptions and presuppositions can be seen in the expectations that our society brings to the various media. As a society we are neither coherent nor consistent in our approach to different media. Our institutional arrangements and regulatory structures reflect less a set of underlying philosophical beliefs and more the exigencies of political and economic circumstances.

Expectations of different media

Social expectations of the different media are expressed through codes of practice, regulatory structures and laws. All media can be said to inform, educate and entertain. For most societies, including our own, regulatory expectations of the media have been built around the balance between those three functions. Dispute and controversy arise when the balance is perceived to have been upset, and the media are felt to be exceeding what are held to be their proper bounds.

One way of examining the relationships among the underlying assumptions and values of the media in our society is by taking each of these functions in turn and examining both expectations and what actually happens in practice. We can then consider how both practice and expectations measure up to what we might consider to be Gospel values and practice.

Information: press freedom and responsibility

Our two major sources of general information and news about the world are the press and broadcasting. Yet as a society we consider the press and broadcasting as very different institutions and make different demands upon them.

The press is organized according to a market model. The market is taken to be the best guarantee of diversity and freedom of opinion. The press is seen as an industry which produces a huge number of different printed products capable of satisfying nearly all tastes and opinions. It is further taken for granted that the press is too powerful an instrument of persuasion and opinion formation to be subject to control or licensing by the state. Yet, at the same time, there are relatively few checks on the power of a few wealthy proprietors to dominate the market, as the case of Rupert Murdoch illustrates.

The assumptions underlying this approach to press freedom and diversity are not fully articulated. Freedom of the press is supposed to enable the press to expose corruption, tell us truthfully what is happening in the world, reveal falsehood and inform us about important issues, people and events. At the same time these expectations tend to come into conflict with other values in British society. Our culture rightly places a high value on personal privacy. Moreover, our political culture is one that has traditionally laid great store by secrecy and discretion. Calls to open up the processes of government to public scrutiny are fiercely resisted by a variety of vested interests. In spite of the efforts of campaigners for freedom of information, Britain has yet to have the principle of open government enshrined in legislation.

In Britain the press issue that arouses most passion is the question of privacy. Privacy is a social value which is deeply impressed in the fabric of everyday life. A sharp distinction is drawn between what is public and what is private, and to cross the line is to risk social ostracism. In the light of the Gospel this has a substantial value. Intrusion into private lives without justifiable cause can do great harm to individuals. Respect for the person demands that their dignity be respected and upheld. Turning lives into the raw material for gossip serves no good purpose.

Yet the very defence of personal privacy which is invoked in denouncing the excesses of a section of the tabloid press reveals the extent to which the public willingly connives in the invasion of privacy. Those newspapers which provide entertaining, but often quite spurious, stories about the private lives of prominent individuals have the highest circulation figures and are thus presumably giving people what they want to read. When these newspapers and their journalists are attacked for confusing gossip with news there is a sense in which they are being made the scapegoats for society's guilt. The demand that these newspapers should be more responsible and less intrusive arises from a public that could ensure such an outcome simply by refusing to buy the more scurrilous titles.

Our society's muddle about privacy and the role of the press is seen also in the fact that though we would like the press to be more responsible about privacy, we are unwilling to grant the press much in the way of rights. Campaigns for a right to privacy and the unwillingness of governments to develop a freedom of information law arouse the suspicion that such a right would unduly restrict the freedom of the press to uncover matters which are of public interest. Unlike the United States of America, the British legal and regulatory systems recognize no special role for the press. There is no equivalent of the idea of the press as the Fourth Estate, with a particular duty to stand against government and legislature as the guardian of the people's right to know. The state of the press and the sharp divide between the so-called 'quality' and 'popular' press reveal our failure as a society to find ways of reconciling freedom, privacy, responsibility and the right to know.

Information: broadcasting bias and objectivity

The way broadcasting is supposed to operate in the realm of news reveals much of the same confusion of attitudes and values. Radio and television have been regarded as the most intrusive and influential of the media. That belief, in addition to the perception that the radio spectrum was a scarce national resource to be exploited in the public interest, is the reason why the ideology of the market has, until quite recently, been explicitly rejected as the basis for the regulation of broadcasting in Britain. Broadcasting is instead treated as a public service, and is subject to a high degree of regulation and to a number of formal demands about how the news gathering and presentation process should be conducted.

Bias in the press is something we deplore but tend largely to take for granted as the necessary price for press freedom. We do not expect newspapers to be wholly objective in their news coverage. We assume that the editorial stance of the paper will have some bearing on the stories that are covered, the events that are highlighted and the conclusions that are drawn. If we do not like or approve of a particular paper's editorial stance we can choose to buy another.

Nevertheless, there is an underlying public unease about press bias which tends to surface at times when newspaper coverage is felt to have become too blatantly one-sided. The press itself attempts to cope with this tendency towards bias by invoking the distinction between fact and comment. The Newspaper Society, which brings together newspaper editors, observes, for example, in its Code of Practice that 'Newspapers are free to be partisan but they should distinguish between comment and fact. Conjecture should not be elevated into statements of fact.' This, of course, begs the question of how one is to establish what is fact. When so much of the 'facts' which newspapers report is speculation, rumour and inference it is often difficult to discover what the 'facts' are in any particular case. This is particularly obvious when statements or opinions are attributed to people who subsequently deny having made them.

The complexity of these issues makes it all the more surprising how confidently we have institutionalized the ideals of objectivity and impartiality in the broadcasting of news. In our regulation of broadcasting we have enshrined the idea that radio and television news are not to have a particular editorial bias. The BBC news guide states quite boldly, 'The BBC has no editorial opinions of its own. It has an obligation not to take sides; a duty to reflect all main views on a given issue.' There is an epistemological assumption here, that if the correct procedures are followed and the right rules are devised, there can emerge an objective and socially acceptable view of the news event in question. The expectations assume that somehow broadcasting can provide a transparent window on the world. This is not, as we have noted, an expectation brought to the press.

This expectation places a huge burden on individual journalists in broadcasting. For, of course, the broadcasters, however diligent and careful, are bound to fall foul of such expectations. Broadcast news is always going to be subject to bitter criticism, just as the press will always be accused of wilful distortion. The process of selecting and presenting the news cannot, in the end, be other than a subjective process, however carefully monitored and regulated. As Sir Alastair Burnet has said, 'The very selection of the news involves bias, there is some bias in every programme about public policy; the selection of the policy to be discussed and those to discuss it means bias.'[2]

The inevitability of bias means that one has eventually to trust the journalist to be animated by a desire for the truth and to be honest enough to recognize his or her own biases and prejudices.

This belief in the integrity and professionalism of the journalist does, however, depend upon a certain common understanding and acceptance of what constitutes news. The critics of broadcasting hold to an ideal of objectivity which embodies a conception of news which understands it as the reporting of politics, economics and other serious cultural and social issues. This is a narrower conception than that employed in the rough and tumble of working journalism. For the practising journalist, news is any piece of information or story which is new, interesting and true. It must also be relevant to the journalist's intended audience.[3]

Broadcasters also tend to argue that their task is simply to place the microphone or point the camera in such a way that represents the interests of a supposedly disinterested listener or viewer. The idea of objectivity is conflated with that of neutrality.

This stance is well expressed by Linda Gage in her practical guide to working as a journalist in independent radio. She writes:

> Objectivity is an important concept in journalism but difficult to achieve in practice. To be truly objective we would need to divorce ourselves from our backgrounds and prejudices. There is a long-standing debate about whether this is possible, but you should at least know your own prejudices and confine them to a part of your mind that becomes inoperative when you are doing your job. You will find it easier to interview people who do not hold the same views as you do, simply because you will be able to think of the opposing arguments more quickly. Remember that is always your job, to find the opposite point of view and put it. There are very few one-sided issues. If for some reason you are forced to give only one side of a story, you owe it to the listener to explain why.[4]

This emphasis on presenting conflicting views is often attacked as a distortion of the news gathering process. It is argued that broadcasters are hindering the search for truth by turning all issues into gladiatorial combats with the broadcaster as a referee. In their defence broadcasters feel that they must reinforce their neutrality against those people who argue that objectivity must have limits. For example, critics, including many in government, argue that broadcasters ought not to be neutral in presenting the statements of terrorists, especially when those claims contradict those of the legal authorities. Broadcasters fear such arguments because they see them as attempts to capture the news on behalf of particular vested interests. The truth of a claim cannot be determined simply by reference to the worth of the source from which it comes. Broadcasters see the collection and presentation of conflicting views as a kind of guarantee of their objectivity and neutrality, and ultimately of the possibility of discovering the truth. Broadcasters also point out that conflict is endemic in the world. They would hotly deny that broadcast news manufactures conflict and would claim to be simply reporting that which already exists. Yet, in the end, broadcasters themselves know that they cannot escape their responsibility for choosing what to show and how to show it simply by invoking an ideal of objective detachment.

Another criticism is that objectivity, despite the best efforts of the broadcasters, is simply a code-word to cover a structural bias in favour of the established sources of news. When government departments, public relations agencies and highly organized political and commercial interests are constantly feeding the broadcasters with news it is difficult for the less well organized and less articulate to have their voices heard. Journalists have actively to seek out under-represented views if they are to reflect opinions from more than a narrow powerful section of society.

The ideal and practice of objectivity is, then, fraught with difficulty for the broadcast journalist. It is also fraught with difficulty for the viewer and listener. No-one can live in complete scepticism all the time. It would make ordinary living intolerable. Yet how is the audience to choose among competing versions of the same news story? Which presentation can be judged to be the most objective and reliable? Who is to be believed and on what evidence?

Research has indicated that media audiences are well aware of the possibilities for bias and distortion in the news. At a popular level this is expressed in phrases such as 'You can't believe anything you read in the papers'. Audiences, however, cannot constantly suspend belief; they have to make judgements about the honesty and integrity of the sources which supply them with the news.

A recent study by the Glasgow University Media Group, on the 1984–85 Miners' Strike, for example, indicates how the power of the news media to shape perceptions and carry conviction depends upon the audience's access to alternative versions of events. Television audiences with no direct experience of the event largely assimilated the 'objective' view of the strike presented by television news programmes. By contrast, those people who did have direct experience to call upon, or who were exposed to alternative sources of information and comment, were able and more likely to contest this 'objective' view in favour of what they took to be a more truthful account.[5]

Education: liberal and secular

The educative function of mass media has been most clearly seen in broadcasting. When radio broadcasting began in Britain under the guidance of John Reith, there was no doubt that broadcasting was seen as a powerful educational tool. Reith's own philosophy was quite explicit about the mission of the BBC to promote and inculcate certain values. He wrote in 1924:

> As we conceive it, our responsibility is to carry into the greatest possible number of homes everything that is best in every department of human knowledge, endeavour and achievement, and to avoid the things which are, or may be, hurtful. It is occasionally indicated to us that we are apparently setting out to give the public what we think they need—and not what they want, but few know what they want, and very few what they need. There is often no difference. One wonders to which section of the public such criticism refers. In any case it is better to over-estimate the mentality of the public, than to under-estimate it.[6]

That view has largely shaped the substance and form of British broadcasting until the present time. It rests implicitly upon a belief in the permanent truth of certain unspoken values, largely associated with what has come to be called 'high culture', which are considered to be worth promoting. As late as 1965, Oliver Whitley, Chief Assistant to the Director-General of the BBC, could write:

> Culture can be boring. Its apostles and agents can be pedantic or supercilious. But when all is said and done, culture still is *a good thing*. Good things have a way of being slow and hard. Culture is an architecture, not a casual kaleidoscope. It needs persistence and takes a long time . . . Culture surely is not an absolute but a process, an enrichment. There are some sophisticated arguments for keeping monetary wealth in the hands of an elite. But they have been long since abandoned in favour of the theory at least of egalitarian, or at any rate, mobile society. So with cultural wealth. To promote it widely has become an imperative, no longer a choice; a moral imperative, come what may . . .
>
> I am a missionary . . . for culture and for the BBC as its discriminating but determined carrier.[7]

Broadcasting today, like society at large, lacks the certainty and assurance about such matters which is evident in Reith's or Whitley's statements. Here is the Annan Report of 1977, advocating a more detached stance:

> John Reith, who created public service broadcasting in this country, was undoubtably determined to use broadcasting as a means for making a better society. Yet much of what people today consider to be good broadcasting would have been rejected by his definition of that term . . . We do not accept that it is part of the broadcasters' function to act as arbiters of morals or manners, or set themselves up as social engineers. In politics, for instance, the

broadcasters should not elbow Parliament aside . . . The broadcasters' duty is to see that the different policies which purport to solve our problems are given an airing. It is not their function to decide how society should develop and run that particular policy for all it is worth: for it may not be worth all that much. In saying this we do not mean that they, or the Broadcasting Authorities which are responsible to Parliament for the public interest, can be indifferent to morality or to the good of society. Far from it. Indeed one of their objectives, which they achieve all too rarely, should be to inspire producers in their programmes to ruminate upon the most profound spiritual values. Nor do we doubt that men of good will across the spectrum of opinion would agree on the values which should inspire programmes. But dissension would appear immediately those values began to be interpreted and expressed in a programme. Nor should the broadcasters usurp the function of the multitude of individuals and organizations which try to persuade men and women how best to live their lives. Broadcasters are wiser to see themselves as hosts to these individuals and organizations and, by inviting them to broadcast, help people to understand issues and what, if anything, can be done to resolve them.[8]

With a growing lack of assurance and certainty about the core values of our society has come a profound unease about the influence of broadcasting in general and television in particular. Indeed, concern about the influence of television can be seen as a concern that the cultural values which shape television's output have become less clear and explicit. The idea has emerged that there is a 'hidden curriculum' in television programmes. This 'hidden curriculum' has come to be felt as a potentially disturbing influence on established ways of thinking, believing and behaving.

Public concern about what people might be learning from television has led to numerous and extensive research projects designed to determine television's exact behavioural effects. The effects of television on violent behaviour in children and adolescents has been a particular focus of interest. Yet, in spite of the effort and the vast sums of money spent, all that many such studies felt able to say for certain was that:

For some children, under some conditions, some television is harmful. For other children under the same conditions, or for the same children under other conditions, it may be beneficial. For most children, under most conditions, most television is probably neither harmful nor particularly beneficial.[9]

This circumspect and tentative view has not allayed widespread public concern about television effects. The commonsense view is that television must have effects and that researchers are simply not trying hard enough to find them.

Uncertainty about core values and unease about the supposed effects of television together create a climate which reinforces the tendency of media professionals to interpret their role as observers rather than shapers of culture.

For the commercial broadcaster, this tendency to detachment can be rephrased in terms of simply giving the people the programmes that they want. This begs many large questions about what people really do want, but it provides media practitioners with a convenient and populist justification for whatever programming policy they might wish to pursue. This policy also has the advantage of being measurable by a supposedly 'objective' yardstick—the audience ratings for particular programmes.

In Britain, however, this populist ideology, though increasingly promoted, is even now relatively restrained. Commercial television, unlike commercial radio, is still expected to provide a certain (undefined) proportion of programmes of cultural and educational merit. The original obligation as stated in the Television Act of 1963 was that commercial television should be 'a public service for disseminating information, education and entertainment'.[10] That expectation is now much weakened, but the fact that education is considered to have a place in the commercial system testifies to the enduring strength of the feeling that television can, and should, be more than solely a medium of mass entertainment.

Even for broadcasters who work in non-commercial public broadcasting, the issue of the place and value of educational programming is complicated by doubts about which values to maintain and promote. While echoes of Reithian certainties might inform the rhetoric of broadcasting policy, the working producer or journalist is forced to communicate with an audience that cannot be presumed to share either moral or cultural values. Yet public broadcasters continue to feel an obligation to extend as well as to serve public tastes and interests.

Public service broadcasters, therefore, have sought to construct a self-identity which can balance the ideal of the broadcaster as a detached, neutral observer with that of the broadcaster as a pioneer in extending the bounds of public taste. The broadcaster, in this view, as a reporter and commentator stands apart from the prejudices and partisanship that produces social conflict while casting a critical eye over established ways of thinking. This liberal, professional ideology of objectivity and detachment has been best articulated by the former BBC Director-General, Hugh Greene. His views, though enunciated over twenty years ago, are still to be discerned as among the underpinning core values of present-day public service broadcasting. These are the values which are currently being challenged by those who propose that consumer choice be the core value of the broadcasting system.

Hugh Greene summed up his basic attitudes to broadcasting in a speech in 1965 to UNDA, the International Catholic Organization of Broadcasters. He said:

> The main purpose of broadcasting, I suggest, is to make the microphone and the television screen available to the widest possible range of subjects and to the best exponents available of the differing views on many different subjects to let the debate decide or not decide as the case may be, and in Cardinal-Elect Heenan's words 'to emerge with a deeper knowledge'.
>
> The presentation of varying views does not mean that the BBC merely seeks to foster an equivocal attitude towards all that is broadcast, to attach an ubiquitous, unanswered question mark to everything it touches in religion, culture, politics or education. But it does mean in my opinion, that the BBC should encourage the examination of views and opinion in an attitude of healthy scepticism.
>
> I say 'healthy scepticism' because I have a very strong personal conviction that scepticism is a most healthy frame of mind in which to examine accepted attitudes and test views, which in many cases have hitherto been accepted too easily or too long. Perhaps what is needed, ideally (though we cannot all—I certainly cannot—achieve the ideal) is what T. S. Eliot described as 'an ability to combine the deepest scepticism with the profoundest faith'.
>
> It follows that in its search for truth—indeed, in whatever it undertakes—a broadcasting organization must recognize an obligation towards tolerance and towards the maximum liberty of expression . . .
>
> But although in the day-to-day issues of public life the BBC tries to attain the highest standards of impartiality, there are some respects in which it is not neutral, unbiased or impartial. That is, where there are clashes for and against the basic moral values—truthfulness, justice, freedom, compassion, tolerance, for example.[11]

The other major set of presuppositions which underpin the self-identity of public broadcasters concerns their interpretation of their educative role. As an educator, in the widest sense of the word, the broadcaster promotes the values of tolerance and understanding, preferring to bracket passionate and extreme views within clearly marked slots for minority programmes. As a cultural explorer, the broadcaster seeks to give space for new forms of expression, from alternative comedy to expressionist drama, testing the established consensus of public taste.

Charles Curran, again twenty years ago, was the BBC Director-General who was able to express these presuppositions most forthrightly and clearly. His view of the BBC stressed its educative role:

It is a question of stretching the capacities of the audience to take in new kinds of enjoyment or to experience more intensely forms of entertainment which are already known to them. There is a substantial element of the educative function in this concept . . .

The BBC's position is one of quasi-judicial impartiality. Just as most public law reflects the general will of the public, and just as some law reflects not simply that minimum standard which the public wishes to protect, but also what it would like as an ideal, so the BBC's programme philosophy seeks to display what the world is like, and to present what might be . . .

And so once more we return to the essentially educative function of the BBC. It is a matter not simply of educating the public in general, but of educating the public as listeners and viewers to choose and to enjoy what they intend to hear and view.[12]

Education, religion and secularism

In the area of values, some of the most contentious public debates have been about the broadcasting of religion. The sceptical views which inform the educational ideology of most contemporary broadcasters tend to reinforce a decidedly secular approach to religious issues and religious values. Religion is, more often than not, bracketed with those issues which are in some way contentious and disruptive. Indeed, religion is very often seen as a cause of social conflict and a cloak for deep-seated racial or social prejudices. The religious claim to truth, especially to an exclusive truth, is difficult to assimilate in a media system that has elevated tolerance and impartiality above nearly every other virtue.

Another factor tending to reinforce secular attitudes within the media is the perception that religious organizations are either hostile to the media or determined to use the media for their own ends. In other words, religious organizations are seen as simply another set of special interests seeking to capture the media for their own purposes. On the other side, religious organizations and Churches tend to have an ambivalent attitude towards the mass media. On the one hand, they see the possibilities of using the mass media to spread their views more widely, but on the other hand, they are fearful that the mass media are inexorably undermining their influence over public culture. Religious groups have always seen the need to have a stake in the educational system, and many bitter battles have been fought, and continue to be fought, over religious influence in schools. It is not surprising, therefore, to find some of the same battle cries being raised in relation to broadcasting and the press.

Moral and cultural certainty was the distinguishing characteristic of the first Director-General of the BBC, John Reith, the son of a prominent

Scots Presbyterian minister, who regarded his appointment as a 'calling' from God, and was determined to make broadcasting into a fit instrument for the Divine purpose. Because of this moral orientation, Reith saw religious broadcasting as having a central place in the BBC's output. For him the aim of religious broadcasting was to provide the nation with a 'thoroughgoing, manly and optimistic' Christian message.[13]

Reith's influence meant that in the first three decades of the BBC's existence the Corporation could be regarded as actively promoting a Christian point of view. Indeed its Christian stance was a source of much complaint from non-Christians. After the Second World War, however, the Corporation began to reflect the increasingly secular and sceptical spirit of British culture. The new Director-General, William Haley, no longer saw himself as committed to making the nation more Christian, though he was still committed to what he saw as the preservation of core values associated with Christian belief. This position was later adopted by both independent television and radio.

The treatment of religious values and ideas in the media has undergone a number of substantial changes during the course of the century. In broadcasting, particularly, there has been a significant shift away from the direct promotion of religious beliefs towards a more or less detached exploration of religious beliefs, behaviour and values. In this respect religious broadcasting mirrors the more general movement away from moral and cultural certainties.

In a public service system the pressure is to produce religious programmes which reflect what might be termed the safe middle-ground of belief and practice. What that middle-ground is of course varies over time. In Britain, the major Churches, through the Central Religious Advisory Committee (CRAC), have had some influence on defining what religious broadcasting ought to be. At one period in the BBC's history the dominant influence was that of a mildly evangelical Protestant Christianity; today, especially now that CRAC is no longer exclusively Christian, the middle-ground is represented by a generally socially-conscious ecumenism.

The middle-ground is not necessarily a bad place to stand. Where there is no middle-ground, there is little possibility of dialogue and mutual understanding, and a tendency to exalt the firmness of one's belief above the search for truth. Broadcasters face a real difficulty, however, in accommodating those religious views which challenge or confront the dominant ethos. It is hard to make programmes which neither ignore such views nor patronize their adherents. The controversy over *The Satanic Verses* and its coverage by the media is a case in point. The degree to which Muslims feel outraged and upset by Rushdie's book is almost impossible to understand within the prevailing frame of reference.

It is important, however, to recognize that British radio and television, especially public broadcasting, devote a good deal of time to religious matters. Worship programmes on radio and television are still broadcast on a regular basis. Reflections and short meditations on religious matters are broadcast on a wide variety of stations every day. Though critics might quarrel with the quality of this output and scoff at its shortcomings, the very fact of its existence reveals that broadcasters and audiences alike regard religious broadcasting as making a valuable contribution to the overall quality of the broadcasting system.

Today few British broadcasters would think of themselves as promoting specifically Christian values. As far as most broadcasters are now concerned, religion is a subject like any other and it is the business of the broadcasters to put Christian and other religious beliefs under critical scrutiny. Religious broadcasting is becoming ever more broadcasting about religion, rather than broadcasting of religion. The public culture, despite the presence of an Established Church, is not regarded by the media as a religious culture. This attitude has given rise to an ever widening gulf between the expectations of many believers and the professional ideology and practice of the broadcasters. While the broadcasters accept, and indeed endorse, the pluralistic multi-racial multi-faith nature of modern British society, many religious people, especially conservative Christians, are fighting to maintain what they consider to be the essentially Christian nature of British culture.

Despite these problems, however, there are grounds for claiming that Gospel values still have some influence in broadcasting. There are also grounds for claiming that religious ideas and values, albeit not always in an easily recognizable form, are to be found throughout the media.

The public service ethos, though less obviously confident, is still a major factor in influencing the practice of broadcasters in both the public and private sectors. The undoubted fact that most British broadcasters still value and adhere to some version of the public service ideal is an indication that they have a concern for the dignity and integrity of the person. The public service ideal expresses this concern by striving to treat the viewer and listener as responsible and rational beings. The virtues of tolerance, impartiality and objectivity, for all their limitations and however difficult to realize in practice, are at least noble ideals to set before media professionals. All these values offer points of connection with the Gospel. It is easy, and foolish, to deride such values as merely humanistic.

Residues of a former Christian culture, or expressions of a secular humanism, are values worth preserving and fighting for, especially as today they are being challenged by far less 'Gospel-friendly' values in the shape of an all-embracing commercialism.

Entertainment: a variety of realities

Religious broadcasts tend to address a religious public, and communicate through a language laden with formularies and replete with expressions that presuppose an acquaintance with traditional religious teachings. For the bulk of the audience this language is almost incomprehensible. Most of the audience now professes a mixture of secular attitudes and a certain yearning for an experience of the transcendent which might be described as a diffused religiosity. While traditional religious programming finds it ever more difficult to communicate with the wider audience, a good deal of the content of popular entertainment precisely captures this blend of secular and religious attitudes and feelings.

At first glance, there seems little evidence of religious values in mass entertainment programmes. In these programmes organized religion is often an object of ridicule or patronizing condescension. The stereotype of the ineffectual vicar is well established in television comedies and drama. When characters are presented who have high moral and ethical standards, these standards are rarely related to specific religious beliefs. More common is the character who acts in a prejudiced or intolerant manner because of a particular religious orientation. There is no doubt that the world of television drama finds it natural to present adherence to specific religious doctrines as a problem rather than as a personal and social benefit. In addition, producers generally take it for granted that the basic social reality within which serials and soap operas operate is one in which an adherence to a particular Church or religion is a minority practice with little relevance to the mass of ordinary people.

Together the secular perspective and the growth of commercialism make it ever more difficult for religious ideas in their traditional form to find a secure place in the media. From a pluralistic viewpoint all media messages should be treated with a high degree of scepticism; from a commercial viewpoint all media messages are selling messages. The combination of viewpoints means that traditional expressions of religious ideas and values are easily regarded as promotional packages, neither more nor less valuable or interesting than any other.

Yet the religious dimension cannot be excluded completely. In his recent book, *Wrestling with an Angel*, Colin Morris puts the point thus:

But even in a secular society, certain archetypal themes run through the life and experience of believers and unbelievers alike. Their lives are touched by dread and glory, unearthly fears have to be subdued and some sort of response made to the ultimate questions of life and death. People still need to locate themselves in the universe, in society and in their own heads.

The human spirit-life does not wither because official religion is enfeebled. It still feeds on the raw material of religious experience wherever it may be found. And television is one such source which offers a store of stories, images, models and symbols to keep in trim what could be called the human religious muscles—awaiting a higher manifestation of the Spirit on which they might be exercised . . .

Thus, if the religious muscles of secular man and woman are not exercised by traditional religion, they will be brought to bear on this other world of humanly created meaning, television, for we cannot survive without drama, pageant, play and fantasy. When formal religion is privatized and becomes preoccupied with esoteric imagery and ritual that is inaccessible to the generality of society, a popular piety springs up, searching for other ways of expressing faith. The starved imagination, like the empty belly, is remarkably catholic in its tastes. Writes Gregor Goethals, 'Until institutional religion can excite the serious play of the soul and evoke the fullness of human passion, television will nurture our illusions of heroism and transcendence'.[14]

Ethical and moral issues are the stuff of television and radio drama. One might say that the television and radio serials and soap operas are the morality plays of modern life. Their stories are primarily explorations of personal relationships and their plots are an endless examination of the complexities of family life. Religious values are present, but in a diffused or residual form. The staple of soap operas and serials is the battle between light and darkness, good and evil, heroes and villains. The explicit connection between morality and religion has been largely severed, but the focus on moral dilemmas, on issues of honesty, integrity, truthfulness, compassion and love, provides a significant point of contact with Gospel values. In broadcast morality plays good is expected to triumph over evil. Even though the villain, male or female, is often the most striking character, the audience expects and knows that their schemes will ultimately be thwarted and that social harmony, albeit a temporary harmony, will eventually be established.

Through these entertainments, the soap operas, situation comedies and game shows, the real and enduring power of the media is shown. That power is the power to shape perceptions. The stories told through the media constitute a variety of frames, or to change the metaphor, a multitude of mirrors which reflect back to us a variety of, more or less distorted, images of our world. The mass media present people with alternative ways of seeing and making sense of social reality. Soap operas and serials like *EastEnders, Coronation Street, Dallas* and *Neighbours*, and the private and public life of their stars, provide an endless supply of stories of scandal and gossip to the popular press. For the millions who follow such programmes part of the pleasure lies in the fact that they are endlessly discussed and reported in their daily papers. Television and the press together constitute a world of shared experience and common discourse. Some people find the world of the soap opera becomes, in some sense, more 'real' than the everyday world of ordinary living; for most it provides a valued and socially acceptable form of daily 'escapism'.

Commercialism and the media

Underlying all our discussion so far has been a more or less explicit discussion of the tension between the commercial orientation of the media and their more public service functions. There is no escaping the fact, however, that the commercial nature of the media is not easily constrained. As Eldridge and Davis note, the media are fundamentally a complex of industries and businesses.[15] As a consequence, most media institutions are organized as industrial operations, media messages are treated as commercial goods and audiences are regarded as consumers. This commercial orientation even makes its mark on an institution like the BBC which holds to a public service philosophy and is organized as a public corporation. The BBC could not continue to fulfil its public service remit if it allowed itself to ignore audience ratings and the commercial competition to concentrate solely on producing worthy programmes. It would soon find little political support for the licence fee and would end up relying on government subvention or advertising.

The basic commercial orientation of the media means that media owners and producers are understandably afraid of upsetting their customers or patrons. In the case of the BBC, for example, the adherence to the kinds of educative philosophy espoused by Charles Curran is constantly being balanced against a concern not to upset unduly the sensibilities of government or large audience groups. In both the commercial and the public sector, broadcasters and journalists are always being accused of betraying the ideals of detachment and impartiality by advertisers, owners, politicians and audience members representing special interests.

Such pressures tend to encourage broadcasters and other media producers to structure their output in terms of majority taste and to define that majority taste in terms of commercially viable products. Commercially viable, more often than not, means products which will offend the least number of people. In order to find a place in the mainstream of media culture programmes have to conform the dominant ethos. Distinctive voices and alternative points of view get lost. As a result very large minority groups often feel that mass media fail to satisfy their tastes or meet their expectations.

Another consequence of commercialism is the tendency of the media to assimilate all forms of media content into a form of mass entertainment. It is not that information and education should not be presented entertainingly, it is that entertainment values can, if given too much weight, distort and trivialize more serious issues. This problem is seen in a particularly acute form in television news.

News organizations are not detached from the imperatives that drive the media as a whole. The need to win audiences, to improve ratings and, in the case of commercial companies, to please advertisers, means that a clear line cannot be drawn between news and entertainment. As the tabloid press has demonstrated, people are attracted by stories about people. The sharp distinction which is made by the high-minded between mere gossip and 'hard news' is not a distinction which seems to be relevant to the majority of the public.

Television communicates through visual images. Television news rooms and television journalists have to structure their news stories around the images available. Television journalists, therefore, have the task of making complex and intractable news stories intelligible to mass audiences who look upon television as an entertainment medium. People watch television as a leisure activity and they do not, on the whole, want to feel that they are being lectured.

To be entertaining television news needs a steady stream of interesting pictures. The more dramatic and arresting the image the more likely it is to be used. When a news story about a complex political or economic issue, for example, is not intrinsically visual, television news editors tend to look for striking personalities who can present differing points of view. Personal or group conflict of opinion, real or imagined, can often become the staple ingredient of news stories. In addition, television producers and journalists can tend to look for dramatic images because of their professional sense that such images will make it easier to hold the attention of the audience.

Critics argue that this quest for dramatic visual images tends to bias television coverage towards those stories which have the most interesting visual content. Indeed, in some cases it is argued that this gives too much opportunity for various groups to set the news agenda. Some events are carefully staged for the cameras. An army of public relations consultants has worked out the right ways to ensure that their client's activities are sufficiently newsworthy to attract television coverage. Political campaigns are obviously and unashamedly designed to maximize television exposure. More dangerously, both legitimate protesters and terrorist groups have been known to adjust their behaviour to the presence or absence of the cameras.

A second criticism is that the emphasis on finding strong pictures can obscure the important issues at stake in a particular news event, leaving the viewer only with a sequence of striking impressions. The result is that the viewer may remain fundamentally ill informed about the issue or event being covered. Analysis can be easily downgraded or even abandoned in favour of a superficial and misleading presentation.

Gospel values in a media culture

One of the urgent tasks of the Christian Churches today is to offer the possibility of integration of personhood and wholeness of spirit to people who are living in fragmented and incoherent societies. As we have seen, the media are a major factor in the promotion of this cultural fragmentation. Unreflecting immersion in media consumption tends to increase the difficulty of finding a coherent vision of life. The messages are so diverse and contradictory.

John Reith and the pioneers of public broadcasting in Britain attempted to build a broadcasting tradition which would encapsulate a moral vision, a common idea of the good. That tradition is still not quite dead, but it has been severely undermined, as a variety of social changes, including the growth and diversity of the media, have undermined 'our sense of being part of a single moral community in which very different people are brought together under a canopy of shared values'.[16] For a time television was commended as a medium which could help in sustaining, if not actually building, this sense of communal values. But the fragmentary nature of the television experience and the sheer number of new channels has made this dream seem increasingly utopian. *At the heart of the modern media is a vacuum of meaning and in this the media are faithful reflectors of modern society*. The media professionals concentrate on defining and policing the rules which allow certain views, opinions and ideas to be expressed through the media. In the place of shared meanings is a multitude of opinions and behaviours. The danger is that the centrifugal forces of modernity so evident in television and other media will propel us into a future in which the medium of public discourse will be the advertising slogan and the 'sound bite'.

Christians have the task of resisting this process and, however haltingly, working to strengthen those elements in the media which bring people together rather than drive them further apart. The Gospel is alive where human beings are respected and celebrated. The assumptions and expectations which underpin the ideologies of objectivity and professionalism, or of commercialism and the market, are inadequate because they fail to engage fully with the human person. They are instrumental ideologies quite compatible with an instrumental view of the media—but not compatible with a view of humanity that celebrates the Word made flesh.

Despite their negative aspects, however, the media do offer some possibilities for personal and spiritual growth, but only if we can disengage from the media flow long enough to be able to see and hear clearly. Programmes of media awareness and critical study of the media are valuable because they help us place the media in perspective. Above all, they emphasize that the media are cultural and commercial institutions and products, made by human beings for human purposes, not natural powers to which we must quietly submit. The view of the world presented by a news programme, a soap opera, a film or a Sunday magazine supplement is not inevitable, straightforward or transparently neutral. It needs to be looked at carefully and with a certain detachment. We need to identify and celebrate those times and places where Christ is suddenly glimpsed in and through the media.

In the early days of BBC television, broadcasters were worried by the immersion of people in media realities. They deliberately created interludes between programmes in order to encourage people to break out of the media flow. Viewers and listeners were urged not to listen or watch continuously, but to be selective about their viewing and listening. There was clear recognition that involvement with the media should not be a substitute for other forms of activity. Today that view would be deemed quixotic. In the pursuit of ratings broadcasters do all they can to hold on the audience for the longest possible time. In our present culture we have to create our own media interludes to break the media flow.

Interludes allow us to appreciate as well as criticize. We can take time to consider which news programmes are, most of the time, reasonably truthful and honest accounts of the world. Media professionals are not all charlatans and deceivers. We may become more aware of those storytellers whose films and plays, humour and music reveal beauty and truth. We would, after all, be intellectually and culturally impoverished without the media. We can discern more clearly when television, radio and the press afford us glimpses of other peoples, new ideas, events and personalities that we can be thankful for. We can be aware of when they make us laugh, cry, think and sometimes provoke us to action.

Prayer, meditation and critical judgement are tools for discerning the traces of the Gospel in the media. Those activities demand a measure of silence, solitude and detachment in one's life. These are precisely the conditions which the mass media threaten constantly to overwhelm. We need to develop the attitudes and skills that will help us and our children to live in a media culture without being absorbed by it and, with God's grace, to find ways of transforming it in the light of the Gospel.

Notes

1 Jonathan Sacks, 'The demoralisation of discourse', *The Listener* (22 November 1990), p. 10.

2 Alastair Burnet, Richard Spriggs Memorial Lecture 1970; quoted in Andrew Boyd, *Broadcast Journalism* (London: Heinemann, 1990).

3 Linda Gage, *Guide to Independent Radio Journalism* (London: Duckworth, 1990), p. 49.

4 Ibid., p. 50.

5 University of Glasgow Media Group, *Seeing and Believing: The Influence of Television* (London: Routledge, 1990).

6 J. C. W. Reith, *Broadcast over Britain* (London: Hodder and Stoughton, 1924), p. 34.

7 Oliver Whitley, *Broadcasting and the National Culture* (London: BBC pamphlet, 1965).

8 *Report of the Committee on the Future of Broadcasting* (Cmnd 6733) (London: HMSO, 1977).

9 W. Schramm, J. Lyle and E. B. Parker, *Television in the Lives of Our Children* (Stanford, CA: Stanford University Press, 1961).

10 Television Act 1963 (11 & 12 Eliz. 2 c.50), clause 2.

11 Hugh Greene, *The Third Floor Front: A View of Broadcasting in the Sixties* (London: Bodley Head, 1969) pp. 94ff.

12 Charles Curran, *Broadcasting and Society* (London: BBC, 1971).

13 Kenneth M. Wolfe, *The Churches and the British Broadcasting Corporation, 1922– 1956* (London: SCM Press, 1984).

14 Colin Morris, *Wrestling with an Angel* (London: Collins, 1990), pp. 175, 177. The quotation is from Gregor Goethals, *The TV Ritual* (Boston: Beacon Press, 1981). p. 84.

15 Howard Davis and John Eldridge, 'The Gospel and our "media culture" ', unpublished paper.

16 Sacks, op. cit.